TRUTH BE TOLD

INTERSECTIONAL RHETORICS

Karma R. Chávez, Series Editor

TRUTH BE TOLD

WHITE NOSTALGIA AND ANTIRACIST QUEER RESISTANCE IN "POST-TRUTH" AMERICA

Laura Elliot Tetreault

THE OHIO STATE UNIVERSITY PRESS
COLUMBUS

Library of Congress Cataloging-in-Publication data available online at https://catalog.loc.gov

LCCN: 2025022596

Identifiers: ISBN 9780814215968 (hardback); ISBN 9780814259580 (paperback); ISBN 9780814284421 (ebook)

Cover design by Brad Norr
Text design by Juliet Williams
Type set in Adobe Minion Pro

♾ The paper used in this publication meets the minimum requirements of the American National Standard for Information Sciences—Permanence of Paper for Printed Library Materials. ANSI Z39.48-1992.

CONTENTS

INTRODUCTION 1

CHAPTER 1 Black Lives Matter, Violent Imaginaries, and Narrative Activism 31

CHAPTER 2 Activist Relational Knowledge against Digital Disinformation in Black Lives Matter and the Women's March 50

CHAPTER 3 Charlottesville's False Equivalencies: Rejecting "Both Sides" by Refusing to Waste Time 72

CHAPTER 4 Whose Insurrection? Rhetorical Gaslighting after January 6 and the Uses and Limits of Testimonial Acts 89

CHAPTER 5 Anti-Trans Disinformation and t4t Care through Joy and Spite 112

CONCLUSION 133

Acknowledgments *143*

Works Cited *147*

Index *163*

INTRODUCTION

On a sunny morning, thousands of armed white men wearing red traveled from near and far to fill the streets of a Southern US city. Their goal was to "take back" what they believed was theirs, politically and economically. Black politicians, though still a minority, held public office to a greater extent than ever before. The city, though still segregated like most American cities, had become known for the strength of its Black middle class, with several business owners locally renowned as success stories in a difficult environment. Many members of the white working class mingled with the Black working class, finding a basis for solidarity. However, the white people who joined the rally that day feared that they had lost jobs to Black candidates and perceived the increasing Black presence in politics as a threat. The white supremacists did not appear out of nowhere; their presence was the result of a coordinated disinformation campaign across both grassroots and established media outlets at the local and national levels. To prime audiences to think the coming violence was justified, this disinformation campaign hinged on arguments that Black activists had become increasingly violent, too radical, and were planning a riot. Several prominent influencers used the rhetoric of "protecting women" to stoke fear of a dangerous threat. The next US presidential election was still a couple of years away, but local elections were coming up, and those who supported the rally also engaged in a sophisticated voter suppression and intimidation campaign designed to disenfranchise Black voters and others who might support progressive candidates.

The white supremacists engaged in violence and property damage, but afterward, the media downplayed this impact as the actions of an unfortunate few bad actors who disrupted a gathering that was generally more civil, in stark contrast with examples of Black protest where acts of defense had been exaggerated into mob violence. Reporters from mainstream national news outlets, who traveled to witness the aftermath of the rally, encountered a political scene where local leaders were attempting to maintain civility against an increasing tendency for public discourse to dissolve into emotionality and uncivil behavior. Black writers attempted to counteract these distorted portrayals by circulating their own reporting, especially in independent media. However, a broader profit-driven media infrastructure worked against them. Dominant platforms tended either to limit the reach of marginalized perspectives by labeling them as "fringe," or to amplify these perspectives in a decontextualized way, which only further inflamed white rage. The US president did nothing to condemn the white supremacist rally, its violence, or the longer disinformation campaigns that enabled it.

Contemporary readers may assume this example refers to the 2017 Unite the Right rally in Charlottesville, Virginia, or perhaps another similar rally in the years since, but it does not. Above, I am actually describing the 1898 white supremacist massacre and coup in Wilmington, North Carolina—only recently labeled by historians for what it is, rather than the obfuscating term "race riot." The red clothing in this example refers not to MAGA hats, but to the uniforms worn by the Red Shirts, a white supremacist paramilitary arm of the Democratic Party in the late nineteenth century. At the time, Wilmington, then the largest city in North Carolina, was remarkable in the South for its Black majority population, multiracial government, prominent Black figures in the local economy, strong Black middle class, and working-class neighborhoods that were less segregated than in comparable cities. In the immediate aftermath of an economic depression, the 1896 election had been momentous, with white supremacists losing control of the state legislature for the first time. This shift in the balance of power represented the success of a regional, coalitional labor movement in which poor white and Black Southerners united against economic exploitation. Angry about losing power, white supremacists used media disinformation and voter suppression tactics to set the stage for a violent coup, whose violence would then be covered up by further disinformation about who acted "violently" and who acted "civilly." The coup succeeded on November 10, 1898, when white supremacists seized power at the city and state levels, with ramifications for generations to come. In Wilmington in

1898, the Black population was 56 percent; in 2020, it was 18 percent. A Black person did not serve on the Wilmington city council again until 1972. No Black person served in Congress from North Carolina again until 1992.[1]

In 1898 the platforms were newspapers and the influencers were charismatic orators; white supremacy was overtly named and championed, not disguised through coded appeals; and electoral politics were entirely and overtly patriarchal, as only men could vote. Structures have changed, but their logics endure. Throughout American history, disinformation and white supremacy have been co-constitutive; "civil discourse" is often part of the problem, not a solution; and the structures of US liberal democracy readily allow for white supremacist interests to gain and maintain power—and, when oppressed populations previously excluded from deliberation make gains toward altering these structures, those who benefit from white supremacy react with violence both material and epistemic, for which they are not held accountable. This book examines all these issues and more, arguing that "post-truth" is old news because distortion, obfuscation, and political control of the "truth" are how white supremacy has always functioned, with effects that have always been especially dire for Black, Brown, Indigenous, trans and queer, disabled, and otherwise marginalized communities. While it may be tempting to think we are dealing with a new crisis of truth, it is important to foreground what is old: the systems of domination long ago programmed into the foundations of our society, which change shape over time but retain their central function.

Post-Truth and Crisis Rhetoric

In the US today, post-truth is usually associated with the presidency of Trump as well as the increasing centrality of digital media, especially social media, to politics. Trump is often framed by political commentators as exceptionally disdainful of "truth," more than any other politician, despite acknowledgment that most politicians lie to some extent (Wang). This is clear in many examples of political commentary published in 2016 by major news outlets:

> There is no doubt that even in the quadrennial truth-stretching that happens in presidential campaigns, Trump has set records for fabrication. (*The Washington Post*)

1. For a much more detailed history of the 1898 Wilmington massacre and coup, from which this summary of events is drawn, see Zucchino, *Wilmington's Lie* and "'Wilmington's Lie.'"

> Never in modern presidential politics has a major candidate made false statements as routinely as Trump has. (*The LA Times*)

> Donald Trump's dishonesty . . . is qualitatively different than anything before seen from a major-party nominee. (*The Atlantic*)[2]

These framings of post-truth politics as new and uniquely Trumpian invoke a rhetoric of crisis, rhetoric that has been expressed by liberals and conservatives alike. As historian Daniel Steinmetz-Jenkins writes, since 2016, media and political discourse has been full of claims about crises—whether the "crisis of democracy," "the crisis of liberalism," "the climate change crisis," or "the crisis of higher education," but without answering "Whose crisis? Which democracy?" (2).

Implicit in crisis rhetoric is a kind of nostalgia for a precrisis past—much like we see in the opening example to this book—and in the context of post-truth politics, this nostalgia often manifests as a longing for an imagined time of civil discourse. This nostalgia is best exemplified by political commentator David Frum's 2016 article for *The Atlantic,* in which he outlined the seven "guardrails of democracy" that Trump shattered—namely:

1. expectations about how a candidate for president should speak and act
2. the expectation of some measure of trustworthiness in politicians
3. the expectation that a potential president should possess deep—or at least adequate—knowledge of public affairs
4. the guardrail of ideology, captured by a candidate's coherent and consistent political platform
5. the primacy of national security concerns
6. a belief in tolerance and non-discrimination
7. and a belief "in a common creed of 'Americanism.'"[3]

---

2. Cillizza, "How the Heck"; Finnegan; Frum.

3. To represent the "guardrail" of "belief in tolerance and non-discrimination," Frum cites the 1980 Republican policy platform: "The truths we hold and the values we share affirm that no individual should be victimized by unfair discrimination because of race, sex, advanced age, physical handicap, difference of national origin or religion, or economic circumstance." This is the same party that spent the entirety of the following decade, under the Reagan administration, systematically destroying Black, Brown, queer, and disabled communities. Frum also neglects to include the two sentences that follow the excerpt from the above policy platform: "However, equal opportunity should not be jeopardized by bureaucratic regulations and decisions which rely on quotas, ratios, and numerical requirements to exclude some individuals in favor of others, thereby rendering such regulations and decisions inherently discriminatory. We pledge vigorous enforcement of laws to assure equal treatment in job recruitment,

Frum's seven "guardrails" represent a remarkably white framework for understanding American politics and the differences between past presidents and Trump, as the "settled norms" he points to are just the ideals of white liberal democratic rhetoric, which has always enacted oppression under the guise of civil language (Mills). The nostalgic rhetoric of this article represents a broader American delusion sustained by both conservatives and liberals: that there was something else before what we now call post-truth politics. Nostalgia is often weaponized effectively by the right wing, represented in Trump's campaign slogan, "Make America Great Again" (taken from Reagan before him). What often goes unsaid is that liberal nostalgia for a time before post-truth is actually the other side of the same coin, and both forms of nostalgia are very much a *white* nostalgia. Nostalgic liberal calls for civil discourse can be just as damaging for marginalized people as conservative disinformation attacks. Understanding how these work together is key to challenging what is now termed post-truth politics, but what is really just the latest manifestation of white supremacist rhetoric.

I understand the allure of nostalgia and the attractiveness of the assumption that if people just knew more or communicated more civilly, if there were less disinformation out there or if it were fact-checked better, or if politicians would debate more respectfully, then we would not have the oppressive conditions we have now in the US. It's a nice fantasy that a more informed population would immediately result in better lives for currently marginalized people. To some extent, it is true that being better informed—especially through relationships with people from marginalized groups—can change minds, and that this can be the beginning of greater political advocacy for individuals who would otherwise be privileged enough to look away. As a

---

hiring, promotion, pay, credit, mortgage access, and housing" ("Republican Party Platform"). As we still see in American politics today, arguing against "equal opportunity" on the basis of opposing "quotas, ratios, and numerical requirements to exclude some individuals in favor of others" is just a veiled call for the elimination of affirmative action and other programs meant to address systemic inequities, and "vigorous law enforcement" is a euphemism for anti-Black violence. The year 1980 is long before post-truth, but this distortion of oppressive policies through the rhetoric of "equality" certainly does not represent "truth" either. In the context of the 1980 policy platform, we can specifically see the seeds of neoliberalism, the ideology that would come to dominate US and UK politics in the following decades, in part by presenting itself as what Lisa Duggan terms a "nonpolitics—a way of being reasonable and of promoting universally desirable forms of economic expansion and democratic government globally" (177). A pre-Trump political era characterized by "reasonable" deliberation is actually part of the political process that made Trump's rise possible (i.e., through increased privatization and divestment from public services, rising gaps between the wealthy and the impoverished through the ongoing mechanisms of racial capitalism, etc.), and one among many examples throughout American history of people in power enacting violence using polite words.

scholar and teacher of rhetoric and writing, I am not against informing people of the truth, checking facts, analyzing and challenging fallacious arguments, or speaking against disinformation in other ways. However, these strategies alone are not enough to achieve liberation within a society designed to maintain power for some by oppressing many. While in some cases, a receptive audience may have an opinion changed when informed of the truth, what happens more often is that oppressed people are forced to make case after case proving their oppression and arguing for its end, exhausting their rhetorical resources trying to persuade a dominating audience who long ago decided never to listen.

As a white person who grew up as a well-meaning liberal, believing in a progress narrative that American society was more or less on an improvement trajectory toward greater equity, who gradually started seeing the holes in this narrative the more I learned, and who was shocked by Trump's election in 2016, I had to let go of the conviction that if "we" (who?) could just, once and for all, find the right words at the right time and arrange them in the right order to show "them" (who?) the truth, then society would improve. After all, that's why I first became interested in rhetoric, finding almost nothing more satisfying than deciding on the right words at the right time to communicate an idea, a feeling, or an experience. I believed more or less in the rhetoric of liberal civic deliberation and was saddened by its perceived decline, infuriated by the unwillingness of some amorphous "them" to just listen or face the truth—to finally agree to act as an audience for "us," who know better.[4] Naively, I was just learning what many who have more directly experienced oppression have known all along: The root problem is not ignorance but domination, not a lack of knowledge but a lack of solidarity.

As Dana L. Cloud writes, what we term "reality" is always complex, rhetorically mediated, and rooted in power dynamics. Rather than beginning by debating different truth claims, it is useful to ask who has the power to set the terms for debate. Cloud explains that there are better and worse ways of responding to the "reality crisis," and that what has proven ineffective is the assumption that when shown the correct information, society will debate rationally (14). However, dissolution into full relativism is not politically useful (14). Cloud provides another way forward, rooted in rhetoric's understanding of "truth as standpoint-based and perspectival," by arguing for a "rhetorical realism" wherein communicators can bring knowledge from marginalized perspectives into common sense, and truth claims that circulate as

4. See Chadwick for an example of this frustrated rhetoric about a population who "just won't listen to the truth" about oppression.

common sense are evaluated on the basis of their degree of fidelity to the experiences and interests of the oppressed and exploited (15). On the left, we should neither reject reality nor "wield facts like hammers"; instead, we can ask deeper questions about whose reality and whose truth claims circulate, to what extent, on whose terms, with what incentives and motivations, and with what consequences for whom (Cloud 35).

When the terms of debate are set by those in power, activists challenging that power may find themselves in a double bind. Engaging only on the terms of dominant social reality further entrenches the perceived truth of that reality. However, complete refusal to "engage the reality frames of the powerful" can make "activists unintelligible and boring at the best of times and profoundly terrifying at the worst" (Cloud 4). In the US, the dominant terms for political exchange are the terms of racial liberalism: a rhetorical trap. Activists must make strategic choices about how to resist and what they are willing to give up in the process. In this work, I build upon Cloud's analyses of movement counterdiscourses and make the case for focusing on rhetorical strategies that multiply marginalized activists use to navigate this difficulty—including some that may seem unintelligible, boring, or terrifying on dominant terms but that are vital for activist survival because they help to sustain community epistemologies.

I argue that liberal counter-disinformation strategies are insufficient against fascist manipulations of truth because liberalism's racialized yet abstracted ideal of civility actually plays into fascism's hand. Tracing the history of racial liberalism and its interconnected roots with fascism reveals that the past *is* important to contemporary discussions of post-truth politics, but not the imagined past conjured by white liberal appeals to a bygone era of civil discourse. Instead, social movement histories from the perspectives of oppressed people, especially the rhetorical traditions of multiply marginalized communities, provide more effective frameworks for resistance beyond the limits of liberalism. Thus, I also argue that it is necessary to begin with the knowledges of the oppressed to develop strategies for surviving the disinformation environment within which fascism thrives. I use the word "survival" here intentionally, as these strategies may fail to bring about any large-scale liberatory change when measured in the short term. However, they provide rhetorical means for people to see each other, to affirm each other's truths even when those are suppressed, and to enact forms of care that are necessary sustenance for long-term social movements. Movements take generations, but people in the here and now also need moments to hold onto.

As I write this in 2024 in the US, the daily violence is overwhelming, yet many people scrolling through headlines feel disempowered to do anything about it—disempowerment that is also by design.[5] This nation is defined by ongoing systemic white supremacy and anti-Blackness, colonial domination, ever-escalating militarization, deliberately organized legislative attacks on transgender and queer people, violent ableism exacerbated by the COVID-19 pandemic, ongoing misogyny and sexism, the economic exploitation required to drive capitalism, and other intersecting forms of oppression, manifesting in the denial of life chances to people oppressed by these systems. Activists working for intersectional liberation must not only fight such attacks using the means of persuasion made available on terms set by dominant power (such as through the mechanisms of US deliberative democracy like the electoral and legal systems), but must also develop ways to sustain their own ways of knowing and caring for their communities in a threatening environment (involving rhetorical work that is often at odds with the available means of persuasion offered by dominant power). These rhetorical negotiations are made even more challenging when part of the goal is building and sustaining intersectional movements—requiring the cultivation of not only on-the-ground strategies for working across differences but also a shared liberatory imagination to keep movements united despite inevitable conflict. However, activists are especially effective at seizing opportune moments to contest the conditions of post-truth politics when they draw from their own community epistemologies, rather than fully accepting dominant terms for political engagement, which were designed from the beginning to deny oppressed people the ability to be recognized as rhetors in the public sphere. Sometimes activists must compromise with these terms strategically in service of certain goals, but in those cases, pairing this strategic engagement with a heightened affirmation of community epistemologies for an in-group audience is especially necessary.[6]

From an intersectional, racial justice, and queer perspective, this book understands activist rhetorical efficacy as that which takes advantage of opportune moments to advocate for oppressed communities while also refusing to sacrifice these communities' shared ways of knowing and relating in favor of making appeals on the terms set by dominant power. How and to what extent to work within dominant terms is a negotiation that activists make

5. See Manne.

6. Activists who aim *only* to work within the available means provided by dominant power usually end up reproducing that power and leaving behind coalitional solidarity toward more liberatory goals (see the mainstream LGBTQ rights movement's abandonment of the mid-twentieth-century anticarceral and anti-imperialist queer activism led by trans women of color in favor of the rainbow capitalist "love is love," and "we're just like you" neoliberal gay activism of the early twenty-first century).

case by case, depending on the immediate context and community needs as well as longer-term visions. But there are always limits to such negotiations. "Compromise"—a lauded tenet of liberalism, along with "crossing the aisle"—is not actually possible when there is epistemological incommensurability. This is why the act of trying to persuade dominant power to listen to the oppressed so often results in a feeling of "banging one's head against a brick wall" (Sara Ahmed 26)—one is experiencing the limitations of the available means but may not know where else to turn, either for additional strategies or just for relief.

In our contemporary context of post-truth politics, it may be tempting to double down on liberal rhetorics of facticity (Won't "they" listen to what is so clearly the truth? Didn't "they" read the fact-checking of that politician's lies?) and nostalgia for civil discourse (Why can't people be more civil to each other on social media?). However, there are many more and much richer troves of rhetorical resources available if we look beyond the limits of liberalism. In responding to post-truth politics, rhetoricians must move past liberal approaches to free speech, civility, and fact-checking, which attempt to solve the problem using the available means set by dominant power and in doing so often devalue the rhetorical practices of oppressed communities. In doing so, we must begin with the counter-knowledges of the oppressed and work in solidarity with oppressed people to develop survival strategies in a disinformation environment. This book works toward this goal by identifying moments in American politics from 2013 to 2023 that represent specific disinformation threats, historicizing these, describing their rhetorical form, and analyzing how activist individuals and communities working for racial and gender justice responded to these moments of threat. By choosing not to engage on the terms of liberal civil discourse or strategically twisting these terms for the purposes of both immediate survival and long-term liberation, activists refuse disinformation and insist on the validity of their own knowledges as a form of community care.

In this introduction, I first detail the problem by framing white supremacy as the real ongoing crisis in the US. With this context, I then explain further why white nostalgia is the more pressing problem of the contemporary age termed post-truth, unpacking why liberal approaches to disinformation are insufficient because of the history of racial liberalism and its ties to fascism. I detail the limitations of civility-based rhetorics with this context in mind, and further trouble approaches to the digital that rely on liberal ideals rather than liberatory goals. Then I describe my methods of analysis, grounded in an intersectional approach to racial rhetorical criticism with a queer studies lens, and I introduce the chapters.

White Supremacy: The Real Crisis

Especially from the perspective of Black and Indigenous people, the United States *is* a crisis—a settler colonialist power built upon slavery and genocide that continues to oppress much of its population as well as populations abroad, especially through militarized policing, surveillance, and incarceration.[7] Though white supremacy is commonly represented in the contemporary US as a fringe ideology, as sociologist Jessie Daniels illustrates in her study of white supremacist groups, it is actually "a central organizing principle of social life" (11). White supremacist oppression is not a bug but a feature of American politics, and it is not new. For many people of color, the "epistemological, ontological, and axiological uncertainty" now termed post-truth "is not just familiar territory, it is violent territory" (Mejia et al. 113).

"Race" itself is a fiction invented by European powers in order to seize land and resources to grow that power (Daniels 13; Omi and Winant 3). James Baldwin pinpointed in his 1984 essay "On Being White . . . and Other Lies" that America "becoming white" was a story told to justify Black subjugation (2). As Ersula Ore details in *Lynching: Violence, Rhetoric, and American Identity,* anti-Blackness was literally structured into America's beginnings through explicit and implicit definitions of who was considered part of civil society and who was not, with citizenship laws "guided by appeals to an 'us' that figured 'the people' as a racially homogenous group and 'them' as a collection of subhuman nonwhite others" (32). Despite subsequent reforms, the imperfections of American democracy continue to "strategically target members of the polity not originally conceived as members of the polity" (Ore 26). This helps to explain the persistence of anti-Black violence and connected forms of oppression in the US.[8] White civic identity is consolidated against

7. In this book, I have chosen to focus on moments of resistance by contemporary Black, Brown, queer, and feminist public rhetors, with much of the focus placed on Black rhetors, and this choice of focus may unintentionally occlude Indigeneity (while also acknowledging that the former categories and Indigeneity are not mutually exclusive). I do not mean to sideline the role of genocide and settler colonialism to the formation of liberal democracy and white supremacy in the US but did not have space to engage all these complex intersections, nor did I have an extensive enough scholarly background in Indigenous studies to give informed enough attention to examples of Indigenous resistance. For excellent studies of Indigenous digital resistance, I recommend the work of Cindy Tekobbe, especially her book *Indigenous Voices in Digital Spaces.*

8. Though a deeper engagement with the Afropessimist tradition is outside the scope of this project, it is worth noting that the term "anti-Blackness" also has a specific usage and history in this body of work. In Afropessimism, anti-Blackness describes the ontological position of people racialized as Black: that of impossible subjects, the negation of whose humanity the West and specifically the United States are built upon (Patterson; Wilderson). As thinkers in

those deemed "other" through the maintenance of a hierarchical, oppositional binary of whiteness and Blackness, with non-Black people of color also implicated (Hill Collins, *Black Feminist Thought* 90). A binary gender system defined in relation to heterosexuality is also a mechanism of control (Butler 141), with both gender and sexuality racialized from the start (Hill Collins, *Black Feminist Thought* 69).

Racism and anti-Blackness have never gone away, but they have changed shape over time. Hortense Spillers argues that despite the abolition of slavery, the American civic imaginary retains its "originating metaphors of captivity and mutilation" (447). The symbolic order, or underlying "grammar," of American society remains violently anti-Black. Following Spillers, Saidiya Hartman traces the "afterlife of slavery" to show how, after emancipation, Black inferiority was no longer an official legal standard but state racism continued to produce "a subjugated and subordinated class within the body politic, albeit in a neutral or egalitarian guise," transforming racial slavery rather than fully ending it (10). The post–civil rights era saw the rise of what Eduardo Bonilla-Silva terms "colorblind racism," where "racism" is associated with overt individual violent or discriminatory behaviors rather than the structures of society itself, a logic rooted in the Jeffersonian liberal ideals of liberty, individualism, and equal opportunity. In practice, such abstractions systematically disadvantage people of color by ignoring history and emphasizing the choices of individuals without examining "the multiple historical and contemporary structural and state-sponsored practices preventing people of color from the liberty of making individual life choices in pursuit of happiness" (Martinez 15). Today, digital technologies extend historical practices of surveillance and policing, constituting what Ruha Benjamin terms a "New Jim Code," made even more dangerous when disguised by tech companies'

---

this tradition argue, only this degree of nonrecognition can explain the ongoing, brutal, yet everyday violence that Black people experience. In this formulation, the "inability to recognize Black humanity" (ross) is paired with the need for Black people to exist in an exploited position in order to sustain the nation, which also depends upon the ability to racialize some populations as white and some as non-Black people of color (who also have specific experiences of oppression and relations to dominant power). Beyond understanding anti-Blackness as the originating crisis that the US depends upon, the Afropessimist tradition goes further to argue that there is no full redress possible for Black people's oppression using the mechanisms of American civil society, which are anti-Black at their core. This is why Frank Wilderson writes that "a Black radical agenda is terrifying to most people on the Left because it emanates from a condition of suffering for which there is no imaginable strategy for redress—no narrative of redemption," at least not within liberal political frameworks. "Civil society," or Western liberal democracy, depends upon anti-Blackness while at the same time insisting that Black people use the discourses and institutions of civil society to undo their own oppression—an impossible trap.

messages of benevolence (139). Critical race theoretical approaches aim to make such hidden practices and histories visible, and it is telling that such approaches have come under heavy attack by those who benefit from systemic racism's invisibilization. The foundational problem remains though its manifestation shifts yet again.

The Problem of Liberalism

Liberalism and Racialization

When post-truth is framed as a novel crisis originating with the contemporary American right wing, it is assumed that "only this new concept of the post-truth could explain how a racist, misogynistic, neo-nationalist member of the economic elite could win a presidential election," which leads to a "cottage industry" of liberal media offering solutions in the form of "information literacy and fake news guides" (Mejia et al. 110). Many high-profile liberal news outlets, such as *The New York Times* and NPR, have tended to blame an ignorant population for the problem of Trump and to posit more information as the remedy. A wealthy, racist, misogynistic neo-nationalist ascending to the presidency is framed as a strange mistake that happened because of voters' lack of knowledge or vulnerability to online disinformation, rather than as a logical outcome in a political system designed with racism, misogyny, nationalism, and capital at its center.

The problem is thus not that there was a different era before post-truth, but that the structural violence of American politics has, through liberal appeals, been hidden from those racialized as white, who are encouraged to ignore this violence. Charles Mills argues in *Black Rights / White Wrongs: The Critique of Racial Liberalism* that liberalism, as an "ideology of individual rights and freedoms" emerging in the seventeenth and eighteenth centuries, should be historicized as "a *racial* liberalism, in which conceptions of personhood and resulting schedules of rights, duties, and government responsibilities have all been racialized" (29). Only through a racialized understanding of "individual rights and freedoms" can we reconcile what Ruha Benjamin pinpoints as the founding contradiction of American society, which "extolled 'liberty for all' while holding millions of people in bondage" (36). This only makes sense when historicizing the ideals of liberal democracy in their racialization. Many people were denied this liberty because they were not legally considered "people" at all. Liberal nostalgia in the post-truth era represents a white longing for an imagined era of rational deliberation and civil engagement in the political sphere, without interrogating the racialized dynamics of who gets to be recognized as "rational" or "civil."

Liberalism and Fascism

During the first Trump administration and immediately afterward, it became common for political analysts, journalists, and scholars to debate whether he technically qualifies as a fascist while nevertheless warning that America could sink further into fascism (Bender and Gold; Dickinson; Lehmann; Leingang; Marantz; McNamara; Tisdall; Tomasky; Ward; Wolf). Pointing to the increasingly open authoritarian, xenophobic, racist, sexist, and antiqueer stances of contemporary right-wing politicians, commentators frame this new wave of leaders as more severe and dangerous than those of previous politicians (Young). American studies scholars Bill V. Mullen and Christopher Vials locate contemporary American fascism in "a predominantly white, racist, nationalist, middle-class 'backlash' that finds its expression in a politics of resentment, victimhood, xenophobia and anti-leftism traditionally associated with classical fascism," built on histories of white supremacy and settler colonialism (2). Fascists gain power partly by using rhetorical strategies designed to obfuscate the violence of their positions, such as coded language that hinges on a victimization and purification logic (Crick 5).

What the liberal alarm about America's perceived creep toward fascism today often fails to reckon with is that the experience of many Black people in the US has already been close or identical to living in a fascist state. Langston Hughes wrote in 1936 that "fascism is a new name for that kind of terror the Negro has always faced in America" (Toscano). A fascist state and a liberal democracy have different structures of power, but "the experience of racialized rightlessness within a liberal democracy can make the distinction between it and fascism murky at the level of lived experience" (Mullen and Vials 271). The interconnected roots of fascism and liberalism become visible through tracing these histories of racism and colonialism. Political philosopher Sabeen Ahmed locates the fascist logic of "ethno-nationalist supremacy" in white liberalism, as "it is precisely the liberal subject with which fascism identifies: the sovereign, self-transparent, self-conscious subject of property right; a subject who was defined in opposition to those others who were not sufficiently 'rational' or 'developed,'" as colonized and enslaved people were defined ("Provocations" 7).

Resisting American fascism has long been part of the Black radical, Marxist, and anticolonial traditions. In the period before, during, and after World

War II, when "fascism" was associated with the rise of Hitler, Mussolini, and other European dictators, Black writers and activists sought to draw attention to the ways in which fascism was already widespread in the US and other places colonized by European nations. After all, Hitler was inspired by US strategies for the land theft, resettlement, and forced sterilization of Indigenous people, and the Nazi police state was partly modeled on the United States' Jim Crow policies of racial oppression (Miller; Whitman). Drawing from Cedric Robinson, Robin D. G. Kelley historicizes early twentieth-century radical Black intellectuals' understanding of fascism not as a surprising turn away from the liberal "march of progress," but as "a logical development of Western Civilization itself . . . a blood relative of slavery and imperialism, global systems rooted not only in capitalist political economy but racist ideologies" ("Poetics" 20). In *Discourse on Colonialism* (1950), Aimé Césaire grounds the origins of fascism in colonialism, not as an ideology that emerged suddenly in Europe in the early to mid-twentieth century. Césaire argues that Europeans tolerated "Nazism before it was inflicted on them, that they absolved it, shut their eyes to it, legitimized it, because, until then, it had been applied only to non-European peoples" (19–20). European colonial domination is not commonly portrayed as fascist only because those impacted are Black, Brown, and Indigenous people in parts of the world colonized by European nations.

This tradition of Black antifascism continued in the second half of the twentieth century. The Black Panther Party, locating fascism in "the power of finance capital" (Spencer), held a "United Front Against Fascism" conference in 1969, attracting 5,000 activists from a variety of organizations with the goal of building a national coalition responsive to "the basic desires and needs of all people in fascist, capitalist, racist America" (Spencer). Angela Davis wrote from Marin County Jail in 1971, "The only effective guarantee against the victory of fascism is an indivisible mass movement" led by "Blacks and other Third World peoples[,] . . . the first and most deeply injured victims of fascism," while embracing "all working-class people, for the key to the triumph of fascism is its ideological victory over the entire working class" ("Political Prisoners" 19–20). Also writing from prison in 1971—months before being killed by guards—Black revolutionary activist George L. Jackson argued that fascism changes shape over time but is best defined through "its capitalist orientation and its anti-labor, anti-class nature," identifying "the U.S. as a fascist-corporative state" (134). As these thinkers and activists show, from the Black radical perspective, fascism has always been present in the US, and further, the only way to overthrow it is through the power of a broad and intersectional movement that includes all people exploited under capitalism but is led by those most harmed.[9]

Troubling "Civil Discourse"

Césaire had an especially damning indictment for bourgeois liberal Americans who uphold this everyday fascism: "I am not talking about Hitler, or the prison guard, or the adventurer, but about the 'decent fellow' across the way; not about the member of the SS, or the gangster, but about the respectable bourgeois" (47). Under the guise of liberal calls for "decency" and "respectability," everyday Americans have long contributed to the perpetuation of oppression. Liberal responses to post-truth politics today continue this practice when invoking nostalgia for a supposed time before this political era when politicians were more "civil," that is, engaging in fact-based discussion with politeness and respect as a form of "civic engagement" idealized in liberal democracies. In a 2018 NPR / PBS NewsHour / Marist poll, 74 percent of respondents said that "the overall tone and level of civility in Washington between Republicans and Democrats" since Trump's 2016 election had "gotten worse." Another poll shows 68 percent of Americans in 2019 indicating there is a "major problem with civility in America today" (Weber Shandwick et al. 2).

Many educational initiatives, including some that were founded as a direct response to the 2016 election and alleged civility crisis, frame the teaching of "civil discourse" as a remedy for our troubled times. In these frameworks, civil discourse is what will "enhance our community's skills to engage in respectful and robust debate" when "good citizenship is perhaps especially important at this time of widening ideological divides and growing political polarization" (Harvard, "Civil Discourse"); "make headway on the many pressing problems that we face only if we're able to talk about them openly, vigorously, and respectfully—especially when we disagree" (The Ohio State University); "contribute to the renewal of our society's ability to engage in intelligent disagreements and productive dialogue between people who hold opposing views" (University of Denver); and "cultivate a love of and the skills for listening and communicating across differences" (American University).

9. The history of Black thought about fascism and antifascism is long and rich. I invoke this history here for context, though a more in-depth exploration is beyond the scope of this project. For further detailing of this history as well as contemporary Black resistance to fascism, see Hope and Mullen; Golstein and Trujillo; Renton.

After the 2016 election, there was also a proliferation of popular books and online think-pieces about "crossing divides," "healing the nation," or using the power of civil discourse to solve "polarization," such as Lilliana Mason's *Uncivil Agreement: How Politics Became Our Identity* (2018) and Ezra Klein's *Why We're Polarized* (2020).

The key rhetorical move common to these arguments is to frame "polarization," or stark ideological difference, as itself the problem with America today—rather than the fact that many are fighting for the liberation of the oppressed, and many are fighting against this liberation. The assumption here is also that if political groups could "meet in the middle," tensions would vanish—but it is not clear how this compromise would improve conditions for those currently oppressed. Also, in failing to mention any of the specific contexts or histories that construct systems of belief, initiatives for "civil discourse" instead point to abstract "differences," "ideologies," or "opinions," assuming that encountering ideas that are "different" from one's own will be a helpful exercise and that detached and rational discussion will allow people to think of the best solutions to political "issues." Such "issues" are abstracted into vague ideological debates, rather than what they are: decisions about the allocation of choices and resources, made according to whose lives are valued more and whose are valued less.[10]

Civility is an ideal of liberal US deliberative democracy that assumes a decontextualized, dehistoricized public sphere in which all people can make arguments and those most logical and persuasive will prevail. Civility is also a mechanism of control—rhetors must make their arguments in a "civil" fashion in both tone and content. The privileged tone is unemotional, logical, assertive, but not threatening—with "tone" *perceived* more than enacted, as marginalized rhetors are often automatically perceived as threatening before saying anything. Rather than being neutral, civility and civilizing discourses are "racialized technologies of the flesh" (Baez and Ore 331), with US citizenship itself conceived according to "norms of urbanity, whiteness, heterosexuality, maleness, ability, and middle-classness" (Chávez 13). In the US, liberal notions of "progress" are tied to the ability to assimilate into these citizenship norms and to perform civility as they dictate.

10. Having discussions across differences can only be useful when people share the same values and commitments; for example, activist communities are full of conflict and require ways to navigate that conflict in service of larger goals. In such situations, pedagogical strategies designed to negotiate differences can be valuable. However, these are not the situations that the initiatives referenced here are designed to address; instead, they point to debates across conflicting political commitments and opposing values as that which "civil discourse" is meant to mediate.

Rhetoric as a discipline is implicated in these assumptions about civil discourse. Civility is a foundation of the Habermasian public sphere, long criticized for its illusion of democratic deliberation while actually structured to serve the interests of a new capitalist ruling class (Cloud 21). When we say rhetoric is the study and practice of effective communication, there are many assumptions embedded into what "effective" means and for whom (McKerrow). For example, ideas about locating the "appropriate" means of persuasion implicitly exclude rhetors "whose ideas, voices, or bodies are considered inherently inappropriate (whether by rule or convention)" (Law and Corrigan 327).[11] Civility, or what M. Remi Yergeau refers to as diplomacy, is often equated with rhetoric itself or what it means to be a rhetorical agent, with oppressed people rendered nonrhetorical for "failing" to adhere to dominant communicative norms (150–51).

Just as the liberal democratic public sphere has never been neutral, contemporary spaces for deliberation such as social media platforms are structured for power and profit. Politicians like Trump have been especially successful in exploiting the affordances of profit-driven social media (Mercieca). Social media platforms claim to be modern democratic public spheres but are products of corporations with a profit motive (Beck et al.; Gelms and Edwards; McKee). User engagement generates capital for the companies that own these platforms, and such engagement is easily manipulated in favor of technocrats and their wealth-hoarding goals. Look only at Elon Musk, the richest person in the world and a key figure in Trump's second presidential campaign and administration, whose purchase of Twitter and transformation of the platform into X in 2023 has greatly influenced American politics (Conger and Mac). Long before events like Musk's Twitter takeover, the use of targeted advertising online had already become central to political campaigns, solidifying the relationship between politicians and technological elites (Cadwalladr and Graham-Harrison; Schmidt et al.). The rise of increasingly sophisticated artificial intelligence (AI) technologies can make it difficult to determine what material online is produced by real people and what is produced by machines, which also perpetuate human-created systems of oppression (Benjamin; Noble). Further, AI technologies are built upon colonialist practices of extraction and require the exploitation of the earth's natural resources and of a large population of low-wage information workers kept at the bottom of the hierarchy in order to generate even more profit for those

11. The concept of invitational rhetoric was developed as a feminist alternative to traditional persuasion (Foss and Griffin), but it has been criticized for adhering to civility norms in its own way by as valorizing a nonconfrontational approach and assuming an even field between interlocutors, rather than a power differential (Lozano-Reich and Cloud 221).

at the top (Crawford). These problems all require material solutions and systemic changes to current power structures, especially the ability of elites to amass wealth while the majority of people suffer.

Social media platforms are intimately tied to the post-truth phenomenon in the public imaginary and often paired with nostalgia for a time before these technologies allowed "fake news" to proliferate or users to become trapped in "filter bubbles," the algorithmically constructed digital feedback loops that encourage users to interact with content that is familiar to them (Barthel et al.; Pariser). Rather than challenging power at the intersection of politics and tech capital, asking *whose* interests are served by what (dis)information circulating where, commentators on digital media and post-truth tend to blame social media users for being uninformed and to suggest surface-level fixes to platforms that would diversify users' feeds and prompt more civil discourse. This tendency is especially clear in a 2017 *BBC Now* feature on "Lies, Propaganda, and Fake News: A Challenge for Our Age" (Gray). The tech experts and scientists quoted in the BBC article make some telling nostalgic assumptions about political debate and the nature of the public sphere: "On page one of any political science textbook it will say that democracy relies on people being informed about the issues so they can have a debate and make a decision" (Lewandowsky qtd. in Gray). "In the past it was harder for relatively fringe opinions to get their views reinforced. If we were chatting around the kitchen table or in the pub, often there would be a debate" (Moy qtd. in Gray). "A major issue most people face without knowing it is the bubble they live in. If they were shown views outside that bubble they would be much more open to talking about them" (Fletcher qtd. in Gray).

There are several connected flaws in the logics of these claims. Here, "fringe opinions" has a negative connotation, but an opinion being viewed by the mainstream as "fringe" may or may not communicate useful information about its content; as the perspectives of marginalized people have often been framed as "fringe," context is always necessary. Seeing "all sides" of an issue is presented as a neutral process, and it is assumed that people have an individual capacity to make a "decision" based on encountering information about these "sides" and evaluating its merits, but information itself is never neutral. Simply being exposed to a wider variety of ideas is framed as an effective tool against people's online "self-radicalization": "Firms like Amazon could offer up films and books that provide an alternative viewpoint to the products a person normally buys" (Lewandowsky qtd. in Gray). The reference to an undefined and universal "person" reveals an assumption that "alternate viewpoints" are automatically valuable. Under this model, would a scholar who often purchases books about the Black rhetorical tradition then begin to be shown books by white supremacists, as the Amazon algorithm attempts to offer up "an alternative viewpoint"? Further, "radicalism" is framed in an automatically negative light, without defining who gets to determine what views count as "radical," and in what ways, when, why, and with what consequences for whom. Encountering varied "information" or "different perspectives" is unhelpful when this information and these perspectives are detached from a deeper analysis of context, history, and power.

Beginning from Marginalized Knowledges

In contrast with liberal ideals of civil discourse, activists from a resistance tradition grounded in intersectional values of racial and gender justice, including but not limited to Black, Brown, queer/trans, and feminist rhetors, insist on the importance of multiply marginalized peoples' embodied experiences, emotions, needs, and rhetorical practices. Given the foundational forms of oppression programmed into American civil society, academic and activist communities debate whether and to what extent an end to oppression is possible using these systems, such as electoral politics and the courts. The question of whether to work within or outside systems is another limiting binary built on a flawed metaphor that assumes a clear boundary between "outside" and "inside." The reality of activist work is much more nuanced and context-dependent (Bessette; Chávez). Some people might work through structures like the legal system as a form of harm reduction or to make specific people's lives more livable. Others may work toward large liberatory goals by focusing on small, localized changemaking practices—for example, working toward the goal of abolition by developing community safety protocols and forms of mutual aid against carceral logics (Davis et al.; Kaba). Whatever one's strategies of resistance are, it is more powerful to look creatively forward to a liberatory future for those currently oppressed, rather than accepting the meager reformist concessions we may be given under the terms of liberalism, or looking nostalgically backward to a past that only ever existed in the imaginations of those in power.

In addition to envisioning possible futures, beginning from oppressed people's perspectives offers another way to think about uses of the past in digital rhetoric. For instance, scholars including Safiya Umoja Noble, Ruha Benjamin, and Simone Browne detail how contemporary technologies continue histories of surveillance and policing that have always oppressed Black people in the US. Other scholars explore how people draw from community-based rhetorical traditions to engage online, often as a subversion or "strategic occupation" of platforms not built for them (Russell). For instance, Moya Z. Bailey explores how Black queer and trans women build community and circulate counterdiscourses on platforms such as YouTube, Facebook, and Tumblr. Catherine Knight Steele historicizes twenty-first-century Black women's digital practices in Black feminist writing from the nineteenth and twentieth centuries, in the process decentering white supremacy in narratives of technological competence. Adam J. Banks centers the DJ as a figure of Black rhetorical excellence in order to situate digital practices such as remix in a longer tradition of African American storytelling, and André Brock Jr. places Blackness at the center of internet culture. In these and other contexts, people draw from collective histories and look for rhetorical resources outside the available means provided by dominant power, or twist these terms for their own purposes. Additional examples include rhetorics of impatience (Carey, "Necessary Adjustments"), refusal (Abraham; Bey, *Them Goon Rules*; Shaye), glitch (Russell), and remix (A. Banks; Martin and Licona).

What interests me the most are the ways in which activists use rhetorical strategies grounded in their community epistemologies and movement traditions to open up moments of resistance to the dominant social order—which may be small, temporary, or incomplete, and may fail according to some measures, but which nevertheless remain essential for sustaining an activist imaginary in service of broader liberation. This book takes an emergent view of social change, following adrienne maree brown, who offers emergence as a framework to "notice the way small actions and connections create complex systems, patterns that become ecosystems and societies" over a long time scale (*Emergent Strategy* 2). Emergent strategy is also relational, starting with small interactions as building blocks for the creation of patterns and systems to live by and work toward (brown, *Emergent Strategy* 1). Activist counter-disinformation strategies for survival and resistance are emergent, glimmering in small, intentional moments of action and connection that sustain individuals and communities in both the short and long terms.

In my engagement with digital disinformation, I attend specifically to disinformation strategies enacted with the goal of "rhetorical exhaustion," defined by Jonathan L. Bradshaw as involving "active means of circulating rhetorical material to halt discourse, redirect the rhetorical trajectories of public discourse, or demoralize publics" (2). The goal of rhetorical exhaustion is not to persuade audiences to accept a particular political position, but instead to wear them down to the point of disengagement (Bradshaw 3). This strategy of wearing down audiences is well suited for social media platforms, as it works through accumulation and amplification. Discrete pieces of (dis) information matter less than the cumulative effect of sharing and circulating an overwhelming volume of material.

Responding directly to specific instances of disinformation, even to correct them or point out inaccuracies, often helps the disinformation spread further, feeding into accumulation (Bradshaw 5). Social media platforms read any interaction with content as "engagement" that drives profit, with no functional differentiation between positive or negative interaction. Further, claims made with a larger goal of rhetorical exhaustion are not always false in a way that could be fact-checked, but instead are hyperbolic, rendering a "fake news" paradigm inadequate (Bradshaw 9). To counter rhetorical exhaustion, Bradshaw advocates for "rhetorical specificity" and "an ethic of self-care" for digital rhetors (3). Because accumulation-based disinformation strategies work through modes of generalization and abstraction, including sensationalizing, rhetorical specificity can help slow their circulation (10). Self- and community care involves knowing when and how to *dis*engage, not to give in to rhetorical exhaustion but instead to prevent its effects. This distinction is similar to the difference between silence as a rhetorical strategy used purposefully by marginalized groups and the experience of being silenced as a tool of oppression (Smilges).

A liberal civil discourse approach is especially ill-equipped to intervene in rhetorical exhaustion. Directly debating claims often misses the mark and only serves to waste time. Because rhetorical exhaustion makes extensive use of abstraction, the tendency of liberal civil discourse to engage in discussion on abstracted terms feeds it rather than countering it. In contrast, activist counter-disinformation rhetorical strategies rooted in the community epistemologies of oppressed groups are often better suited for challenging rhetorical exhaustion. Such strategies refuse to play on the terms of liberal civil discourse, or play *with* those terms strategically. Rhetorical exhaustion is more affective than rational, rendering rational deliberation less relevant in this context (Bradshaw 6). Activist counterstrategies lean into the affective in their uses of imagination and narrative genres. They also involve a refusal to waste time, which can be powerful when time-wasting is a key element of rhetorical exhaustion. As the remedy for exhaustion is rest, activist counter-disinformation strategies also prioritize recovery and community care.

My Approach

Methodology

This book participates in a larger project in rhetorical studies of looking beyond a white rhetorical tradition rooted in Western liberal democratic discourse and toward the creative rhetorical theorizing done by activists working across intersections of oppression today, and by contributing a focus that is not identity-bound, but intersectional. It is necessary to question what cultural frameworks of understanding are considered neutral and capable of crossing contexts, and what frameworks are considered limited to one context—for example, by disrupting the assumption that rhetorical theories developed by white Europeans can be mobilized to understand the practices of any community, while frameworks emerging from specifically marginalized communities, like Black rhetorics, are framed as only relevant to these communities (Cultural Rhetorics Theory Lab; Ono and Sloop 40). Here, I ask what might change about post-truth criticism and counter-disinformation efforts if we move away from white liberal assumptions and instead center the meaning-making practices of activists working for intersectional liberation.

I use the term "intersectional" as a framework meant to emphasize the interconnected nature of systems of oppression. Patricia Hill Collins writes that intersectionality is challenging to define because it is by design a flexible framework, but it can be operationalized through its central "critical insight that race, class, gender, sexuality, ethnicity, nation, ability and age operate not as unitary, mutually exclusive entities, but rather as reciprocally constructing phenomena that in turn shape complex social inequalities" ("Intersectionality" 115). Moving beyond analyses of post-truth rhetoric that fail to attend to intersecting modalities of power, and that neglect to center white supremacy and anti-Blackness as central to American politics, this book builds upon a "critical disinformation studies" approach, as advocated by scholars Alice Marwick, Rachel Kuo, Shanice Jones Cameron, and Moira Weigal. This approach takes as foundational the view that "disinformation is a key way in which whiteness in the United States has been reinforced and reproduced" (Marwick et al. 1). Methodologically, critical disinformation studies "encourage[s] scholars of mis/disinformation to interrogate power differentials more broadly and race specifically when discussing disinformation" (Marwick et al. 1).

To accomplish this, I use the method of racial rhetorical criticism, which Lisa Flores defines as "rhetorical criticism that is reflective about and engages the persistence of racial oppression, logics, voices, and bodies and that theorizes the very production of race as rhetorical" (5). As "the art of rhetorical criticism is concerned with politics and publics, with cultural discourses and social meanings, with rhetors and audiences," we cannot ignore how these concepts are racialized (Flores 6). This work is especially important because of the ways in which those in power maintain white supremacy by twisting the terms used to refer to race or by erasing race through appeals to neutrality. Racial violence changes shape across time and place, but "this violence shares a fundamental grammar—a rhetorical logic. Racial rhetorical scholars can trace it and name it" (Flores 17).

This work of naming and tracing the rhetorical logic of racialization takes multiple forms. One focus of racial rhetorical critics is on vernacular discourses, studies of which "figure communities of color as authors and creators of cultural practices and discourses that have been constitutive of their identities, both as members of the nation-state and in opposition to it" (Flores 11). Importantly, rather than telling a narrative of inclusion or exclusion, "vernacular studies may well be theories of multiplicity, (in)coherence, and intersectionality" (Flores 12). In addition, Flores points to racial rhetorical criticism that "traces the representational politics of race," including "analyses of dominant discourses and the figurations of race within," with the goal of uncovering "the racial and racist ideologies that pervade dominant discourses and public vocabularies" (13).

Racial rhetorical criticism is a historicizing project with a dual mission: chronicling the forms of meaning-making used by communities of color in a way that aims for fidelity to those communities' rhetorical traditions and critiquing dominant discourses by contextualizing specific components of these discourses in their racialized histories. In this book, I operationalize this dual focus. In each chapter, I analyze the racialized and gendered aspects of specific examples of contemporary American political discourse that make use of disinformation or distortion, and I detail how activists take advantage of moments of public visibility to respond to these instances of distortion in ways that are rooted in their own communities' vernacular discourses and rhetorical traditions.

Because "race is not an isolated but intersectional, multivocal concept" (Flores 17), I have chosen activist examples based not only on the identities of the activists but also on their stances of solidarity with people impacted by intersecting systems of racialized and gendered violence. While acknowledging that centering the voices of communities of color is extremely important to racial rhetorical criticism, I also want to avoid framing any identity as easily categorizable or definable, and as a scholar of digital rhetoric I am also especially attentive to the ways in which discourses can circulate across communities and contexts. To attend to these nuances, I add a queer lens to my use of racial rhetorical criticism. Beginning from the generative instability and contingency of identity, queer rhetoric locates its critique in terms of dominant relations to power rather than stable identity categories (Alexander and Rhodes). Karma Chávez frames queerness as "a coalitional term, a term that always implies an intermeshed understanding of identity, subjectivity, power, and politics" (7). In using this approach, I emphasize when activist rhetors are working from a shared relation to power as well as when they negotiate power differentials, and how that complicates their rhetorical strategies.

Rather than organizing around a shared identity alone, a coalitional stance asks how we might work across positionalities in service of common goals, which is especially important to me as a white queer scholar engaging in racial rhetorical criticism. Cathy Cohen argues for "a politics where one's relation to power, and not some homogenized identity, is privileged in determining one's political comrades" ("Punks" 438). Building on Cohen's work, Marquis Bey argues for shifting away from identitarian discourse "that considers blackness, transness, and feminism to be possessed identities from which politics emerge (i.e. 'I *am* black,' 'I *am* trans,' 'I *am* a feminist')" and more toward "how we might rally around subversive politics, which then serve one's identity as such" (*Black Trans Feminism* 7). Importantly, this is not an argument for an erasure of identity but a rethinking of the relationship between one's identity and politics, with shared political commitments rather than shared identities as a basis for transformative work.[12]

Further, in addition to my focus on rhetorical practices aligned with oppressed communities' vernacular traditions rather than dominant discourses, I work from a queer methodology of looking for that which may be considered strange, not fully effective, or even a failure according to the terms of the dominant (Alexander and Rhodes; W. Banks et al.; Waite). I also engage in the queer and Black feminist practice of challenging binaries, especially those rendered as oppositional (Hill Collins, *Black Feminist Thought*), including old/new, assimilation/resistance, and success/failure, arguing that everything is always more complicated. Some of the examples of resistance that I analyze may not be considered "successful" or "effective" according to the terms of dominant political rhetoric (such as measuring efficacy in terms of a specific policy victory). However, on the terms of communities' own cultural rhetorical practices, "efficacy" may be understood in different ways (for instance, an example of public activist rhetoric that does not lead to a measurable policy change but that affirms community epistemologies in a time when they are under threat). Inspired by queer theorist José Esteban Muñoz, I understand a queer future as that which we cannot in our current political context even fully conceptualize. However, when we look to the creative rhetorical practices of those currently oppressed. we can see "glimpses" of other possibilities that refuse the narrow terms set by dominant power (Muñoz 23). Such glimpses work to sustain what Muñoz calls "an economy of desire and

12. I also want to be careful to note that not all spaces need to be coalitional. It is also very useful for people who share an identity or experience of oppression to have spaces just for them (e.g., Black spaces, queer spaces).

desiring" (26). Desire sustains our resistance to the current social order, as it is "always directed at that thing that is not yet here, objects and moments that burn with anticipation and promise" (Muñoz 26). Thus, I am more interested in moments of glimpsing, glitching, and desiring than in a more narrow understanding of efficacy defined by a direct and measurable connection between activist rhetorics and political outcome (though also acknowledging the importance of activism with more targeted goals).

In doing antiracist and queer work, it is also necessary to discuss my positionality as a white queer person. I benefit from white supremacy and will never experience racialized oppression, and any marginalization I experience through hetero- and cissexism and misogyny is greatly mitigated by the power and privilege I have as a white, middle-class academic. I am not part of all the communities whose practices I am analyzing; however, I believe that scholars can do rhetorical criticism about groups that do not share their identities, and that doing so can enrich our scholarship when we approach it with reflexivity and awareness. As a queer person, I also know there is no gender liberation without an end to racist oppression. In this project, I do not claim authority over the cultural forms and modes of engagement that make up, for instance, the Black rhetorical tradition; instead, drawing from a cultural rhetorics approach when discussing Black rhetorics and other community-based practices, I rely on the work of scholars who are part of these communities and who are experts in specific areas of their rhetorical traditions in order to historicize and contextualize my analyses.

I do not have a map or set of steps outlining what is required for liberation, nor do I have recommendations for movements' way forward. I am a scholar and not a community organizer and so would not presume to know better than the people working on the ground every day.[13] Though I am a rhetorician, I also do not believe that rhetoric alone will save us. However, through my use of racial rhetorical criticism combined with a queer lens, and my broader commitment to intersectional solidarity with currently oppressed communities, I contribute a way for fellow critics to consider how we might fight rhetorical exhaustion not with the ineffective tools of liberal civil discourse, but with a wider repertoire of strategies developed by and for

13. As Ruha Benjamin also points out, "As with abolitionist practices of a previous era, not all manner of gettin' free should be exposed. Recall that Frederick Douglass, the philosopher of fugitivity, reprimanded those who revealed the routes that fugitives took to escape slavery, declaring that these supposed allies turned the underground railroad into the upperground railroad. Likewise, some of the efforts of those resisting the New Jim Code necessitate strategic discretion, while others may be effectively tweeted around the world in an instant" (161).

oppressed people, including those rooted in Black, feminist, and queer resistance traditions.

Selection and Analysis of Materials

Each chapter focuses on a moment in American politics during a ten-year period from 2013 to 2023 that has been connected in the US mainstream media to post-truth because of the ways in which those in power mobilize lies, distortion, misrepresentation, decontextualization, or other forms of disinformation. Initially, I planned to focus this project on the shorter period of the first Trump presidency (2017–21) given Trump's centrality to the construction of post-truth. However, I found it necessary to expand this focus to show that these moves are not restricted to Trump and to emphasize that he is a symptom, not the cause, of oppressive rhetorics in the US. I chose to begin with 2013 because this year represents the formal beginning of the Black Lives Matter movement as the most visible activist movement currently resisting anti-Blackness in the US. Several chapters do focus on events during the first Trump presidency, but the final case study engages with events afterward, culminating in 2023. This period (2020–23) included rapidly escalating legislative attacks on queer and trans people in the US, which set the stage for the second Trump administration's immediate anti-trans executive orders upon his return to the White House in 2025. This book does not detail events during the second Trump presidency, but its earlier focus will still help to contextualize such events.

Some chapters focus on a specific event traceable to a time and place, such as Trump's remarks following the Charlottesville, Virginia, Unite the Right white supremacist rally, while other chapters analyze a more diffuse spread of disinformation strategies, such as the final chapter's analysis of anti-transgender legislation and the role played by unfair standards of evidence. For each event, I began by reconstructing the story of what happened—how the example(s) of disinformation originated and spread through research methods informed by digital circulation. Attending to rhetorical circulation involves locating meaning-making not with a singular author or audience, but on movement across contexts and a diffuse and unpredictable sense of "consequentiality" (Gries 47). Within a circulation framework, rhetorical acts are not bounded one-time utterances but unfolding phenomena, which may have unintended effects, reach unexpected populations, and be taken up and recomposed by different audiences over time (Chaput; Edwards; Gries; Ridolfo and DeVoss). Through a racial rhetorical criticism and queer studies lens, I specifically work to historicize how circulating rhetorical acts are connected to longer histories of racialization and gendered oppression. Thus, I treat examples of disinformation not as static one-time utterances but as evolving rhetorical acts that carry racialized and gendered logics.

After detailing the rhetorical form of each disinformation event, I turn toward resistance by detailing examples of counterstrategies used by activists from intersectional leftist traditions that prioritize racial and gender justice (especially foregrounding the work of Black activists, but also including some examples from non-Black people of color and occasionally white activists who take an intersectional approach). I focus especially on kairotic moments when activists take advantage of moments of public visibility to enact resistance in a way that is connected to their communities' rhetorical traditions. I analyze a variety of digital and print materials, such as a public-facing online writing and art project; activists' perspectives in the form of social media posts, interviews in media sources, and documentary footage; activist memoirs; and examples of testimonial genres, both given in person and video recorded for circulation on social media.

For each chapter, I chose activist responses to analyze using a few central criteria. For one, I needed to be able to find enough information and context about what activists were doing, including public acts like writing, speaking, or creating media, as well as additional context through sources like media interviews or documentary footage that allowed me to gain a fuller picture of activists' thought processes. I chose examples that I found to be not only rich texts in terms of activists' rhetorical savvy and communicative ability, but also *atypical* on the dominant terms of American political engagement, especially in their use of strategies that are not completely aligned with or that run in direct counter to liberal rhetorics. Thus, for each case study, I was looking for the exceptions and not the rules in terms of how people tended to respond to a disinformation event.

Chapter Summary

Chapter 1, "Black Lives Matter, Violent Imaginaries, and Narrative Activism," focuses on the ways in which the Black Lives Matter (BLM) movement has been misrepresented and villainized in political and media discourse, in service of a white supremacist agenda that rhetorically constructs Black activists and those who stand in solidarity with them as violent, using liberal tropes to frame violence as a universal moral negative. The chapter analyzes rhetorical artifacts by BLM activists, including memoirs by the movement's founders as well as a digital project, *Black Futures Month*. The analysis of these materials focuses on BLM rhetors' use of narrative activism to tell their own stories and connect individual and community-based experiences to systemic oppressions. I explain how these rhetors resist villainizing distortion campaigns through Black queer feminist strategies of truth-telling and affirmation. Importantly, these are not just strategies for representing marginalized experiences, but rather accountability- and movement-building strategies rooted in the difficult work of constructing a coalitional imaginary.

Chapter 2, "Activist Relational Knowledge against Digital Disinformation in BLM and the Women's March," focuses on the components of activist resilience to disinformation attacks. In response to disinformation circulated by a Russian agency hired by the Trump campaign in 2016 that attempted to target Black Lives Matter, among other social movements, I analyze examples when BLM activists countered disinformation events by mobilizing their relational knowledge: the experiential, networked knowledge of activist communities. In the second half of the chapter, I use a complementary example of the digital aftermath of the 2017 Women's March on Washington. I examine how disinformation spread after the march in order to exacerbate existing divisions and tensions within the movement, and how in contrast to BLM, the Women's March lacked a strong enough foundation of relational knowledge to endure these attacks. I use these examples to foreground the counterintuitive need for slowness in a disinformation environment characterized by speed. In the case of the BLM activists, it was the forms of relational knowledge built slowly over time that allowed them to respond quickly to disinformation in the moment. For the Women's March, the movement had not had enough time to build this base of knowledge, and it was more vulnerable to disinformation attacks.

Chapter 3, "Charlottesville's False Equivalencies: Rejecting 'Both Sides' by Refusing to Waste Time," engages with the aftermath of the Unite the Right rally in Charlottesville, Virginia, specifically the rhetorical strategies invoked by Trump when he remarked that "both sides" (i.e., the white supremacist Unite the Right participants and the antiracist counterprotesters) were equally to blame for the violence that transpired. "Both sides" is not only a distortion strategy but also a trope of liberalism, based in false equivalency and reliant on decontextualization, a tactic of manipulation that attempts to use "logic" as a weapon against the situated and contextualized knowledges of oppressed populations. Drawing on a variety of materials such as documentary footage, news coverage, and online materials by local activists, I frame "both sides" as specifically a time-wasting strategy, and analyze activist responses that refused to waste any more time, using strategies of naming and historicization against the abstraction of "both sides."

Chapter 4, "Whose Insurrection? Rhetorical Gaslighting after January 6 and the Uses and Limits of Testimonial Acts," analyzes the white supremacist insurrection at the US Capitol building on January 6, 2021, during which Trump supporters stormed the Capitol in an attempt to prevent the counting of electoral votes that would certify the victory of President Elect Joe Biden in the 2020 election. This chapter focuses on the rhetorical strategy of gaslighting as used by politicians in the aftermath of the insurrection. I also invoke structural gaslighting to describe the ways in which US liberal democracy works to obscure its own roots in white supremacy, and how this contributed to the uptake of nostalgic nationalist rhetoric by both Republican and Democratic politicians after the insurrection, rather than an engagement with the white supremacist motivations of the insurrection. I situate gaslighting in relation to testimonial injustice and analyze an example of testimonial by New York State Representative Alexandria Ocasio-Cortez that both capitulated to and subtly resisted the nationalist rhetoric of the Democratic mainstream. I also point to the ways in which Ocasio-Cortez's intervention is limited by her position within the system of American politics, as well as the broader limitations of testimonial exchange when one group is not only treated with a credibility deficit but is rendered as outside of the social order, thus ineligible for testimonial exchange altogether. In this context, I turn to the history of Black insurrection to critique politicians' choices to condemn the January 6, 2021, insurrection because it was an insurrection, not because it was white supremacist, which also allows for the surveillance and control of Black insurrectionary action against white supremacy.

Chapter 5, "Anti-Trans Disinformation and t4t Care through Joy and Spite," turns attention toward attacks on transgender people during the 2022 and 2023 legislative sessions across the US. I situate anti-trans disinformation in a longer history of politicians using implicitly racialized and gendered representations of childhood innocence to justify antiqueer and anti-trans policies. I focus on one specific anti-trans disinformation strategy that involves setting an unreachable standard for evidence and explain its roots in both medical and legal conceptions of transness. I also analyze how the strategies for resistance offered through the mechanisms of liberal democracy are limited due to their incompatibility with trans phenomenology. I analyze two examples of contemporary trans youth activists using media and public performances to do one specific type of counter-disinformation work: t4t (trans-for-trans) community care as a way to create spaces of rest and recovery from disinformation attacks, choosing to prioritize trans modes of being and resisting rather than performing trans pain on the terms set by dominant power for deliberative discourse in the legislative sphere.

Against other conceptions of post-truth as an isolated phenomenon rooted in a lack of media literacy, in new digital technologies, or in societal "polarization," this book treats contemporary post-truth politics as a logical manifestation of white supremacy in the US, and it analyzes recent examples of disinformation, especially those circulated with the goal of rhetorical exhaustion, through this lens. Instead of only focusing on developing "new" solutions to post-truth, rhetoricians should look to the activist communities who have already developed ways of responding to the distortions and lies at the heart of the US itself, long before post-truth was a buzzword. Because approaches to disinformation that fail to reckon with systems of power will only reinforce oppression, I contribute a set of conceptual tools that scholars may use to analyze disinformation contexts and sites of resistance.

CHAPTER 1

Black Lives Matter, Violent Imaginaries, and Narrative Activism

Black Lives Matter activists are among the most recent in a long line of Black changemakers who have been the targets of surveillance and disinformation campaigns. Throughout US history, politicians and lawmakers have constructed Black activists as violent threats to the state, often by using the liberal rhetoric of civil discourse to frame activists as "uncivil" and to bar them from public deliberation. Further, rhetorical sleights of hand divert public attention from the actual violence of anti-Blackness. Real acts of violence, such as the police murder of George Floyd, are reframed by politicians and media as a "mistake," as the actions of one "bad cop," or as a justified action by a white individual in the face of a falsified violent threat from a Black individual. Though these anti-Black rhetorical strategies may now be critiqued using the framework of disinformation in the post-truth age (Coburn et al.; Corley), they are much older than this political moment and part of a longer white supremacist strategy designed to construct a national imaginary that excludes Black truths.

Like other post-truth rhetorical strategies, restricting imagination involves decontextualization: divorcing events from their history and context and treating them as isolated incidents. Much of the US population is kept deliberately uninformed about histories of systemic racism and its intersections with other forms of oppression. Individuals are often blamed for problems rather than systems, which works because individual people have been abstracted from their societal and historical contexts. For example, in cases of gun violence in the US, shooters are commonly framed as individual bad actors detached from societal structures of misogyny and racism, key parts of the environment that produces more gun violence than anywhere else in the world. Similarly, disinformation actors use decontextualization to remove individual acts of police violence from their context and to de-historicize acts of protest and activism.

The anti-BLM disinformation playbook centers rhetorical moves that represent Black victims of violence as violent themselves. Black Lives Matter, now an abolition-centered foundation, began as a grassroots movement in 2013 after Trayvon Martin, a seventeen-year-old Black high school student, was killed by George Zimmerman, a neighborhood vigilante with a history of racism who was acquitted in the case after claiming he acted in "self-defense" because he perceived Martin as "suspicious" and "threatening" (Smith). Eric Garner, killed in a police chokehold in 2015 while crying "I can't breathe," was represented through the frame of a threatening Black male stereotype ("6 feet 2 inches tall and 395 pounds," "hard to miss," "lumbering") (A. Baker et al.). In Cleveland in 2015, police shot twelve-year-old child Tamir Rice two seconds after assuming Rice's toy pellet gun was a real gun, and this fatal assumption was used in media coverage as a justification for the officers' brutality (Rice). Sandra Bland was pulled over by a police officer in 2015 for the minor act of not signaling a lane change, and she was found dead by hanging in a jail cell three days later. The officer who pulled her over claimed he felt threatened, but it took four years for Bland's cell phone video of the traffic stop to be released, showing the officer yelling and pointing a gun in Bland's face (Montgomery). The police officers who shot Breonna Taylor five times in her own home in Louisville, Kentucky, in 2020 were able to dodge accountability in part because Taylor's boyfriend, believing it to be a home invasion, fired one shot into a police officer's leg (Oppel et al.). Rather than being assumptions or evidence of "bias," these choices of framing are acts of *violence*, rooted in a white supremacist agenda of maintaining control over the American national imaginary.

Restricting Imagination as a Disinformation Strategy

Disinformation actors, today and throughout American history, construct Black people as violent for the purpose of diverting attention and blame from the actual violence of white supremacy. The maintenance of a white supremacist social order requires ongoing rhetorical work to normalize the extreme violence of our political condition (Ore), partly by controlling public imagination about what "violence" is. By using "violence" as a trigger word, politicians subtly encourage audiences to agree with certain definitions of what counts as violent. For example, after the 2021 insurrection at the US Capitol, Trump claimed that this attack was "nonviolent," compared to the alleged "violence" of the uprisings against racial injustice after the killing of George Floyd in summer 2020: Those attacking the Capitol were "great patriots who have been badly & unfairly treated for so long," while he called BLM protesters "thugs and terrorists." In defense of Trump after the Capitol attack, Republican Representative Matt Gaetz of Florida said, "[Trump] was far more explicit about his calls for peace than some of the BLM and left-wing rioters were this summer when we saw violence sweep across this nation" (Watson). In these examples, "violence" is defined according to images of property damage, "rioting," "thug" behavior, or "terrorism," all terms constructed within the popular American imaginary to carry a negative connotation (and erasing the context that, in the case of these protests, police often instigated the violence that protesters were later solely blamed for). Here, "violence" is *not* defined as the insidious, epistemic, rhetorical, and physical violence that Black people experience daily.

The political work of restricting imagination also involves setting limited, presentist, and nonintersectional terms for what is desirable and debatable for a public at a given moment. This work is not only the domain of the contemporary political right but also has roots in liberalism. The limited political imaginary of liberalism is often disguised under calls for pragmatism and expediency, which frame more radical and intersectional imaginaries as impractical and unachievable. For example, queer of color theorist José Esteban Muñoz famously critiques "the erosion of the gay and lesbian political imagination" into a narrow, assimilationist, and presentist "gay pragmatism" (21). The left's restricted imagination is also visible in regular headlines in liberal media strongholds like *The New York Times* framing prison abolition as a novel and impractical idea (Bazelon), not a long-standing and richly theorized tradition or a historical reality that existed in many places worldwide before the rise of modern-day incarceration.

The Black queer feminist messaging of BLM is often made unintelligible according to the standards of liberal civil discourse, wherein arguments for political change are expected to be tailored for dominant audiences, made palatable through assimilationist messaging, and stripped of more radical content. Further, the organizational structures and rhetorical strategies of BLM are often erased or overwritten by commentators who do not understand its purposeful intersectional messaging and misread it as disorganization or lack of a unified agenda. For instance, a 2017 *Chronicle of Higher Education* article claims that "if you want to know what that [BLM] movement is about, you won't find a Black Power-like treatise on its philosophical foundations. You'd have to cobble it together from various sources," and states that Black Lives Matter has a "scattershot ideology" and "leaderless structure" that "threatens the movement's future" (Parry). These assertions were made in spite of the fact that founders Patrisse Khan-Cullors, Ayọ Tometi, and Alicia Garza had outlined on the BLM website a unified set of guiding principles and indicated the movement was designed to challenge patriarchal models of hierarchical leadership (Black Lives Matter, "About").

Beyond the disinformation specifically targeted at BLM, the larger problems are the lies, delusions, and diversions of white supremacy in the US. Post-truth is not just a contemporary, isolated political phenomenon, but an unsurprising outgrowth of the fact that white supremacy has always needed an environment of distortion to function. Populations have always had to be deluded to believe that white supremacy is a naturalized condition, like the air that we breathe rather than a structure that people in the past chose to design and people today choose to maintain. As such, Black activists and their accomplices have always had to resist the violent delusions of white supremacy to envision better futures and act toward those possibilities. They do this while also facing disinformation attacks targeted directly at their activism. Because of this already existing environment of untruth that Black activists have been navigating for centuries, they have developed strategies for addressing, resisting, and healing from disinformation attacks. These are the communities best prepared to guide responses to contemporary post-truth politics, which must start by imagining in a more capacious way than the liberal political imagination allows. Black Lives Matter is a massive and certainly imperfect movement;[1] however, one thing this movement has always done well is sustaining a shared imaginary and cultivating cultural rhetorical resources rooted in Black radical and intersectional traditions.

Narrative and Imagination as Counter-Disinformation Activist Rhetorics

Instead of engaging in a futile debate with those who choose to circulate anti-Black disinformation, activists narrate their own truths rooted in the movement's philosophy of valuing Black life, which is also an act of community

1. BLM at the national level has been criticized in recent years for a number of issues that affect many large-scale movements, such as a potentially uneven distribution of resources across chapters, lack of donor transparency, and questionable property purchases by some of its leaders (Morrison).

care. They often refuse to engage with derailment tactics that seek to discredit and divert attention away from the movement and instead work to establish the terms of a different imaginary, rooted in Black liberation. Rhetorician Miriam F. Williams found in a study of #BlackLivesMatter Twitter discourse that derailments such as "All Lives Matter" or "black-on-black crime" are common disinformation tropes that users deploy against BLM, but despite the persistence of these disinformation attacks, BLM activists often choose not to engage directly, instead doubling down on their message and mission; in doing so, they refuse to cede ground to the idea that "Black lives matter" could be a debatable claim.

Choosing not to engage directly with disinformation can be an effective strategy in digital spaces. As the design of social media platforms does not differentiate between a user interacting with content because they agree with it or because they disagree, all interactions are just engagement, which drives profit. Thus, direct engagement with disinformation on social media, even for the purpose of correcting it, can cause the disinformation to circulate more widely. Instead, activists may choose to circulate counternarratives that do not engage directly with disinformation but seek to drown it out (e.g., encouraging a high volume of #BlackLivesMatter posts with narratives of Black life, rather than arguing directly with a post about "black-on-black crime"). BLM activists' strategies are influenced by de-escalation, a method of resisting abuse tactics and preventing violence. Through their rhetoric, they de-escalate and defuse disinformation claims by bringing the focus back to their mission. Further, BLM uses narrative on a broader scale in order to create and sustain a shared movement imaginary that affirms Black experiences without homogenizing them and insists on critical connections between personal narratives and larger oppressive systems. This specific yet capacious imaginary helps the movement sustain accountability to its abolitionist vision.

As BLM cofounder Patrisse Khan-Cullors explains: "We're trying to re-imagine humanity and bring us to a place where we can decide how we want to be in relation to each other versus criminalising our neighbours or being punitive towards them" (Wahlquist). This "re-imagination" and corresponding use of narrative has deep roots. As Robin D. G. Kelley details in *Freedom Dreams: The Black Radical Imagination,* imagination and creative praxis have always been a vital part of Black movements. As one example, the Afrofuturist tradition uses imagination as a form of creative activist praxis (see Carrington; brown and Imarisha; Jackson and Moody-Freeman; Nelson; Womack). Literacy education scholar Ebony Elizabeth Thomas points to an "Afrofuturistic renaissance of the late 2010s" including Jenna Wortham and Kimberly Drew's multimedia anthology *Black Futures,* Natasha Marin's work *Black Imagination:*

Black Voices on Black Futures, science fiction writer N. K. Jemisin's collection *How Long 'til Black Future Month?,* and many others. Importantly, imaginative work is not separate from movement-building. For example, activist adrienne maree brown draws from Afrofuturism and science fiction in her organizing, writing, and facilitating, using the theory of "emergent strategy" to ask "how we intentionally change in ways that grow our capacity to embody the just and liberated worlds we long for" (*Emergent Strategy* 3).

Compared with such a focus on radical imagination, many currently dominant approaches to challenging disinformation are normatively presentist and limited by a white liberal imaginary. They focus largely on solutions that can be used in the present moment or the short-term, immediate future to respond to discrete pieces of misinformation (i.e., live fact-checking of a debate, which is important but unlikely to be read by those who already believe disinformation), or approaches that look to the immediate future but not very far (i.e., a new media literacy curriculum in a school). There is nothing inherently wrong with focusing on present or short-term tactics, but without a larger, more radical future vision, there is no way for these to become part of larger systemic change. Many responses to the post-truth condition suffer from a failure of imagination.

It may seem counterintuitive to offer "imagination" as a counter to disinformation. Post-truth politics trade in imagined realities constructed by fictions, lies, and distractions, so the logical opposite would be facts and hard evidence. However, imagining is also a key tool for questioning dominating systems and thinking otherwise. As Jacqueline Jones Royster and Gesa Kirsch explain, "Imagination functions as a critical skill in questioning a viewpoint, an experience, an event, and so on, and in remaking interpretive frameworks based on that questioning" (83). Such work involves questioning the origins of truth claims and situating them within particular imaginaries, asking who has the power to decide how something is defined (such as the concept of violence, or the parameters for what kinds of social change are considered possible). The idea of imagining a better future sounds like an obvious component of activist rhetoric, with a feel-good connotation, but in practice, it is more complicated. Whose future gets imagined and how? Who gets to do the imagining? How do imagined futures guide practice in the present, by whom, and for whom?

Imagination involves narrative work, both in terms of narrating present or past conditions and narrating possibilities for the future. In addition to narrative's broader history in rhetorical studies (Cloud 43), Black feminist, queer, and critical race approaches to theory and activism have always engaged narrative and imagination as key strategies for analysis and social change (Atwater; Baker-Bell; Carey, *Rhetorical Healing*; Martinez; Richardson; Royster). Storytelling is central to the rhetoric of BLM (Browdy 17), part of not only the organization's genesis but also its growth, as the claim "Black Lives Matter" encourages the composition and circulation of stories about specific experiences of Black life. In its messaging, BLM chooses to center complex narratives of Black life that are often erased, including Black queer experiences, and to underline the importance of telling Black stories on Black terms; as rhetoricians Elaine Richardson and Alice Ragland write, "BLM expands upon Black language traditions and creates its own semiotic system and literacy practices to signify pride, resilience, and affirmation of all Black humanity" (29).

Narrative as an activist rhetorical strategy holds a complex position in relation to disinformation and post-truth politics. It is important to listen to the personal experiences of people experiencing oppression in the ways they choose to narrate these experiences. Activist and theoretical traditions with roots in Black, queer, and feminist struggle foreground embodied and experiential knowledge as a form of authority, working against the many ways in which those invested in oppressive systems deny the knowledge claims of oppressed populations in order to maintain power. At the same time, narrative does not automatically accomplish activist work, and the narratives of marginalized people may also be co-opted in order to maintain systems of power. For example, Karma R. Chávez engages with activist Yasmin Nair's critiques of personal narrative under neoliberal capitalism, in which political groups use the stories of oppressed people to prompt audiences to "feel bad" about the circumstances of those people; in this case, affective responses of "'feeling good' about helping an individual in a bad situation stand in place of a critique of the labor conditions and capitalist expansion that have created the bad conditions in the first place" (60). Relatedly, Sujatha Fernandes points to a "contemporary boom of storytelling" in political contexts, where "those relating their stories are individuals rather than members of a class or community," entering into conflict with other individuals rather than with "dominant classes or patriarchal structures" (6). In such cases, personal narrative can work against social change because such change is not possible when the focus is kept on the individual rather than on systems and structures.

While acknowledging the validity of these critiques, I also want to shift the focus here away from narratives that are told for dominant audiences or for the purpose of persuading people in power to sympathize with the suffering of oppressed people. Narrative also serves an important function *within* oppressed communities working for change, when the goal of narrative is not to appeal to a dominant audience but instead to construct a social movement imaginary capable of valuing community experiences without homogenizing these experiences. Such an imaginary must account for individual community members' truths without aiming to eliminate friction between those truths, and this process of negotiation is key to building accountability in intersectional movements such as BLM.

The work of honoring the experiential knowledge of marginalized people should be done without sanitizing it for dominant audiences, reducing members of an oppressed group to the same shared experiences, or treating one or a few members of that group as the only people with authority to narrate experiences of oppression. All of those moves reinforce a dominating imaginary, not only through misrepresentation but also by erasing the real conflicts and tensions that exist within activist communities. Especially in intersectional movements, decisions about messaging are far from straightforward. When deciding what messages to circulate, activist groups grapple with friction between representing real complexity (often for the benefit of audiences with shared identities and experiences, who can feel affirmed by seeing their complexity reflected) and simplifying representations to accomplish specific goals. In order to tease out these tensions and complexities, here I treat narrative not only as a relaying of one's personal experience, but as part of a larger imaginative and dialogic process that activist groups use to create shared knowledge. This shared activist epistemology, developed through imaginative work, becomes an important basis for countering disinformation. While I do not have access to the behind-the-scenes decisions that went into the works analyzed in this chapter, I focus on public-facing materials created by writers and artists associated with BLM in order to analyze their narrative and imaginative rhetorics, including memoirs by its founders and a digital project featuring a wider variety of BLM voices.

Narrative Activism in Black Lives Matter Memoirs

Several activists connected with Black Lives Matter have written memoirs where it is possible to see their orientation toward narrative activism and building accountability as a movement strategy, and the relation between these ideas. This section focuses on two of these: Patrisse Khan-Cullors's *When They Call You a Terrorist: A Black Lives Matter Memoir* (coauthored with asha bandele) and Alicia Garza's *The Purpose of Power: How We Come Together When We Fall Apart.* These works show BLM activists theorizing about the role of narrative in building and sustaining intersectional movements, and about the relationships among narrative, imagination, and accountability.

Khan-Cullors forwards a personal account of her activism and a theory of storytelling in *When They Call You a Terrorist.* It's easy to see the connection to post-truth rhetoric and disinformation in the title itself, where Khan-Cullors takes on the widespread disinformation designed to villainize Black Lives Matter. Khan-Cullors situates activist storytelling as both a form of resistance to and recovery from the trauma caused by right-wing disinformation attacks. As rhetorician Ronisha Browdy writes, Khan-Cullors's approach to countering the "terrorist" label is emblematic of one way BLM deals with disinformation attacks. In response to the claim "you are terrorists," her response is not "we are not terrorists"; instead, in the text of the memoir, it is the more unexpected move of "we are stardust" (Khan-Cullors 1). Browdy situates this rhetorical move as part of a strategy grounded in Black feminist storytelling (17). By fighting back in this way, Khan-Cullors signals that she does not intend to argue with a dominant audience on its own terms, which would mean implicitly agreeing to entertain the "terrorist" claim; instead, she aims for fidelity to the mission of BLM to value Black lives.

In her memoir, Khan-Cullors reframes "terror" as an element of racial trauma, using her own life narrative to contest the white supremacist imaginary wherein Black activists fighting violence are constructed as "terrorists," a term meant to consolidate national identity against those deemed to be outside "threats"—eliding the state-sanctioned violence that caused the need for an activist response. First, she frames the experience of being called a "terrorist" as a traumatizing event. She narrates how in 2016, after a sniper later identified as Micah Johnson who falsely claimed to be associated with BLM opened fire at a protest in Dallas, Texas, a petition circulated to the White House asking for BLM to be designated a terrorist organization. Khan-Cullors situates this "terrorist" accusation in a history of disinformation targeted at Black activists, "a tactic from the way back that has continuously been used against people who challenge white supremacy. We will remember that Nelson Mandela remained on the FBI's list of terrorists until 2008" (7). She then relates the personal trauma of having this label weaponized against her community: "Even still, the accusation of being a terrorist is devastating, and I allow myself space to cry quietly as I lie in bed on a Sunday morning listening to a red-faced, hysterical Rudolph Giuliani spit lies about us three days after Dallas" (7). Immediately after this, Khan-Cullors invokes the word "terror" in a way that moves its definition away from a white American nationalist imaginary wherein "terror" is a threat to the state, and into a Black imaginary, where what is "terror" is the daily violence of anti-Blackness: "Like many of the people who embody our movement, I have lived my life between the twin terrors of poverty and the police" (7).

She invokes "terror" in this way throughout the book, rhetorically shifting the term out of the control of those who would call BLM activists terrorists and placing it in its proper context: the terror of white supremacy. She narrates the story of her brother, Monte, who is incarcerated and tortured by police, and who does not receive treatment for his mental illness but is instead criminalized for it. Monte is charged with terrorism, a fact Khan-Cullors will return to throughout the book to emphasize the violent misuse of this term. After a fender bender with a white woman driver, who calls the police, "although his mental illness was as clear as the fact that he was Black, he was shot with rubber bullets and tased. And then he was charged with terrorism. Literally" (116). Khan-Cullors details the enraging arbitrariness of the charge: "If someone alleges that you have said something threatening to them and causing them to fear for their life, you can be charged, as my brother, who was in a full manic episode, was charged, with terrorism" (116). This charge of terrorism is considered logical within a dominant imaginary wherein it is accepted that a white woman is justified in feeling "threatened" by any interaction with a Black man, and that the Black man is the one to blame for this perceived threat. However, as Khan-Cullors reveals here, the charge is illogical when considered within a different imaginary wherein a Black man is experiencing a mental health crisis (likely exacerbated by racial trauma itself) and is in need of help.

After shifting the framework to define this charge as absurd rather than logical, heightened by Khan-Cullors's detailing of its devastating impact on Monte's life, she returns repeatedly to "terrorism" contextualized in white supremacy, as it has shapeshifted across time: "At the moment Jim Crow's back was broken, American politicians found myriad other ways—all legislated, all considered legal—to ensure that the terrorism that had always been the primary experience of Black people living in the United States continued" (209). Khan-Cullors concludes the book with an invocation of a new generation who will also have to fight the "terrorist" label, who will also know it is a violent example of disinformation designed to obscure the real terrors of living in an anti-Black society: "Terrorism is being stalked and surveilled simply because you are alive. And terrorism is being put in solitary confinement and starved and beaten. And terrorism is not being able to feed your children despite working three jobs. And terrorism is not having a decent school or a place to play" (283). Here, by the end of the memoir, "terrorism" has been redefined in a way that begins from Black experiences and imagines a future without these daily terrors. Further, against a white imaginary that takes as its foundational assumption the state as an entity worth protecting from "terrorist" threat, Khan-Cullors situates personal narratives within their historical context of anti-Black oppression, extending the timeline and scope of the story beyond the limited terms set according to the priorities of the state. In this framework now firmly grounded in a Black imaginary, it is meant to seem obvious that "terror" has always actually been anti-Blackness and other intersecting forms of state-sanctioned oppression.

Relatedly, in her book *The Purpose of Power,* BLM cofounder and longtime community organizer Alicia Garza offers a theory of political power in relation to narrative. Garza explains that contemporary conservativism has been very effective at constructing and circulating narratives, especially by using narrative strategies to unite large factions of people coming to conservatism for different reasons (e.g., those motivated by religion as well as those motivated by economic interests). People with a variety of specific motivations are able to come together under "the right's narrative: The story of America is about perseverance, rugged individualism, faith, and hard work" (192). This narrative requires other narratives that define people of color as outsiders to this "story of America":

> The right has invested in new narratives about communities of color, specifically about Black people and immigrants of Latin descent. Black women became welfare queens taking advantage of the government; immigrants became dangerous predators; Black men became angry gun-toting radicals who wanted to disrupt our way of life. Women finally inching toward breaking that glass ceiling became the reason and the rationale for broken homes and families and a changing way of life. (192)

Here, Garza specifies some of the "controlling images" (Hill Collins, *Black Feminist Thought*) that conservative movements have used to distort reality and demonize populations. The right—made up of coalitional alliances among various factions of conservative culture—unifies under a common narrative that is rooted in white supremacy as the same time as it obscures these roots.

While Garza focuses this part of her critique on the contemporary political right, the left also has its own controlling images. When liberal political groups use narratives, these are often simplified and sanitized narratives that attempt to appease dominant power, at the expense of those most marginalized by that power. In using these strategies, liberal movements fail to work toward substantive, transformative change that centers Black, queer, poor, and disabled communities. As Garza writes, it may be necessary for radical leftist movements to form coalitions with liberals, but not at the expense of complex narratives. Instead, radical storytelling can work in more powerful *and* nuanced ways to create truly coalitional movements, not just bland calls for "unity." Instead of using narrative as a medium for the spread of disinformation, radical narrative is rooted in the truth-telling of people experiencing oppression and in building relationality between people so they can unite against that oppression. One of the keys to using radical narrative to build coalitional movements is accountability—determining to whom and for what a movement should be answerable, in what contexts, and how.

Imagination as Narrative Activism in *Black Futures Month*

In addition to using narrative activism to connect personal experiences to larger systems and to ask how definitions change when removed from a white imaginative framework and understood within a Black imaginary, BLM activists also use narrative to imagine futures as a movement strategy. The act of imagining futures is one strategy to create accountability models that imagine what a world could look like if activist movements worked toward addressing the roots of interconnected oppressions with a focus on those most threatened by these oppressions. Imagining what a world without these deep-rooted oppressions could look like can act as an invention strategy for movement-building; in imagining this world, activists must ask whose struggles must be alleviated and what systems of power must end in order for this world to become a reality. They must also engage with a variety of narratives from community members with different positionalities and experiences, reckoning with potential friction among these rather than homogenizing them into one easily consumed story. In the process of this invention, a movement can build more accountability to its most vulnerable community members by centering its goal on the changes necessary to make a better world for those communities, rather than accepting the liberal charge to assimilate into the values and modes of engagement favored by dominant power, which at best only improves circumstances for those made less vulnerable by those systems.

Black Futures Month is one project that engages with these complex processes through its multiplicity of voices and the multimodal nature of its rhetoric. This project ran as a collaboration between the Black Lives Matter Global Network and the online *Huffington Post* Black Voices vertical for several years, from 2015 to 2017. The project became increasingly multimodal, beginning with writing, then pairing writing with visual art, then adding video and audio content. Each February during these years, the series published a daily post by Black creators, focused on the concept of Black futures. This was meant to shift attention away from Black *History* Month in the US, where

Black activism is often framed as something of the past and for which media coverage and education are often sanitized for a white audience. In contrast, the purpose of *Black Futures Month* was to represent radical, intersectional visions for Black liberation that invoked histories in order to imagine futures. By featuring writing and art from many different Black creators, the project increased its circulation potential beyond the preexisting audience of any one individual creator, and it also enacted the BLM ethos of valuing a multiplicity of voices (which other genres, like the memoirs by movement founders, are less equipped to do). In its partnership with a large digital media platform, *The Huffington Post, Black Futures Month* also had built-in infrastructure for publishing and circulating daily content. This content was likely to reach more audiences because of the exigence of Black History Month, and in the process aimed to challenge audiences to think outside a white imaginary that consigns Blackness to the past or that asks Black people to make concessions for survival in the present, but instead within a Black imaginary that is both historically grounded and future-oriented.

In *Black Futures Month,* images work as visual representations invoking an aesthetic and ethos tied to Black queer feminist futurity. The images do not only represent the topic of each day's post, but they also generate an aesthetic language for *Black Futures Month* and work across each other to make critical connections to other topics and the intersectional mission of *Black Futures Month* in general. Pragmatically, the images serve as the primary means of circulating each day's post on social media sites Twitter, Tumblr, Facebook, and Instagram while encouraging viewers to click through to the full post. Artworks are often associative and imaginative, representing specific Black struggles in the present or visions that invoke liberatory Black futures, with Afrofuturistic imagery especially common. In the written pieces, activists representing a variety of intersectional Black experiences write both in broad and specific terms about issues facing their communities and use the space to imagine what could be different in the future, and what conditions would need to change to help bring that about.

Shanelle Matthews, director of communications for the Black Lives Matter Global Network, writes in a 2017 *Black Futures Month* post about challenging white imaginaries:

> White people have long tethered the humanity of Black people to the whim of white imagination. The stories policymakers and racists tell about people like us and the places from which we come are predicated on assumptions imagined long before we were born by people who meant us harm. Those stories may be true for some individuals, but are untrue for whole

> communities. Those stories may have shaped the way people understand our place in the world, our trajectory and our value—but we do not assent.

Matthews ties the power of white imagination to a violation of consent. By saying "we do not assent," Matthews establishes anti-Black stories as a violation. By invoking a "we," Matthews is not only writing about her own experience but invoking a larger community. Not assenting is most effective as a collective act, making this framing of "we" especially important. Activists can challenge dominant imaginaries, but they must first come together to share experiences and in the process cocreate their own imaginaries. Matthews continues, "When we use dreaming and radical imagination as a strategy—like organizing, like communications, like fundraising—we can set concrete goals based in our highest visions and work in tandem to realize them." Imagining futures is framed here not as an abstract concept but as a deliberate choice, alongside organizing, communications, fundraising, and other strategies key to activist movements. Specifically, imagining futures operates as an invention strategy to maintain accountability to vulnerable communities by focusing on what needs to change for whom in order to work toward that world.

Imagining futures has generative potential, especially in light of the fact that oppression works in part by limiting imagination. In the 2016 post "Why Black People Must Hold on to Our Dreams," Black femme performance artist Kiyan Williams explains:

> Systems of domination wage wars against our psyches and imagination, constantly presenting us with realities in which, to put simply, Black people are dying in the present and have no possible future. The psychic oppression we experience as a result of anti-black state violence disallows the possibility for a world wherein Black people can live, let alone thrive. Under systems of domination, during times of hopelessness and pessimism, what compels us to keep fighting, to keeping on keeping on?

As Williams argues, one of the ways oppression works is by disallowing the possibility of imagining a future. Systems of domination control the movement of bodies and the movement of minds, placing limits on what it seems possible to imagine. In response to this "psychic oppression," Williams frames imagining Black futures as an intervention that is vital to activism:

> In order for me to be alive right now I had to be able to dream and conjure images of resistance, presents wherein my people fought and resisted police violence, futures beyond white supremacist cis heteropatriarchy that

> I wanted to inhabit. Our imaginations nurture the fire of liberation. They allows us to experiment and explore alternative realities like: what does a world without police and prisons look like? And how can we exist and love outside of the gender binary, transmisogyny, and systems of domination[?]

This rhetoric insists on the necessity for intersectional messaging in the invention of activist futures—or else we are limited to thinking only of minor adjustments but remaining within an oppressive imaginary.

Instead of only sharing personal experiences of oppression in the present, *Black Futures Month* creators engage in imaginative work that connects specific individual needs with the end of larger oppressive systems, revealing the bleak state of our current world through expressions of desire for another one. As Biko writes in the 2016 post "Black Trans Lives Matter Too":

> I dream a world in which all black lives matter. A world where we are not poisoned by the water and genetically modified foods. I dream a world where our black bodies are not criminalized because of sex work or HIV/AIDS. I dream a world where we have complete and total access to the entire universe without barriers or borders. I envision a world without prisons and without police. I envision a world that supplies our basic needs like . . . housing and medical care for all people.

Here, Biko moves between registers: the specific and tangible (not being poisoned by the water) juxtaposed with the broad and intangible ("the entire universe," no "barriers or borders"). She also connects the ability to access certain things (like housing and medical care) with the necessary absence of existing systems that block that access (like prisons and police). She also makes an implicit argument that the ability to envision a world without oppression begins by asking what currently oppressed people need the most, especially those oppressed by intersecting systems of power such as Black women, girls, and queer and trans people, whom Biko's specific examples focus on (as Black trans women, for example, are a population currently most likely to be criminalized for sex work). Imagining better worlds for these communities is not just a tool for inclusion; it changes the work itself. Beyond a limited liberal imaginary that can only conceive of change within the terms of the existing social order, what Biko is calling for is a future specifically imagined to meet the needs of those most oppressed by that social order. When meeting the needs of these communities is a prioritized future goal, movements cannot call themselves successful while also leaving these people behind. In other words, narrating the possibilities of imagined futures for those currently oppressed can also create movement accountability in the present.

The accompanying image to Biko's piece, by visual artist Ethan Parker, makes use of Afrofuturistic imagery to portray Blackness and transness as communal technologies of resistance. The image features two people who are physically linked at the shoulders. On the left is a Black person with pink hair, piercings, and a third eye on their forehead; on the left is another Black person with blue hair and a visor covering their eyes, gauged earlobes, and green lips with a piercing. They are also linked behind their heads by a box full of wires, with some of the wires cut and others growing into DNA strands above the two interlinked figures; these strands also contain lines of computer code. In front of the figures is an overlay of text: "We are Black & Trans," with the hashtag #BlackLivesMatter below. The image emphasizes community and technology through the interconnectedness of the figures, the interwoven DNA strands, and the computer code and wire imagery. It evokes Black transness as not only an individual but also a community experience, mediated by technologies of self- and community creation. Alongside Biko's words, the artwork unites Black trans histories, presents, and futures. As Biko concludes the piece, "Before western concepts of gender bankrupted our social capital, we served as the mediators, the healers and the griots. It's my hope that in the future black trans folks will be loved, respected, included, paid, healthy and free." Here, Biko emphasizes that Black trans communities have always existed, long before a colonialist and white supremacist binary gender system. By framing Black trans people as "the healers and the griots," Biko invokes a history through which they have used the technologies available to them to do the important rhetorical work of community care, narrative, and preservation.

In the 2015 post "Every Breath a Black Trans Woman Takes Is an Act of Revolution," Lourdes Ashley Hunter, national director of the Trans Women of Color Collective, juxtaposes dominant American narratives of history with the truth of colonization: "We were indoctrinated to believe America (stolen land) was discovered (invaded) by colonist[s] (murderers, rapists, thieves) exploring the free world. We are still denied our history to this day." By placing the indoctrination (America was discovered by colonists and explorers) next to the historical corrective of what really happened (America was violently invaded), Hunter begins from an argument based in definition, similar to the work that Khan-Cullors does with "terror." However, Hunter includes another level of historicization by narrating how Black trans women have often been left out of reclamation and redefinition narratives *within* Black communities:

> It wasn't until I was a young adult that I realized that my life would be very different from what I had imagined. I had no idea that I would face brutal violence and structural oppression simply for existing. I had no idea I could be legally denied access to medical care, housing and employment. I never imagined that I would have to fight for basic human rights. These experiences are similar to the ones my mom told me she experienced growing up in the 50's. Similar to the ones the history books [have] re-written for the glorification and commodification of white supremacy. I thought the fight for Black folk to obtain civil rights in this country happened over 45 years ago. What I realized is that fight was not for the liberation of the Black Trans Woman.

Hunter historicizes her experiences of oppression as a Black trans woman in terms of the erasure of colonialist and anti-Black violence in white narrations of history *and* in an elision of trans narratives within Black communities. In response, Hunter makes an argument that Black trans women's experiences should be further historicized for a fuller understanding of the deep-rooted, interconnecting oppressions that emerge from these histories. In an environment where white supremacy benefits from erasing or misrepresenting Black experiences, it is also necessary to refuse homogenous representations of progress and liberation and instead ask more specific questions about whose needs are prioritized when, in what ways, and with what consequences. Such questions reveal friction among different movement members' narratives, but this can become a productive friction rather than one that must be resolved immediately.

In another piece, the 2017 post "Uncaged Black Futures Now," Black Lives Matter Urbana-Champaign organizer Kadeem Fuller narrates the historical timeline of white supremacist domination (from colonization, abduction, and enslavement, to Jim Crow, to mass incarceration), establishing a unified narrative of shared oppression. Then, Fuller shifts the focus to the contemporary chapter of this story, mass incarceration, and complexifies the shared narrative: "The rise of the carceral state has only continued to take the hopes, futures and lives of many amongst us. The United States warehouses 25 percent of the world's prison population and the silhouettes in those cages are disproportionately Black women, Black trans folk and Black men." These people are first framed as "silhouettes in cages," stripped of identity and difference, but Fuller reinscribes their identities as "Black women, Black trans folk and Black men," in the process also working to disrupt the common focus only on Black men—the default silhouette in much public discourse on incarceration—by placing Black women and trans folk first in this sequence of naming. In this way, Fuller also builds a narrative strategy capable of holding shared histories while also reckoning with specificity and difference.

The artwork accompanying Fuller's piece echoes and builds upon the ideas in the writing. The image by Damon Locks features a dark color palette and carceral imagery. At the bottom of the image, three sketched figures appear with their features mostly obscured, staring straight ahead at the viewer. Each figure is portrayed as an arrested subject, holding signs stating "Police Dept. Chicago, IL" and a mostly obscured booking date. Behind the figures, vertical slashes connote prison bars. Above this section of the image is a black space with text written over it, connoting a graffitied wall; the text reads, "We are disappearing behind these walls #BlackLivesMatter," "End mass incarceration," and other related statements. Above this section, at the top of the image, there is an urban skyline emerging from the black wall and then a lighter section where there are silhouettes of birds. The image's progression from darkness at the bottom to a small amount of lightness and space at the top indicates that the people at the bottom are being hidden away, incarcerated behind an impenetrable dark wall, and meant to be forgotten. The graffitied slogans between these people and the city skyline, however, serve as a reminder of why the state is trying to incarcerate them and separate them from public life and visibility. The skyline and hints of birds at the top connote two simultaneous things: a small amount of hope and fresh air at the top of the image, but also a reminder of what is inaccessible to the people at the bottom of the image who are incarcerated. Locks's image reminds viewers that white supremacy benefits from mass incarceration and asks viewers not to look away, but to remember the obscured figures being forced into this system and out of sight; paired with this, Fuller's writing also asks readers not to homogenize this population under "Blackness" alone but also to attend to difference (i.e., how gendered violence manifests differently for incarcerated Black trans women than for Black cis men or another population).

In *Black Futures Month,* artists and writers use narratives of past, present, and future as a way to theorize ways to imagine a society not built upon anti-Blackness, heteropatriarchy, colonialism, and other interconnected systems of domination. By imagining these alternative possibilities, these creators pinpoint ways in which the current order of things is not natural but was built in service of the specific interests of those who benefit from white supremacy, and how people in power maintain that power in part by controlling the public imagination. The writers and artists of *Black Futures Month* denaturalize dominant and normativizing societal practices through their critiques, using creative works to make them strange again. Above everything, these futures center the needs of communities facing intersecting oppressions and imagine, in detail, a world without those oppressions, in order to begin advocating for the conditions where that might be possible.

Imagination, in the creative activist works analyzed in this chapter, is an accountability practice. Through imagining futures, activist communities engage in invention strategies that may also help community members with different positionalities think through both the shared features of and the friction between their narratives. Friction, or moments of narrative difference and specificity, can be a generative signal rather than something to eliminate in service of constructing a shared vision, for example through asking whose needs should be prioritized and why, an essential component of building accountability. This sense of accountability, understood as commitment to a movement's vision for intersectional liberation without homogenization, is necessary for the construction of a shared imaginary. A strong shared imaginary is vital for movements to be able to successfully challenge disinformation. This imaginary—deeper than a shared present reality and set of priorities—can also be the most difficult thing for new movements to negotiate.

CHAPTER 2

Activist Relational Knowledge against Digital Disinformation in Black Lives Matter and the Women's March

It is now well known that the Russian state-sponsored Internet Research Agency (IRA) interfered in the 2016 US presidential election. Agents created multiple Twitter accounts, often linked to a network of other social media accounts, websites, and fake media platforms. These accounts were widespread; according to the US House of Representatives Permanent Select Committee on Intelligence, there are 2,752 suspended IRA Twitter accounts, which likely does not include all of them. Rather than simply posting incorrect information, the IRA infiltration worked by "connecting to cultural narratives that people know, enacting stereotypes, and modeling how to react to information" (Arif et al. 2). These information agents were not just publishing biased information or circulating false narratives but performing a campaign of influence that was more fluid, nuanced, and difficult to counter. The goal of such information operations is "not necessarily to convince someone of something, but to strategically direct discourse in ways that 'kill the possibility of debate and a reality-based politics,'" partly by "strategically and opportunistically tapping into latent social fractures" (Arif et al. 3). Different forms of disinformation had different goals. In the case of conservative-targeted content circulated by RU-IRA agents, the goal of the messaging was usually to accept a pro-Trump stance. However, for other content, especially that which referenced social justice issues, the goal was not such overt persuasion, but rather motivating audiences to disengage through overwhelm and exhaustion (Bradshaw 9). In this context, white liberal democratic modes of engagement like rational deliberation and civic discourse are irrelevant.

As these complicated online disinformation campaigns become more widespread, rhetorical studies has renewed its commitment to understanding how disinformation spreads, and further, what the prevalence of disinformation tells us about the complexity of political rhetoric in an era characterized as post-truth. As Jim Ridolfo and William Hart-Davidson explain, "The militarized deployment of digital rhetoric is now part of our everyday lives—that is, the production and proliferation of mass disinformation campaigns" (4). However, studies of disinformation have often failed to contend with race and racism (Mejia et al. 110). Further, scholarly efforts to counter disinformation campaigns have often ignored how multiply marginalized groups have always had to contend with disinformation and have developed innovative strategies for doing so. In this case, one site of interference was the attempted co-optation of online #BlackLivesMatter discourse, but in many ways, IRA agents got it wrong.

Analyzing some of the strategies that Black activist communities use to challenge disinformation helps to show how culturally specific rhetorical practices can be highly effective in countering disinformation campaigns on a grassroots level. As explored in the previous chapter, BLM as a movement has a strong imaginary and an extensive collection of shared rhetorical resources developed through movement history and negotiation. This chapter will focus in particular on one element of this activist rhetorical imagination—relational knowledge—as an important resource for fighting disinformation. However, as a later example from the Women's March will show, if a movement is new or coalitionally fragile, lacking an agreed-upon shared imaginary and repertoire of cultural rhetorical practices to draw from, this can make the movement more vulnerable to disinformation attacks, which add more noise and distortion to the process of movement identity formation.

Framing social movement imaginaries and rhetorical resources as central to counter-disinformation efforts allows for an exploration of how activists negotiate fraught technological spaces. "Technology" has often been a scapegoat for political disinformation, with a variety of more specific targets (i.e., social media, algorithms, filter bubbles, etc.). It is true that digital technologies such as social media algorithms do foster the rapid circulation of disinformation, and that these technologies have permanently altered politics. As informatics scholar Safiya U. Noble has extensively studied, forms of oppression, including racism and sexism, get encoded into technologies, and this harms multiply marginalized communities. However, as Noble and others also emphasize, it is insufficient to stop at blaming the technology alone.

Instead, we must look at the root causes for phenomena like "algorithmic inequity," including white supremacy, heteropatriarchy, and colonialism (see also Browne; Wachter-Boettcher). Changing technologies without interrogating deeper systems of oppression not only leaves these systems in place, but also allows for what sociologist Ruha Benjamin calls "technological beneficence"—the tendency of tech companies to rhetorically frame themselves as society's saviors while covering up ongoing oppression (36).

When studying disinformation campaigns and how to counter them, the relational knowledge of multiply marginalized activist communities has much to teach rhetoricians. The following section analyzes the IRA's rhetorical strategies in targeting Black Americans and exploiting American racism, as well as how government reports and media coverage frame Black Americans in relation to these disinformation campaigns. Then, I detail a theory of antiracist relational knowledge grounded in Black rhetorical practices, explaining how relational knowledge can work as an activist strategy of countering disinformation. I demonstrate these concepts through an analysis of examples of Black Lives Matter activists successfully challenging disinformation through relational knowledge, both on a local level and through attracting national media coverage for their resistance. In this way, localized relational knowledge became the basis for activists to use media coverage to circulate counternarratives to disinformation more broadly, helping reclaim some control over the narrative. After these examples, I turn to a counterexample of Russian online disinformation that aimed to exploit the fractures of the nascent Women's March movement.

While these movements are too different for a one-to-one comparison, especially in terms of connections between local chapters and a broader movement vision, I present them side by side here to prompt considerations about the pace of movement growth in the context of disinformation attacks. For BLM chapters, their deep and specific rooting in Black activist rhetorical traditions allowed them to react quickly to disinformation and then to achieve media visibility and broader circulation in service of their own goals. However, the Women's March became more vulnerable to similar disinformation attacks partly because it grew too quickly and lacked deep roots in a specific resistance tradition, attempting instead to negotiate a coalitional identity on the fly, facing time-bound pressure as a movement brought into being as a response to Trump's election. These different examples of movements negotiating a digital disinformation environment allow rhetoricians to consider the value of slowness, not only speed, in developing counter-disinformation strategies.

The IRA Campaign's Targeting of Black Americans

As part of a larger campaign designed to tap into American tensions in order to create confusion and disorientation online, Russian IRA agents attempted to co-opt online #BlackLivesMatter rhetoric. To study this infiltration into social media posts related to #BlackLivesMatter, informatics scholars Ahmer Arif, Leo Stewart, and Kate Starbird compiled and analyzed a data set of around 250,000 tweets between 2015 and 2016 containing the terms "BlackLivesMatter," "BlueLivesMatter," or "AllLivesMatter," and that included information about police shootings. In the official government reports and media reporting on Russian interference into the 2016 election, Black Americans are often framed as the targets of disinformation (DiResta et al. 8; Howard et al. 16–17), rather than as agents who were successful in fighting disinformation—even though several groups of Black activists have had success in countering disinformation in their local communities. Such targeting was not necessarily an effort to recruit Black Americans to a particular ideology, but one method in an arsenal of strategies designed to foster chaos and conflict. IRA agents working with the Trump campaign created accounts across the American political spectrum and used them to stage fake conflicts to stoke a sense of "polarization." It is also worth noting that the targeting of Black Americans may actually be a method of indirectly targeting white Americans, who were the observing audience for distorted performances of Blackness. Theodore Johnson, a scholar of Black voting behavior, explains that Russian accounts may have put "black activist language out on social media in order to scare white citizens into thinking their nation was changing, and mobilize white voters in support of Trump. . . . Black folks were not the target for that. . . . I'm convinced the 'Blue Lives Matter' crowd was the target there" (Lartey). Although the reports and media coverage often frame Black Americans as the unwitting targets of Russian disinformation, in actuality, Black Americans are among the most politically sophisticated groups in the US (Cohen, *Democracy*; Tate).

Though it is impossible to fully determine the efficacy of IRA tactics (DiResta et al. 58), it is clear that fake Russian accounts attempted to subtly manipulate people through micro-targeting and playing on emotional associations. For example, as journalist April Glaser reports for *Slate,* "Hundreds of ads were bought about American racism, laser-targeted to people interested in, to take a few examples, 'Understanding racial segregation in the United States,' and 'Martin Luther King, Jr.' and 'Black is beautiful' and the 'African American Civil Rights Movement (1954–68).'" Further, IRA accounts tried to infiltrate racial justice discourse by using the hashtag #BlackLivesMatter on a variety of posts. However, not all these accounts' content was highly politicized. Part of their emotional manipulation strategy worked by drawing in viewers with more innocuous content and building a base audience this way, who would then be there when the accounts posted more politicized content.

Fake accounts "used cultural, linguistic, and identity markers in their Twitter profiles to align themselves with the shared values and norms of either the left- or right-leaning clusters" (Arif et al. 12), and these markers were infused across their profiles—from their choice of profile picture to who they followed to the phrasing of their content. Further, agents aimed to create content that would be difficult to fact-check and often avoided overt acts of political persuasion like presenting arguments and claims, so it would be inaccurate to understand this content as "fake news" (Bradshaw 7). As Jonathan L. Bradshaw explains, the IRA's social media strategies work through accumulation, with the goal of "rhetorical exhaustion," or the "active means of circulating rhetorical material to halt discourse, redirect the rhetorical trajectories of public deliberations, or demobilize publics" (2). Through exhaustion, audiences are persuaded not to take a specific political stance but instead to disengage from political processes altogether, which is why Bradshaw argues the IRA campaign is better understood as voter suppression rather than political persuasion (8).

The Russian accounts made use of textual, visual, and multimodal resources such as memes to engage in mimicry and circulate their content. At first glance, these seem to mimic the rhetoric that circulates in online social justice communities, but to someone immersed in the Black activist tradition, they fall short. For instance, they tend to evoke simplistic understandings of historic figures such as Martin Luther King Jr. and Malcolm X. To counter disinformation like the above examples, a deep racial justice literacy is needed—the kind that Black activist communities have long cultivated and shared through networks of relations. Against the oppressive technology of race, Black activists' relational knowledge works as an antiracist technology. The following section provides a theoretical framework for understanding relational knowledge as a strategy for countering disinformation. Then I offer an analysis of two cases where Black Lives Matter activists in Minneapolis and Baltimore were able to counter an instance of disinformation by mobilizing their relational knowledge at the local level, which also led to media coverage and a wider circulation of their messaging.

Relational Knowledge

Relational knowledge is a specific kind of localized activist knowledge that draws its expertise from community epistemologies, connections with others, and movement histories. BLM is a movement grounded in a Black queer feminist epistemology, which influences the movement's understanding of relationality. Keith Gilyard and Adam Banks explain that much African American rhetoric foregrounds relationality and cocreation, in contrast with the more individualistic worldview of Aristotelian rhetoric. Modalities such as call-and-response require audience participation and co-constructed meaning, rather than "people independently manipulating 'means' to persuade others through 'delivery'" (Gilyard and Banks 47–48). Patricia Hill Collins writes that the four elements of a Black feminist epistemology are "lived experience as a criterion of meaning, the use of dialogue, the ethic of personal accountability, and the ethic of caring" (*Black Feminist Thought* 266), all of which foreground relational ways of being and acting.

Relationality is a key part of radical community activist groups (Licona and Chávez 96; Licona and Russell 2). Adela C. Licona and Karma R. Chávez posit the concept of relational literacies as "understandings and knowings in the world that are never produced singularly or in isolation but rather depend on interaction. This interdependency animates the coalitional possibilities inherent in relational literacies" (96). Scholars have also theorized relationality in terms of cross-community solidarity (Ramos; Del Hierro et al.), as well as coalition-building that foregrounds negotiations across positionalities (Chávez). Further, relational knowledge describes not only activists' relationships with others in the present, such as a local community, but also connections over time. For instance, Eric Darnell Pritchard describes how, in addition to relations with those in the present, relations with movement histories are vital for Black LGBTQ people (103).

The question "Who are your people?" is key to relational knowledge. Civil rights organizer Ella Baker was known for asking this question. It exemplified Baker's approach to organizing, which emphasized community-building and the power of ordinary people to make change, rather than traditional models of top-down charismatic leadership. In radical activism with the goal of systemic change, it is imperative "to find out who we are, where we have come from and where we are going" (E. Baker), a process enabled by relational knowledge. Scholar Barbara Ransby details in her book *Ella Baker and the Black Freedom Movement: A Radical Democratic Vision* that "who one's people were was important to Ella Baker, not to establish an elite pedigree, but to locate an individual as part of a family, a community, a region, a culture, and a historical period. Baker recognized that none of us are self-made men or women; rather, we forge our identities within kinship networks, local communities, and organizations" (14). These networks, communities, and organizations, and the knowledge and modes of interaction they build slowly over time and work to sustain, are key to an activist group's ability to counter disinformation attacks.

Knowing "who are your people" helps activist communities detect who is not being a respectful guest in the movement. A localized activist community is what Jacqueline Jones Royster terms a "home place" (32), and disinformation actors are intruders. Cross-community discourse and coalition-building are certainly possible when respect for others' "home places" is foregrounded. However, communities are rightly suspicious of those who enter "home places" without the necessary respect and knowledge. The ability for community members to detect what is a good-faith effort at connection and what is an intrusion is a function of relational knowledge: the knowledge that an activist community has built up over time, influenced by movement histories, with a deep sense of who each other's people are.

Baker's question of "Who are your people?," combined with Royster's concept of "home places," represent a relational approach to organizing that can be seen in today's Black Lives Matter movement, which is coalitional and nonhierarchical, rooted in localized community-building rather than top-down leadership. Rather than being victims of disinformation campaigns, many Black activists are innovators who develop ways to resist disinformation that are rooted in their lives and worldviews. To these ends, the following section uses two examples to illustrate relational knowledge in action. I start with an overview of how Black Lives Matter responded to reports of Russian interference. Then, I amplify how local groups of Black activists in two cities used relational knowledge to counter attempted IRA co-optation of Black Lives Matter discourse online, and how these efforts also led to wider media circulation of shared movement narratives.

Black Lives Matter Activists' Relational Knowledge

Black Lives Matter's Movement Rhetoric

As Elaine Richardson and Alice Ragland describe, Black Lives Matter is rooted in Black literacy traditions, "through the purposeful use of Black language, communicative practices, and new literacies" (52). At the same time, Black language, cultural practices, and activism are frequently co-opted by other groups, whether through appropriation or distortion. As BLM cofounders Cullors, Garza, and Tometi, among other activists, consistently remind audiences, those seeking to discredit BLM often decontextualize and distort its messaging. In 2016 Russian information agents were just the latest example of bad-faith actors engaged in this mission.

In the official response to the Senate Intelligence Committee reports on Russian interference, Black Lives Matter stated, "The Black Lives Matter Global Network understands that it is a target as we continue to fight for Black liberation across the globe, and we will not be deterred by those attempting to exploit us and the millions of Black folks in America who vote and demand change. We will continue to work tirelessly to challenge white supremacy, injustice, and oppression throughout the world" ("Black Lives Matter"). The statement goes on to reiterate the origins and mission of Black Lives Matter, foregrounding the relations that sustain the movement: "Founded in 2013 by Patrisse Cullors, Alicia Garza, and Opal Tometi in response to the acquittal of Trayvon Martin's murderer, Black Lives Matter Global Network is a chapter-based, member-led organization in the US, UK, and Canada." They foreground BLM's intersectional mission—"We support the lives of the Black queer and transgender communities, the disabled, the undocumented, those with records, women, and all Black lives along the gender spectrum"—and end with its radical imagination: "By combating and countering acts of violence, creating space for Black imagination and innovation, and centering Black joy, we are winning immediate improvements in our lives." BLM's to-the-point response acknowledges the Senate reports but quickly pivots to highlight the actual work being done by BLM activists. They also refocus attention on systemic anti-Blackness, underlining the fact that this, not Russian interference, is the real problem.

Activists in local BLM chapters were able to use similar rhetorical moves to counter specific instances of IRA appropriation. They fight these attempts at appropriating BLM rhetoric by noticing their incongruity with current movement rhetoric, prioritizing care for local communities who may be threatened by the appropriation, and using media attention to attempt to redirect broader audiences' focus away from disinformation and toward the activists' mission of improving the quality of Black lives. As Bradshaw argues in his work on rhetorical exhaustion and Russian trolling, counterstrategies such as sharing an example of disinformation in order to point out its factual inaccuracy are actually ineffective in this context. To a social media platform, any such responses are "engagement," no matter the motivation, and sharing with the purpose of discrediting often only serves to perpetuate the disinformation's spread. Further, because the goal of disinformation campaigns like Russian trolling of American politics is not persuasion through fact-based appeals but rather amplification through the force of accumulation, fighting this accumulation requires a counterintuitive strategy: not more speed and volume, but more slowness and specificity (Bradshaw 11). In the case of the BLM chapters included below, activists are able to respond *quickly* to community risks posed by fake online content because of the *slow* relationship and knowledge-building they and others in the broader movement have already done over a long period of time.

Mobilization of Relational Knowledge by Minneapolis BLM

On July 6, 2016, police shot and killed thirty-two-year-old Philando Castile in a Minneapolis suburb. Castile's girlfriend, Diamond Reynolds, had been recording the police stop, and the shooting was streamed on Facebook. Only a few hours after the shooting, a Facebook page with the name "Don't Shoot" started targeting people living near the Twin Cities and promoting an event called "Justice for Philando Castile," advertised with a date, time, and location in Saint Paul. This profile and the event were eventually revealed to be run by a fake Russian account, which activists did not know at the time, though they found it suspicious enough to investigate (O'Sullivan). The Minneapolis BLM chapter was later featured in a CNN article and short documentary about Russian trolls' use of social media to interfere in American politics.

In the CNN interview, chapter leader Mica Grimm described that something felt wrong about the event because no one in the tight-knit local activist community knew who was running it. Rhetorical awareness was a key part of this felt sense, because the language was off; Grimm thought the name Don't Shoot was a dated formulation at that moment. The phrase "Hands up, don't shoot" was common after the murder of Michael Brown in Ferguson in 2014, but Grimm explains that by 2016, "many Black Lives Matter activists were no longer using the chant because they felt it was submissive and they wanted to focus on language that they felt was more empowering" (O'Sullivan). As Grimm also said during the CNN short documentary, because no one knew the people behind Don't Shoot, experienced activists decided "we need to reach out to these people to make sure they don't put anyone in danger."

Another activist, Sam Tyler, contacted the Don't Shoot page to ask who was organizing the event, and they responded by referencing the names of local groups, but the people Tyler, Grimm, and others knew who were working for these groups also did not know who was behind Don't Shoot. Eventually, as

Tyler described to CNN, "After talking to them a little bit back and forth and realizing that they were completely making up everything that they had been saying . . . we decided to present them either the ultimatum of either handing us administrative access to the event page or we were going to dissuade people, through a press release, through whatever means we had, of showing up to this event" (O'Sullivan). Don't Shoot gave in and handed control of the Facebook event to these activists. Grimm explains, "Our solution was to take over the event and have our own marshals and have our own leaders, and a lot of other organizations helped us do that. Just to make sure that if people were going to show up, that people weren't putting themselves in a position of danger" (O'Sullivan). This example reveals that, although the Russian accounts' use of language and other tropes may seem accurate to outsiders, to insider audiences it often rings false in subtle but important ways.

The Minneapolis BLM activists mobilized a local response to the fake event that focused on protecting their community from potential exposure to risk, and in the aftermath, they used the visibility of the CNN article and documentary to highlight their own expertise and redirect attention back to the real matters at hand: protesting police violence and memorializing Castile. Grimm demonstrates expertise in the current activist rhetoric of Black Lives Matter by explaining the datedness of the "don't shoot" language and pointing out how she used this as a cue for the insincerity of the account. Grimm and Tyler also establish their expertise in organizing when they speak about putting safeguards in place to make sure that those attending the protest would not be put in danger. In a media environment when it is commonly represented that anyone with a digital presence can be an activist, Grimm and Tyler are drawing attention to the extensive skills and experience needed to actually accomplish meaningful community action. In the process, they refute the Don't Shoot account through emphasizing the holes in its performance of activism, which in turn reveal Don't Shoot's lack of expertise.

Further, Grimm and Tyler emphasize the importance of community networks, highlighting the in-person local communities that are essential to activism and pointing out that the digital presence of Don't Shoot is meaningless without an ability to show connections with local groups. In *Unapologetic: A Black, Queer, and Feminist Mandate for Radical Movements,* activist Charlene A. Carruthers draws on that question of Ella Baker's, "Who are your people?," to argue that the work of community organizing requires understanding who one is in relation with, which also depends on one's positionality, *and* the degree to which one enacts accountability to those people (98–99; see also Ransby 14). Through this lens, Tyler, Grimm, and the other activists in Minneapolis are basically asking the Don't Shoot page, "Who are your people?" Don't Shoot's deflection and inability to answer serves as further evidence of inauthenticity. When asked, Don't Shoot cannot name its people. Grimm and Tyler recognize this not only through their experiential knowledge as long-time local activists, but also through the ways this knowledge is informed by the movement history and theory of Black Lives Matter—grounded in the Black radical, queer, and feminist tradition, the movement foregrounds consciousness of positionality and relationality and emphasizes the need to be accountable to those with whom one is in community. By foregrounding these issues when interviewed by CNN, Minneapolis BLM activists take advantage of a moment of national visibility to draw attention to the role of the local, specific, and relational in countering disinformation.

Mobilization of Relational Knowledge by Baltimore BLM

In a similar move to Don't Shoot, a Facebook profile named "Blacktivist," later revealed to be another fake IRA account, created an event for an anniversary march in honor of Freddie Gray, who was killed by Baltimore police using excessive force in an arrest. Criminal charges were filed against the police officers involved, but the charges were dropped (Lopez). Local activists in Baltimore were skeptical of the Blacktivist page claiming to be organizing an anniversary event in honor of Gray because they did not know who was behind it. They mobilized locally in ways similar to the response of the Minneapolis BLM chapter, and also used national media coverage about Russian disinformation to redirect attention back to their mission.

In this case, the efforts of Baltimore BLM activists were covered in an article in *The Guardian* about Russian attempts to appropriate Black activist rhetoric for the purpose of sowing division. While the activists, at the time when they first discovered the Blacktivist profile, did not know it was a fake Russian account, they did know that something was off about it. In the *Guardian* article, local pastor and community organizer Heber Brown III explains that he initially thought the Blacktivist account "was an out-of-town figure trying to co-opt the local movement for publicity," and activist Jamye Wooten thought the account "could be an undercover police officer spying on protesters" (Levin). Both these activists and others knew that there was something inauthentic about the event and the account behind it because of their historical knowledge: They assumed it was a new example of either co-optation of a Black movement by an individual hoping for personal gain or surveillance of a Black movement by police, both processes with long histories.

Like Sam Tyler in Minneapolis, Brown messaged the Blacktivist account on Facebook to find out who was behind it. Soon after the exchange that followed, Brown circulated a screenshot of the conversation in a public Facebook post. Brown began by asking whether the person behind Blacktivist lived in Baltimore: "I'm just hearing that you're not from Baltimore. Is this true? Are you a local organizer/activist or not?" Blacktivist responded, "Me personally—no. But there are people in Baltimore. Volunteers. We are looking for friendship, because we are fighting for the same reasons. Actually we are open for your thoughts and offers." Brown countered by offering a moment of activist education: "But this is not the way to organize. You should have started with the conversations before you organized an event here. The way you're going about this is deeply offensive to those of us who are from Baltimore and have been organizing here all our lives. If you want friendship, come listen and learn before you lead." Blacktivist then apologized and asked what they could do to make it better. Brown reiterated his points about local action: "Post a public apology. Cancel the event and take your cues from those working locally."

In his exchange with Blacktivist, later referenced in the *Guardian* article, Brown highlights relational knowledge as vital for activist organizing. He starts with a variation of "Who are your people?" by asking whether the account is a local organizer or not. When Blacktivist responds with vague gestures toward "friendship" and mentions unknown "volunteers" and "people in Baltimore," Brown immediately detects the inauthenticity and counters with, "But this is not the way to organize." Blacktivist's attempts to perform local connections are clearly shallow and easily detectable lies, compared with genuine activist relational knowledge. Brown highlights "start[ing] with the conversations" and advises the other account to "come listen and learn before you lead" and "take your cues from those working locally," emphasizing the importance of relational processes like local conversations and extended periods of listening.

When he posted the screenshot of this conversation publicly on Facebook, Brown also included his commentary:

> I just conversed on twitter with the "Blacktivist" person trying to organize a #FreddieGray event in #Baltimore tomorrow. Don't have to be mean, but must be direct. You can't bust up in somebody else's house talking about you want friendship and are "open to our thoughts" after you take what you need. If that ain't some settler colonialist, Euro imperial, Christopher Columbus–type occupation mentality I don't know what is! (Let me stop before ya'll have me cussing on Facebook.) I pray that the example of this exchange can help us do better in filtering out unsolicited "support."

Brown invokes activist communities as home places (Royster)—"You can't bust up in somebody else's house"—and connects Blacktivist's actions with histories of appropriation of Black activism, where people from outside the local community say they want to connect but really just extract labor and knowledge without working in real solidarity with the community ("talking about you want friendship and are 'open to our thoughts' after you take what you need"). Brown calls out Blacktivist for participating in a pattern of colonialist extraction: "some settler colonialist, Euro imperial, Christopher Columbus–type occupation mentality" where those outside of local activist groups attempt to occupy these communities and co-opt their labor. Although Brown and his audience for the post did not know at the time that the account was a Russian fake, it was offensive enough on its own because of its rhetoric of co-optation. Later, they use the moment in the media spotlight of the *Guardian* article to draw attention to the broader historical context of such co-optation, indicating to audiences that Russian internet trolls are less important than the larger problem of white supremacy.

Both the Minneapolis and Baltimore BLM activists were able to take advantage of media attention to Russian disinformation in order to circulate their own movement messaging, rooted in their relational knowledge. They were able to act quickly by responding immediately to the local threat posed by fake accounts and later by communicating specific and strategic messages to large media sources like CNN and *The Guardian*. However, they were only able to use rhetorical strategies requiring such speed because of something much slower: knowledge of histories, relations with others, and embodied experiences leading to a felt sense of what rings true or untrue, built over time.

Without this slowness and specificity, a movement is less able to respond effectively and with speed to threats posed by disinformation. The following section details another example where a movement, the Women's March on Washington, was made more vulnerable to disinformation attacks because it had not yet had time or space to firmly establish itself as a complex coalitional movement with a clear set of shared values, histories, and long-standing relationships. These vulnerabilities made it easy for disinformation attacks to target existing tensions in order to undermine the Women's March as it struggled to grow from one event into a lasting movement.

The Women's March on Washington and the Difficulty of Intersectional Coalition-Building in a Disinformation Environment

The January 2017 Women's March on Washington was called at the time possibly the largest single-day protest in US history, with affiliated marches in many

US cities and internationally on every continent including Antarctica (Vick). The marches took place the day after the inauguration of Donald Trump as the forty-fifth US president, after being quickly organized in the months following his election. The Women's March has struggled with many of the tensions that are common in intersectional coalition-building. Its policy platform was called "beautifully intersectional" by some (Vagianos), but the march and resulting movement also had to contend with legacies of white liberal feminism as well as tensions between different organizers' understandings of what is relevant to a "women's" movement.

In this case, the movement required but was also harmed by speed. The Women's March came together very quickly in response to the exigence of Trump's election. The idea for the march began in the Facebook group Pantsuit Nation, a large group in support of Hillary Clinton. When Clinton lost to Trump, several white members of Pantsuit Nation attempted to organize in response to the outrage they felt, but some were inexperienced with political organizing and did not know each other outside this one digital space (McSweeney and Siegel). They later recruited women of color as leaders of the march, but the quickly growing Women's March continued to struggle to establish an identity and purpose—was it a one-day event or a larger movement? Whom was it meant to serve and what was it meant to advocate for (Cauterucci)? To further complicate matters, threatening an already fragile coalition, disinformation played a role in the Women's March, its digital circulation, and its aftermath.

The Women's March and its circulation represent many complex rhetorical actions and it is beyond the scope of this work to analyze all of them, but I focus on a few specific moments during and in the years after the march to illustrate important dynamics. A liberal feminist framework has remained a limitation for enacting the intersectional principles that the march claimed to represent, and a disinformation environment poses additional challenges to complexly mediated activist rhetoric and to the work of coalition-building. High-profile national coalitions attempting to enact intersectional principles may be especially vulnerable to disinformation attacks if these coalitions are fragile and not fully formed, while those more deeply rooted in shared histories, values, and relations are better positioned to mobilize, both to protect local communities and, through moments of media visibility, redirect public attention away from disinformation and toward their own mission.

In response to the harmful legacies of "white feminism"—or feminist movements that privilege the demands of those closest to power, such as white women whose circumstances may be improved through liberal reform and assimilationist political strategies, while neglecting multiply marginalized people who need more systemic and radical change—the Women's March movement attempted to enact intersectional principles and include women of color in its platform and messaging. This was especially important in light of information shared widely shared after Trump's election that 53 percent of white women voted for him while 94 percent of Black women voted against him (Beckett et al.).[1] Media outlets from NPR to *The New York Times, Huffington Post, Vox,* and *USA Today* featured coverage of the march that invoked intersectionality as essential for this movement; on the other hand, some coverage also reinforced decades-old tendencies for white feminists to condemn intersectional approaches as "divisive."

From the beginnings of the Women's March, many women of color were justifiably skeptical about whether this movement would be something new and more intersectional than previous iterations of mainstream feminist movements, or whether it would just be more of the same. The idea for the march actually started out with the name "the Million Women's March," appropriating the labor of the people of color who organized the 1995 Million Man March and the 1997 Million Woman March (Lemieux). The name was changed to the Women's March on Washington, and the march leadership changed, with three women of color named as cochairs: Tamika Mallory (a Black gun control activist), Carmen Perez (a Latina criminal justice reform activist), and Linda Sarsour (a Palestinian American Muslim activist) (Lemieux). While praising this decision, several Black women activists were especially vocal in pointing out that labor again fell onto these women of color to remedy a situation caused by white people. As cultural critic Jamilah Lemieux wrote in her viral *Colorlines* article "Why I'm Skipping the Women's March on Washington," "I'm really tired of Black and Brown women routinely being tasked with fixing White folks' messes. I'm tired of being the moral compass of the United States." And as activist Brittany Oliver pointed out, "Recruiting women of color afterwards is a step in the right direction, but not the answer. The success of individuals don't equate to the masses of people who are suffering." The positions of Mallory, Perez, and Sarsour as the representatives for the march came to symbolize some of these tokenizing patterns in feminist movements.

In 2017 the march's cochairs became the target of several controversies that unfolded on and off social media, with disinformation evolving alongside real

1. The percentage of white women who voted for Trump in 2016 has since been challenged because of its reliance on exit poll data; a broader data set shows the number to be more like 47 percent. This more recent data, however, still shows a dramatic difference between white and Black women, with the number of Black women who voted for Trump too small to show on a chart (Pew Research Center, "Examination").

concerns like those expressed above about what it takes to sustain functional coalitions across differences. A fragile and new coalition, especially one that grows too big too soon in response to high-pressure political exigency (such as Trump's election), is especially vulnerable to disinformation attacks because the coalition is still attempting to establish its identity and relations (made more necessary and more difficult when attempting to unite people with different positionalities and relationships to feminist movements).

In similar ways to those explored in the previous section in the case of online Black Lives Matter rhetoric, disinformation attacks originating in Russian agencies and other contexts targeted the Women's March and worked specifically to put pressure on existing fractures and points of tension. During this time—the immediate aftermath of the Women's March and Trump's inauguration in 2017—the Russian Internet Research Agency that collaborated with the Trump administration was expanding its goals and focus. As journalist Ellen Barry reports for *The New York Times*:

> Accounts at the Internet Research Agency, an organization based in St. Petersburg and controlled by a Putin ally, had boasted of propelling Mr. Trump to victory. That year, the group's budget nearly doubled, according to internal communications made public by US prosecutors. More than a year would pass before social media platforms executed sweeping purges of Russian-backed sock-puppet accounts.
>
> For the trolls, it was a golden hour.
>
> Under these auspicious conditions, their goals shifted from electoral politics to something more general—the goal of deepening rifts in American society, said Alex Iftimie, a former federal prosecutor who worked on a 2018 case against an administrator at Project Lakhta, which oversaw the Internet Research Agency and other Russian trolling operations.

Workers were instructed to look online for any content that seemed potentially "divisive" and that could be exploited for wide circulation: "There was a routine: Arriving for a shift, workers would scan news outlets on the ideological fringes, far left and far right, mining for extreme content that they could publish and amplify on the platforms, feeding extreme views into mainstream conversations" (Barry). During this time period, the Women's March became an obvious target for such work. Similar to the appropriations of BLM discourse, "the job was not to put forward arguments, but to prompt a visceral, emotional reaction, ideally one of 'indignation'" (Barry). The goal of prompting this indignation was to create more and louder noise in the system, distracting people from real political concerns and sustaining confusion, an effective method for discouraging involvement in a movement and creating an environment of information overwhelm and burnout, or "rhetorical exhaustion" (Bradshaw), the opposite of what is needed to sustain political involvement.

Online trolls, though lacking a particular political investment themselves, were again able to exploit American tensions. They observed real social media discourse and sought to imitate and exaggerate this rhetoric. For example, "in January 2017, as the Women's March drew nearer, they tested different approaches on different audiences, as they had during the run-up to the 2016 presidential election. They posed as resentful trans women, poor women and anti-abortion women. They dismissed the marchers as pawns of the Jewish billionaire George Soros" (Barry). Trolls posed as Black women criticized the Women's March for repeating older patterns of white feminism, with the content of these messages at times similar to the real concerns raised by actual Black women (Lemieux; B. Oliver; Obie), but with nuance removed and with a heightened tone of outrage.

These fake performances were not designed to express real critiques or push the Women's March and its resultant movement to do better at putting its intersectional mission into practice; instead, they were solely designed to stoke anger and contribute to social fracturing. For a casual observer, though, it could be difficult to tell the difference. According to the findings of scholars Samantha Bradshaw and Amélie Henle in their study of a data set of 7,056 tweets by state-sponsored disinformation accounts (Russian, Iranian, and Venezuelan) that targeted feminist discourse online, including the Women's March:

> Tweets in our data discussed three main intersectional critiques: that feminism is (1) too White to represent Black women, (2) too liberal to represent conservative women, and (3) too wealthy to represent poor women. In all three cases, the IRA [Internet Research Agency] co-opted the narratives that feminist activists have themselves raised about contemporary feminist movements in both online and offline spaces. . . . Intersectional critiques about racial or political identities were predominantly discussed by Russian accounts, where more than 86% of the tweets came from IRA (66%) or GRU [Russia's military intelligence organization] (20%) accounts. These accounts used discourses about feminism being rooted in "White" and "liberal" values, and that Black women or conservative women are not represented by the movement. (4605)

In these trends, it is possible to see both where these disinformation accounts overlapped with real and valid critiques and where they diverged. For example, two categories—critiques that mainstream feminism "is too White to represent Black women" and "too wealthy to represent poor women"—represent similar critiques to those made by real activists calling for intersectionality in feminist movements. However, the other pattern observed—that mainstream feminism is "too liberal to represent conservative women"—illustrates that these accounts were not actually ideologically aligned with intersectional politics but just posting what they knew, based on previous evidence gathered by observing online interactions, would stoke outrage and achieve wide circulation. The idea that conservative women should be represented in feminist activism illustrates a "both sides" rhetorical tendency that will be explored further in chapter 3 of this book—the ideal of American liberal deliberative democracy that all "sides" of an issue deserve an equal place at the table, an ideal that enables conservative women to claim the term "feminism" just by virtue of being women while actually supporting policies that perpetuate misogynist oppression.

In this environment, march cochair Linda Sarsour became a particular target for these kinds of disinformation attacks online. As Barry reports:

> Russian amplifier accounts began circulating posts that focused on Ms. Sarsour, many of them inflammatory and based on falsehoods, claiming she was a radical Islamist, "a pro-ISIS Anti USA Jew Hating Muslim" who "was seen flashing the ISIS sign."
>
> Some of these posts found a large audience. At 7 p.m. on Jan. 21, an Internet Research Agency account posing as @TEN_GOP, a fictional right-wing American from the South, tweeted that Ms. Sarsour favored imposing Shariah law in the United States, playing into a popular anti-Muslim conspiracy theory that Mr. Trump had helped to popularize on the campaign trail.
>
> This message took hold, racking up 1,686 replies, 8,046 retweets and 6,256 likes. An hour later, @PrisonPlanet, an influential right-wing account, posted a tweet on the same theme. The following day, nearly simultaneously, a small army of 1,157 right-wing accounts picked up the narrative, publishing 1,659 posts on the subject, according to an analysis conducted by the online analytics firm Graphika on behalf of The Times.

These online attacks also affected Sarsour offline, as she began to receive a large volume of hate mail; her in-person appearances attracted large crowds of protesters, at one point led by far-right figure Milo Yiannopoulos; and her family members were also threatened and harassed. As Sarsour describes the mental health impact of all this targeting, "I mean, just imagine . . . every day that you woke up, you were a monster" (Barry).

Rather than contributing potentially valid critiques of Sarsour or other leadership that could lead to productive discussion, these disinformation attacks created an environment of rapid escalation and binaristic thinking where it was difficult to tell what was being circulated by real people with valid concerns and true activist commitments, and what was being circulated by trolls and disinformation agents whose only goal was creating more noise. The fact that disinformation thrives in this environment of overwhelm poses particular problems for a new movement struggling to build a broad intersectional coalition such as the Women's March. Intergroup tensions are common in this kind of work, as activists coming from different backgrounds must contend with their own positionalities and their varied and complex relations to systems of power. It is possible that such tensions may have been resolved over more time, but this was greatly complicated by the march's organization happening under great public scrutiny and while becoming a circulating digital phenomenon in a disinformation environment, where trolls were often watching to see what tensions could be further exploited.

The Women's March movement began to fracture further when several of its leaders were accused of anti-Semitism (McSweeney and Siegel). While actual anti-Semitism is condemnable, the way the term was used in widely circulating digital rhetoric about the Women's March often participated in a dog-whistle political strategy meant to halt critical reflection and negotiation. In this context, a false charge of anti-Semitism is wielded to shut down advocacy by and for Palestinians. Around the time of the Women's March, Democratic presidential candidate Hillary Clinton was using such rhetoric. For example, in a March 2016 speech to the American Israeli Public Affairs Committee, "Hillary Clinton called the Israel boycott movement 'alarming' and characterized BDS [Boycott, Divestment, and Sanctions] activists as anti-Semitic, accusing them of 'bullying' Jewish students on college campuses" but providing no evidence that such bullying actually took place (Shafie and Chávez 33). Such statements equate the acts of making valid critiques of the state of Israel or advocating on behalf of the Palestinian people with "anti-Semitism," diverting attention from the actual content of these messages. Clinton's use of the term "anti-Semitic" in this way points to her allegiances with white feminism, which refuses intersectional attention to issues such as the ongoing oppression of Palestinians because reckoning with this would also require challenging systems that benefit many white women in the US and elsewhere. Clinton was obviously an influential figure because her presidential loss to Trump drew many outraged feminists to the nascent Women's March movement.

As the Women's March continued to grow, claims of "anti-Semitism" were made for a variety of reasons. Some Jewish women expressed feeling excluded from the movement's leadership when Jewish women were not named as a group in the Women's March Unity Principles. Some claimed that at the first in-person meeting for what would later become the Women's March, Perez and Mallory made an assertion that "Jewish people bore a special collective responsibility as exploiters of black and brown people," but the march leaders deny that this happened. As Mallory and another cochair, Bob Bland, recollect, "There was a particular conversation around how white women had centered themselves—and also around the dynamics of racial justice and why it was essential that racial justice be a part of the women's rights conversation," and that "it never had anything to do with Jews" (McSweeney and Siegel).

More publicly damaging than these allegations, however, was the rapid circulation of rhetoric about Mallory's attendance at the 2018 Nation of Islam's Saviours' Day event and a video of it on her Instagram account. At the event, Nation of Islam leader Louis Farrakhan "endorsed a number of anti-Semitic and homophobic conspiracy theories" (North). The Women's March made a statement that "Minister Farrakhan's statements about Jewish, queer, and trans people are not aligned with the Women's March Unity Principles" (North). However, Mallory was criticized for refusing to cut ties with Farrakhan entirely, and in response she wrote an op-ed where she explained that she had attended Saviours' Day since she was a child: "I first went with my parents when I was just a little girl, and would begin attending on my own after my son's father was murdered nearly 17 years ago. In that most difficult period of my life, it was the women of the Nation of Islam who supported me and I have always held them close to my heart for that reason." She wrote that, while she does not agree with anti-Semitic and homophobic views, "Where my people are is where I must also be. I go into difficult spaces." As journalist Anna North reports:

> Mallory's unwillingness to disavow Farrakhan makes more sense in the context of the history of the Nation of Islam, some have argued. The group has a history of providing services in black communities, running child care centers and bakeries, Amy Alexander, a journalist and the editor of a book on Farrakhan, told *Vox*. Many black people in America "kind of respect what they accomplished in neighborhoods that have been underserved for years," she said. "Even though I can condemn Farrakhan for the crazy nonsense and the racist stuff and the bizarre stuff he says, I can also acknowledge that the Nation did great things when they were really needed."

This nuanced point, requiring historicization, contextualization, and the ability to hold multiple truths at once, is exactly what is quickest to get lost in environments of digital disinformation. Because the Women's March was already a fragile coalition that grew too big too fast, lacking a shared imaginary and a strong enough collection of rhetorical resources, it was especially vulnerable to discourse designed to shut down nuance. Several separate events, involving different people, places, histories, and contexts across a multiyear time span, became sloppily grouped together using the dog whistle of "anti-Semitism." This association stuck because of its digital persistence, in an environment where repetition is more important than evidence when persuading audiences to view events as connected. As cultural critic Christina Cauterucci writes in her analysis of the enduring and complex legacy of the Women's March five years after, the circulation of the term "anti-Semitism" in relation to the Women's March says more about a fraught digital media environment and problematic activist celebrity culture than it does about the march itself:

> When Mallory and Perez drew criticism for their support of noted sexist and anti-Semite Louis Farrakhan, it was no big stretch for critics to use the leaders of the Women's March to smear the entire movement. For several months, when the women's groups that had sprung from the 2017 event should have been publicly celebrating the wins of the 2018 midterms, virtually the only media coverage of the Women's March was about the leaders' alleged history of anti-Semitic remarks. Turns out, placing a highly visible hierarchy of self-appointed leaders at the top of a still-fluid grassroots movement is a recipe for defection.

Like in the case of Black Lives Matter disinformation, it is impossible to tell how much of this circulating discourse after the Women's March was "real" and what was the result of disinformation attacks. As Barry writes, "It is maddeningly difficult to say with any certainty what effect Russian influence operations have had on the United States, because when they took hold they piggybacked on real social divisions," and in this case "the divisions within the Women's March existed already." Either way—whether the result of real interpersonal conflicts connected to the difficulty of building an intersectional coalition, or of disinformation attacks, or both—"the fabric of the coalition tore, slowly and painfully. Ms. Sarsour and Ms. Perez stuck by Ms. Mallory, and before long, progressive groups began distancing themselves from all three. Under intense pressure to step down as the leaders, Ms. Sarsour, Ms. Perez, and a third co-chair, Bob Bland, did so in 2019, a move they say was long planned" (Barry). Part of what is now remembered about the Women's March are these divisions and a sense of failed coalition.

However, as Cauterucci emphasizes in her retrospective on the march, it is impossible to fully capture the many complex impacts of the Women's March over time, and despite its troubles, it was not a failure. Cauterucci points to smaller local groups that activists started after meeting at the march or corresponding about it; to people who were galvanized to take part in local actions for the first time or as part of ongoing commitments; and to the heightened public awareness that the march brought to questions of intersectionality and coalition-building. The idea that the legacy of the Women's March may actually lie with local groups points back to the value of slowness and specificity. Large movements that grow too big too fast in order to keep up with a constant environment of shifting political exigencies may burn bright at the start but then burn out or be snuffed out by the environment of confusion and obfuscation that disinformation actors create. In contrast, movements deeply rooted in relational knowledge are more resilient.

CHAPTER 3

Charlottesville's False Equivalencies

Rejecting "Both Sides" by Refusing to Waste Time

On August 11 and 12, 2017, the Unite the Right rally filled the streets of Charlottesville, Virginia, and dominated local and national media coverage for long afterward. Unite the Right was constituted by white supremacist, neo-Nazi, and alt-right groups from across the US. In addition to circulating violent rhetoric, some supporters were physically violent, including one self-professed white supremacist who drove a car into a crowd, injured many people, and killed a counterprotester, Heather Heyer. In documentary interviews, attendees speak of the rally as a show of numbers and power meant to demonstrate that these groups were organizing in real life, not just online. They talk about "stepping off the internet in a big way," showing they are "more than an internet meme," and "starting to slowly unveil a little bit of our power level" (*Vice*).

Footage of the rally shows Unite the Right participants yelling white supremacist chants, marching with lit tiki torches, and instigating violence across town by fighting counterprotesters (*Vice*; "Documenting Hate"). As Charlottesville social justice activist Emily Gorcenski says in an interview with a reporter:

> You could feel how angry they were but also how happy they were to be doing this. To be intimidating people like this and this happy rage. . . . They were cheering, they were running through the streets yelling at people, and

> they walked away and they got away with it. They're coming in here the next day ready to do more. I thought, like, here we go. ("Documenting Hate")

In the national conversation after the rally, Charlottesville came to represent a moment when overt white supremacist groups seemed, to many American audiences, to come into mainstream visibility. That fact, and the immediate notoriety of Trump's remarks about Charlottesville that followed, make the rally a touchstone moment in contemporary US politics.

Trump made his first remarks on Charlottesville as a tweet on August 12, 2017, when he wrote: "We ALL must be united & condemn all that hate stands for. There is no place for this kind of violence in America. Lets come together as one!" He followed this up with a recorded video statement on the same day saying, "We condemn in the strongest possible terms this egregious display of hatred, bigotry and violence on many sides. On many sides" (Johnson and Wagner). In these remarks, Trump lays the rhetorical groundwork for the "both sides" attitude that came to characterize his methods of courting favor with white supremacist movements more broadly. This chapter analyzes the rhetorical scaffolding that upholds the "both sides" remark, going far beyond Trump himself to demonstrate how "both sides," as a strategy of false equivalency, is not only a contemporary right-wing trope but has deeper roots in liberalism.

By setting up false equivalencies, erasing context, and refusing to name the "sides," "both sides" creates the environment of obfuscation that white supremacy needs to thrive, supported by the civic ideals of abstract liberalism. The rhetoric of false equivalencies like "both sides" works by wasting audiences' time, which is visible in liberal responses that accept the premise that all "sides" deserve to be heard in civil discourse. I also analyze activist responses that challenged "both sides" in the aftermath of Unite the Right. Because "both sides" works by wasting time, intersectional leftist activists respond by refusing to cede their time. They use strategies of naming and historicization in an effort to take back control of time and redirect attention to material concerns. However, charges of "incivility" are weaponized against these activists under the guise of liberal ideals.

By fighting "both sides" claims, activists attempt to reclaim control of time by dismissing the abstraction of false equivalency and working quickly to resituate political discussions in the context of oppressed people's material conditions and the histories that have created those conditions. As Tamika L. Carey writes in her work on Black women's rhetorics of impatience, such discursive practices "involve 'talking back,' 'turning it out' and 'calling a thing a thing,' or radical truth-telling, and they reveal a distrust of circular discussion, deflection, or distraction" ("Necessary Adjustments" 270). As opposed to white rhetorics of civility, which set a slow or nonexistent pace for social change and waste the time of oppressed people by asking them to engage in a performance of polite and reasoned discussion with their oppressors, rhetorics of impatience assert that "equity and justice for one's self, Black women, and Black communities is already overdue and, thus, requires speed and decisive action" (Carey, "Necessary Adjustments" 270). Building on this understanding, refusing false equivalencies sets up the groundwork necessary for activists to make demands for accountability, or calls for those in power to be publicly answerable for their actions and their oppressive consequences.

In the following sections, I first analyze Trump's "both sides" remark and its circulation, explaining more about the context and consequences of this specific rhetorical action, and situating it within the framework of false equivalency as a trope of liberal civic discourse, which explains why liberal engagements with "both sides" often work to perpetuate white supremacist oppression. I then analyze how Black leftist activists from Charlottesville responded to this moment in public discourse by refusing to waste any more time on "both sides" arguments, replacing the abstraction of false equivalency with naming- and historicization-based rhetorical strategies. I also explore how activists work to disrupt civility rhetoric as an additional strategy of taking back the terms of debate and the pace of the public discussion when their rhetoric is deemed "uncivil."

The Rhetorical Life of "Both Sides" after Charlottesville

During the media Q&A following a news conference about infrastructure at Trump Tower on August 15, 2017, Trump expanded his "many sides" comment in some unplanned remarks (Jacobs and Laughland). A reporter asked, "Why did you wait so long to denounce neo-Nazis?" Trump responded: "I wanted to make sure, unlike most politicians, that what I said was correct, not make a quick statement. The statement I made on Saturday, the first statement, was a fine statement, but you don't make statements that direct unless you know the fact. And it takes a little while to get the facts. You still don't know the facts." This language shows how insistence on "facts" can be weaponized by precisely those rhetors who regularly manipulate facts for their own gain. When asked about the alt-right's role in the attacks, Trump says, "Well, I don't know. I can't tell you. I'm sure Senator McCain must know what he is talking about, but when you say the alt-right, define alt-right to me. You define it. Go ahead. Define it for me, come on, let's go." As journalists attempt to respond (including by offering definitions for "alt-right"), correct falsehoods, and follow up, Trump holds up a hand and shifts into focusing on an invented entity that he calls the "alt-left" (while calling the reporters "fake news"):

> Okay, what about the alt-left that came charging at [indiscernible]—excuse me—what about the alt-left that came charging at the, as you say, the alt-right? Do they have any semblance of guilt? . . . As far as I'm concerned, that was a horrible, horrible day. Wait a minute, I'm not finished. I'm not finished, fake news. That was a horrible day—I will tell you something. I watched those very closely, much more closely than you people watched it. And you had, you had a group on one side that was bad. And you had a group on the other side that was also very violent. And nobody wants to say that, but I'll say it right now. You had a group—you had a group on the other side that came charging in without a permit, and they were very, very violent. (qtd. in Jacobs and Laughland)

Trump then diverts into the topic of the alt-right organizers' stated goals to protest the removal of a statue of Confederate general Robert E. Lee. After that, he resumes his "both sides" rhetoric, clear in the media transcript below, which I quote at length to illustrate the persistence with which Trump deploys "both sides":

> TRUMP: I am not putting anybody on a moral plane, what I'm saying is this: you had a group on one side and a group on the other, and they came at each other with clubs and it was vicious and horrible and it was a horrible thing to watch, but there is another side. There was a group on this side, you can call them the left. You've just called them the left, that came violently attacking the other group. So you can say what you want, but that's the way it is.
>
> REPORTER: You said there was hatred and violence on both sides?
>
> TRUMP: I do think there is blame—yes, I think there is blame on both sides. You look at, you look at both sides. I think there's blame on both sides, and I have no doubt about it, and you don't have any doubt about it either. And, and, and, and if you reported it accurately, you would say.
>
> REPORTER: The neo-Nazis started this thing. They showed up in Charlottesville.
>
> TRUMP: Excuse me, they didn't put themselves down as neo-Nazis, and you had some very bad people in that group. But you also had people that were very fine people on both sides. You had people in that group—excuse me, excuse me. I saw the same pictures as you did. You had peo-

> ple in that group that were there to protest the taking down, of to them, a very, very important statue and the renaming of a park from Robert E. Lee to another name. (Politico Staff)

Trump then attempts to justify his comments that there were "bad" and "good" people on "both sides" and accuses the protesters on the "left" of not having a permit while the alt-right protesters did, seeking to obscure the content of the groups' messaging through a dubious legalistic technicality. He states, "So I only tell you this: there are two sides to a story. I thought what took place was a horrible moment for our country, a horrible moment. But there are two sides to the country." Here, he shifts the "story" into the language of the "country," escalating "two sides" out of the immediate context of Charlottesville and into a broader claim about "two sides to the country."

In doing so, Trump uses his "both sides" comment not to denounce the events in Charlottesville or the death of Heather Heyer, but to tap into the discourse of nostalgic mourning for a white supremacist past (a pattern clearly repeated through Trump's campaign and presidential rhetoric, including his slogan "Make America Great Again") (Perry 59). In this framework, the Unite the Right protesters have come together to use their state-sanctioned right to protest the removal of "a very, very important statue" with which they feel a nostalgic connection (i.e., covert white supremacy), and a few "bad people" (i.e., overt white supremacists) disrupted this allegedly respectable mission, but ultimately the unpermitted "left," present without permission of the state, were the truly "violent" ones.

Afterward, Trump was thanked in a tweet for his remarks by former Ku Klux Klan (KKK) leader David Duke. A White House memo after the press conference stated that Trump's remarks were "entirely correct—both sides of the violence in Charlottesville acted inappropriately, and bear some responsibility," and that politicians and media "should join the president in trying to unite and heal our country rather than incite more division" (qtd. in Acosta and Diaz). Trump supporters tried to echo his rhetoric of "both sides," often by attempting to villainize the counterprotesters by representing them as violent. For example, columnist J. Peder Zane writes in Miami's *Herald Sun,* "The white supremacists, most of whom were carrying sticks and shields, were largely to blame for the violence. But it is also clear that many of the 'anti-fascists' were itching for yet another fight. That's been true at least since the presidential campaign, when they engaged in violence at Trump rallies." Zane deflects attention from the actual issues behind the conflict by invoking conservative audiences' biases against "antifa," used as a flexible label for any group on the left without specifying what these groups are fighting for. He locates the threat of white supremacists within a specific, material image (some individuals who carried "sticks and shields") rather than in the diffuse ideology of Unite the Right, while he portrays the threat of the left as an abstract and generalized threat that may spark at any moment ("itching for yet another fight," "when they engaged in violence"). This creates a false equivalency between white supremacists and those fighting white supremacy.

"Both sides" has continued to be invoked frequently in the years since the Unite the Right rally. During the first debate in the 2020 presidential race between Trump and then Democratic candidate Joe Biden, moderator Chris Wallace referenced the "both sides" comment and asked if Trump would now condemn white supremacy—which he did not, instead telling the white supremacist group the Proud Boys to "stand back and stand by" (C-SPAN). In the same debate, Trump repeated his rhetoric equating the alt-right with an invented equal on the left by saying the "radical left" and "antifa" were the actual threat. In short, "both sides" has become a touchstone and a shorthand for Trump's allegiances with white supremacists, as well as a cultural touchstone for the ways false equivalencies work in this political moment.

"Both sides" has existed long before Trump and will continue after his presidency. As historian Catherine Baker explains, the rhetoric of "both sides" was used by many political leaders responsible for twentieth-century atrocities, who deploy "the language of relativization" to deny that responsibility ("Want to Know"). In recent years, numerous politicians have invoked the phrase, including Kentucky senator and House Minority Leader Mitch McConnell and Maine senator Susan. R Collins (Barrett). For example, after a series of violent acts where a man mailed pipe bombs to political figures and organizations that Trump has criticized, Senator Collins responded to a question about whether Trump should "lower his rhetoric in the wake of the threatening mailings" by stating, "There is no excuse for inciting violence regardless who is the person doing it. Certainly, there have been people on both sides of the aisle who have been guilty of whipping people into a frenzy" (Barrett). In Collins's formation, Trump does not need to be held accountable for how his words incite violence; instead, she abstracts the violence and diffuses it into a meaningless platitude about "people on both sides of the aisle." The false equivalency hinges around the liberal deployment of "violence" as a universal moral negative, without a definition of what is meant by "violence" or any evidence of specific forms of violence used by whom and against whom, analysis of the context and power differentials involved in acts of violence, and consideration of what the consequences of that violence may be.

"Both Sides" and the Rhetoric of False Equivalency

"Both sides" is a deceptive trope that works through false equivalency. Through the "both sides" sleight of hand, rhetors circulate disinformation that attempts to discredit antiracist groups and others working toward justice, diverting attention from the actual content of these groups' messaging. The imagined leftist equivalent to the alt-right is painted in the public eye as dangerous, a common form of fearmongering. A binary is also established between two unstated but assumed "sides," rhetorically constructed as "us" and "not us," a strategy used to center whiteness as the default and foreclose other options for identification. Any issue is much more complicated than two "sides," but this debate is framed in the American two-party political system. Mimicking this structure, rhetors take advantage of a two-sides conception in the public imaginary to build "both sides" arguments. In the process, public audiences also learn the assumption that "extremes" are bad in any form simply because they are far to one "side" of a political ideology, without having specific conversations about the positions taken by those aligned with the ideologies in question (e.g., the stance of "centrism" makes an assumption that the "far left" and the "far right" are equally "bad" and opposite poles, without defining the beliefs, values, and plans of anyone sorted into various positions along this imagined political spectrum).

As a disinformation tactic, "both sides" diverts attention from the actual issues at hand by stoking moral outrage over invocations of "violence," defined implicitly or explicitly as overt acts of physical destruction such as property damage or fighting, without any context for what caused the violence. Further, the diffuse and everyday violence of oppression is removed from the definition altogether. Debates about whether or not particular protesters acted "violently" obscure the fact that "both sides" is itself a violent rhetorical strategy. False equivalencies, as rhetoricians Chaim Perelman and Lucie Olbrechts-Tyteca explain, hinge on "arguments of reciprocity," in which "quasi-logical argument becomes possible through disregarding everything that makes the situations different and reducing them to what makes them symmetrical" (224). In the case of Charlottesville, what is different about the "sides"—one side fighting for white supremacy and one side against it—is completely disregarded and replaced with a veil of symmetry through the claim that both sides are to blame for some abstracted and morally negative violence.

Rather than originating with the contemporary right wing, false equivalencies are built into the notion of US deliberative democracy itself and the liberal ideal of the American public sphere. False equivalencies are such a common and effective rhetorical strategy in American political discourse because of the deliberative democratic idea that, in civic debate, all sides must be given their fair hearing. Rhetors who invoke "both sides" are aware of this history, and they use it to their advantage. Rooting out the right's false equivalencies is one important step, but to get at the root of the problem, activists need to challenge the exclusionary ideals of deliberative democracy and civic engagement that have always worked to oppress Black people, queer people, and other multiply marginalized communities.

"Both sides" works as an enthymeme, an argument with unstated premises. As another example removed from the immediate context of Charlottesville, "both sides" allows political groups to target social justice curricula in schools for elimination by arguing that advocating for social justice in the classroom does not allow "all voices to be heard" or "all opinions to be respected," an argument built on the assumption of false equivalency between all possible "opinions." Through such uses of "both sides" rhetoric, right-wing politicians turn liberal tropes of civic discourse on their heads, using the language of liberalism (tolerance, respect for differing beliefs) against itself. This rhetoric is often highly effective. For instance, in March 2021, an Idaho right-wing group successfully advocated for Boise State University to shut down more than 200 general-education ethics and diversity classes midsemester, arguing that in these classes "students were harassed because of their personal views" (Richert)—their anti-social-justice views. In another example from spring 2021, Florida Republicans began what would become an assault on antiracist curricula and initiatives in schools, coordinated with increasingly anti-trans and antiqueer policy proposals, by introducing legislation in favor of what they termed "viewpoint diversity" on college campuses, claiming "liberal bias" in classrooms (Luscombe). Such rhetorical strategies are enabled by the logic of "both sides," and after Charlottesville, Trump popularized a pattern of false equivalency that would come to be used by more politicians in the coming years.

"Both sides," like other rhetorical strategies designed to dodge accountability, works through wasting time and erasing context. The liberal ideal of the public sphere is dehistoricized and decontextualized, rendering all "sides" of an issue as equally valid. Since time and context are what give "sides" of an issue their differential values and consequences, erasing history and context renders the "sides" value-neutral and requires no accountability from any actor. In a void, any argument can be made in favor of any "side." Calls to restore history and context are then framed as "biased" moves to insert irrelevant information into the discussion, ignoring the fact that dehistoricization and decontextualization are choices that provide evidence of "bias."

In this political environment, the time of oppressed people—already in short supply—is further wasted. Drawing from Brittney Cooper's concept of the "racial politics of time" and argument that "white people own time," Tamika L. Carey explains that both overt and implicit strategies designed to uphold white supremacy work through control of time within "a system of temporal hegemony where ideological and material structures converge into a culture of hostility that pushes equity for a group further out of reach" ("Necessary Adjustments" 270). "Both sides" as a rhetorical strategy is part of this "system of temporal hegemony." By removing history and context, "both sides" rhetoric maintains white supremacy in multiple ways. Trump can say there was blame on "both sides" without explicitly naming one of the sides as white supremacists and the other side as antiracist counterprotesters and can create a moral equivalency between alleged bad actors (the overt white supremacists contrasted with the supposedly equal but opposite "antifa" or "alt-left"). Then, those who attempt to directly debate Trump or others who use similar false equivalencies are often just further sucked into the internal logic of the false equivalency, which wastes time even more.

In contrast to white-controlled time, scholar Marquis Bey describes a Black queer feminist temporality as "a temporal tense of anteriority noting what will have had to happen in order for the future to be realized" (*Them Goon Rules* 105–6), placing past, present, and future in constant dialogue, with the goal of radical change. Part of this temporality, as Bey explains, relies on a politics of refusal: "We cannot mobilize around, and actualize, the radically different world in which we wish to live until we refuse the one we have been given" (*Them Goon Rules* 106). Activists enact both refusal and generative imagination at the same time. A politics of refusal as a condition for radical imagination also suffuses conceptions of queer time, in contrast to the presentist, assimilationist stance that characterizes mainstream LGBT politics. However, activists also do the difficult work of not discarding the potential for changes *now* by focusing only on utopian potentialities. This is the balance enacted skillfully by rhetors who responded effectively against Unite the Right and "both sides" by choosing not to waste any more time.

Not Wasting Any More Time: Naming and Contextualization

In the aftermath of Charlottesville and the "both sides" remark, activists used moments of public visibility to regain control of time, even temporarily, and to restore missing history and context, countering the abstraction of "both sides" by drawing attention to historical and contemporary oppression in the US. In doing so, they also resist the liberal rhetoric of civility that is foundational to "both sides." Because Unite the Right gained extensive national media attention and "both sides" circulated widely online for a long time after the day of the initial event, activists also used the event's circulation to draw attention to the material conditions of oppression in Charlottesville and in the US more broadly. In circulating claims rooted in the material and specific, they chose not to waste time entertaining Trump's remarks on the abstract terms of liberal civil discourse.

In her analysis of Black women's "rhetorics of impatience" as strategies for enacting refusal and taking back control over time, Carey includes an example from the aftermath of Charlottesville: political analyst Symone Sanders's appearance on CNN after Unite the Right. Sanders appeared alongside Virginia Republican Ken Cuccinelli in an interview on CNN's *New Day,* hosted by Chris Cuomo. When discussing Trump's response to Charlottesville, Cuccinelli attempts to frame the rally as an isolated incident and to decontextualize the event. Sanders refuses to let Cuccinelli continue by insisting that the rally represents a pattern of white supremacy in the US, recontextualizing Charlottesville as an "egregious symptom of what is wrong all over America." Cuccinelli consistently speaks over her, repeating "No, no, no," before saying "Can I finish, Symone? Can you just shut up for a moment?" (New Day). Cuccinelli's interruptions are typical of the rhetoric of misogynoir that Black women face daily (M. Bailey). As Carey explains, Cuccinelli attempted "to invoke conversational civility customs to regulate Sanders" by claiming that his interpretation also deserves airtime. However, "her retaliatory interjections unmask the apolitical rhetoric he was using to deny white supremacy at work" (Carey, "Necessary Adjustments" 281). Sanders does not allow Cuccinelli to continue to misrepresent Unite the Right as an aberration rather than a logical outcome in the context of US histories of white supremacy, just as she does not allow her own speech to be cut off and regulated, enacting a Black feminist refusal to waste time.

Like Sanders, other Black activists responding to Charlottesville were quick to refuse the time-wasting strategy of "both sides." Instead, they waste *no* time on worthless engagement with the futile abstraction of "both sides," instead aiming to refocus attention on naming specific histories and material conditions of oppression. For example, in the *Vice* News documentary *Charlottesville: Race and Terror,* a reporter asks Charlottesville community activist Tanesha Hudson what she thinks of Trump's "both sides" comment. Without hesitation, Hudson states:

> I thought it was a bunch of nonsense. You know, he stood in one of his rallies when he was running, before he was elected, and said, "If they would've did that 40 years ago, they'd have left out on a stretcher." You okayed this activity. This is the face of supremacy. This is what we deal with every day, being African-American. And this has always been the reality of Charlottesville. You can't stand in one corner in this city and not look at the master sitting on top of Monticello. He looks down on us. He's been looking down on this city for God knows how long. This is Charlottesville. (*Vice*)

Hudson quickly dismisses the idea of "both sides" as "nonsense," unwilling to cede any time to engagement with this false equivalency. Her refusal to waste time even engaging with "both sides" enacts a Black queer feminist temporality: There is no time to debate false equivalencies because there is much more important work that needs to be done *now.* Hudson instead chooses to spend her time providing specific evidence that Trump has endorsed white supremacy by pivoting to a quote from one of his campaign rallies. In doing this, Hudson brings the missing context of "both sides" back into play, and through this contextualization, she establishes that Trump's use of "both sides" is connected to his history of white supremacist discourse.

Hudson then expands beyond the context of Trump through saying, "This is what we deal with every day, being African-American. And this has always been the reality of Charlottesville," establishing that white supremacy is not isolated to Trump's remarks or even to the Unite the Right rally but is part of the daily reality of America—for Black people, nothing new. She moves far beyond Trump by emphasizing the materiality of white supremacy, saying, "You can't stand in one corner in this city and not look at the master sitting on top of Monticello," invoking founding father Thomas Jefferson's slaveholding. By framing Jefferson as "the master sitting on top of Monticello," Hudson also brings historical context back into the discussion, after it is erased by the false equivalency and temporal flattening of "both sides." She situates "both sides" back on a historical timeline, disrupting its presentist stance. She ends by saying, "This is Charlottesville," again emphasizing that the violence of white supremacy is not restricted to Unite the Right but is a daily material reality for Black people living in Charlottesville. She refuses the diversion of Trump's "both sides" remark by dismissing it immediately as nonsense and moving into the more important work of challenging day-to-day white supremacy in Charlottesville and more broadly.

Because "both sides" refuses to name the "sides," or mischaracterizes them as opposite poles on an imagined line, activist rhetors use naming as a counterstrategy meant to restore the accountability that is dodged through abstracted language. They name the specific material conditions of white supremacist oppression and connect them to their historical roots. For instance, writer Michael Harriot, in an essay for *The Root,* clearly delineates what Trump and other rhetors actually mean by deploying the "both sides" sleight of hand. Harriot uses naming to demonstrate how, the moment when the "sides" are explicitly named, the logic of false equivalency breaks down. Responding to Harriot by taking a "side" would require being answerable for that choice:

> Some people are wondering what Trump specifically meant by condemning hate and bigotry "on many sides." Allow us to explain:
>
> He means the side that hates people of color, and the people of color who are recipients of hate.
>
> The side that pierces innocent black bodies with bullets, and the side that has the audacity to die from being shot.
>
> He's talking about the 1 percenters whining about a 2 percent tax hike, and people who work a full-time job and still can't afford to pay rent.
>
> He means the ones who complain about affirmative action because they spent thousands on tutoring and practice tests, and the side that knows that, regardless of income, schools with black students are more likely to be underfunded.

In his goal to illuminate how power works in this context, Harriot does not waste any time entertaining the logic of "both sides" on its own terms. He takes the vague rhetoric of "sides" and spells out what beliefs and groups constitute the "sides," shifting the focus away from invisible and amorphous ideologies and toward the material realities of actual people, in the process revealing the violence behind "both sides" claims and revealing who holds power, when, why, and with what consequences. After beginning with these specific examples, Harriot goes broader with his rhetoric, and he invokes the ways "violence" is often tied to "both sides" as a diversion and discrediting tactic:

> When Donald Trump talks about the hate on both sides, he means white America—which holds every economic, social and political advantage in this country and has been metaphorically and literally slitting the throats of blacks, Hispanics and non-Christians for the entire existence of America.
>
> And he's talking about the people who've been getting their throats slit. Because they hate, too. They hate getting their windpipes slashed open. They are bigoted against the neck slicers. Have you heard how loud they scream at the Black Lives Matter rallies just because their sons and daughters are dying? How dare those ungrateful bastards talk shit about white people? I

> know they have no power and they have done absolutely nothing to inflict harm on white people, but who do they think has to mop up all that throat blood from the nice, white marble floors?

Harriot builds an extended metaphor to illustrate how violence works, counter to the rhetoric of "both sides," and how in the US whiteness has always meant power to inflict violence and then blame those harmed by that violence for fighting against the conditions causing them harm. Harriot points out the irony inherent in an accusation of being "bigoted against the neck slicers," in a rhetorical move that is similar to Tanesha Hudson's immediate dismissal of "both sides" as "nonsense." Those who are slitting throats versus "the people who've been getting their throats slit" obviously brings the "sides" into stark contrast, and in doing so aims to reestablish the actual, material terms of debate, rather than a false debate that wastes time by abstracting the terms and obfuscating the mechanisms of power.

Disrupting Civility Rhetoric

The presentism and abstraction of "both sides" are further enabled by the white liberal democratic ideal of civil discourse. As detailed in the previous section, after Charlottesville, Black activist rhetors consistently challenged an implicit claim behind "both sides" rhetoric: that civil discourse requires listening to all sides of an issue. In doing so, however, some encountered pushback from liberal politicians seeking to uphold "civility."

In Trump's use of "both sides" and many other invocations of this trope, the daily violence of white supremacy is erased. This erasure is easy to achieve because white supremacy is often represented as a fringe ideology rather than a structuring principle of the US itself (Daniels). The rhetorical work of associating "white supremacist violence" with specific instances of destruction enacted by individuals who proudly claim affiliation with groups like the KKK allows for the larger system of white supremacist oppression to continue unchallenged. As rhetoric scholar James Chase Sanchez explains, Trump communicates in a way that "winks" (borrowing Charles Morris's term) at white supremacist groups, including the KKK, but that also allows him deniability. He dodges accountability by using terms that are easily interpretable as white supremacist tropes by those "in the know"—such as "patriotism," "heritage," "safety," and "security"—but that he can also pretend are innocent because of the abstraction of the terms (Sanchez 50). The versatility of abstraction as mobilized in white supremacist rhetoric allows the same exact language to be used "as a call of arms for members of the KKK on one hand, and . . .

presented as civil on the other" (Sanchez 55). By saying that Trump's white supremacist rhetoric can be presented as "civil," Sanchez points to a strategy that Trump and other rhetors use to express white supremacist ideas under a veneer of deniability enabled by the liberal ideal of civil discourse. This strategy is also not Trump's alone. Legal scholar Ian Haney López, in his work on coded racial appeals that he terms "dog whistle politics," investigates how politicians use "a steady drumbeat of subliminal racial grievances and appeals to color-coded solidarity" in attempts to foreclose the possibility of white people standing in solidarity with people of color. This allows politicians to make promises "to protect supposedly embattled whites" from constructed threats of a racialized other, deflecting attention from the threat of their own policy choices "combining dramatic increases in wealth at the very top along with severe strains for almost everyone else" (I. López 2–3).

After Unite the Right, civility discourse played out in Charlottesville in major ways. An episode of an NPR series titled "Civility Wars," which covered Charlottesville city council meetings in the aftermath of the violence, reports that Democratic city mayor Mike Signer "struggled to maintain order as people in the gallery would shout down speakers and use other disruptive tactics including crinkling water bottles" (Elliott). Signer states that "there has been a lot of very strong emotion expressed in our chambers by people who are deeply traumatized. . . . How do you have that happen when you also need to do the public's business?," framing "trauma" and "emotion" as opposite to "business" or the running of a city. Charlottesville organizers and residents aimed to use this venue to call for accountability from local officials for not doing more to stop Unite the Right. Against representations of Charlottesville as "a charming college town," activists sought to bring attention to the material conditions of oppression that Black residents already experienced before Unite the Right. From their perspective, the problem had been going on for a very long time—centuries—and they were fed up and unwilling to waste any more time on niceties. However, from the perspective of the mayor and some other councilmembers, these people's responses were examples of sudden and disruptive outrage prompted by Unite the Right, and that outrage had to be controlled before real "deliberation" could begin.

Activists in city council meetings were shut down for expressing emotion under the silencing tactic of "civility." Signer's positionality here is complicated, and I do not mean to frame him as the source of the problem for civility rhetoric; however, his deployment of it, even from a marginalized position himself, points to the need to think more critically about when civility is deployed and which multiply marginalized populations are shut out. As Signer explains to a reporter in the PBS/Frontline documentary *Charlottesville: Documenting Hate,* he was also the victim of harassment and violent threats as the mayor and as a Jewish man. At the same time, Signer is framed in media coverage as someone who favors rules of conduct that fit a white liberal civility ideal: "As mayor in 2017, Signer's answer was to enforce rules—the standard Robert's Rules of Order—and then some ground rules for how long people could speak and prohibitions on heckling, harassment or foul language. In other words, he sought to pursue civility" (Elliott). As Signer defines it to NPR, "I see civility just as an instrument to let people, with very strong opinions, very strong emotions, be in the same body to get things done" (Elliott), again framing "very strong emotions" (the repetition is his) as an obstacle to being part of the same public and "getting things done"; thus, emotions must be controlled via "instruments" like civility.

But as BLM activist Jalane Schmidt counters in the NPR article, "Civility is actually used to shut down discussion. . . . It is often a way to 'tone police' the folks that don't have power and that don't speak in four-syllable words" (Elliott). Council member Wes Bellamy also disrupts the division between emotion and political discourse:

> I could have a conversation with you and because my vernacular is not the same, and because a topic makes me more emotional and I'm more passionate about it, it doesn't mean that I'm not being quote-unquote civil. . . . It could just mean that when I was talking to you in a way that you may deem civil, you refused to listen to me. So now you're going to have to hear me by any means necessary. (Elliott)

Bellamy gestures to the double bind that many marginalized rhetors experience, where they are told to use "civil discourse," but this does not mean they are listened to, so their attempts to follow the rules of civility are likely to waste time that they do not have. Since activist rhetors are regularly shut down when deliberately or inadvertently challenging civility discourse through their words, actions, or emotional expressions—or even just their bodies in a space—then they must use any means necessary to be heard (Alexander et al.). Schmidt's statement points to the available means of persuasion, but with a twist: Activist rhetors are not only using the means available to them as governed by white liberal civility norms, but they are making their own means, including, in the Black resistance tradition, "making a way out of no way."

Implications

In 2021 Charlottesville residents and counterprotesters brought a civil suit against fourteen people and ten white supremacist organizations involved in the Unite the Right rally (Elamroussi). The defense used strategies of obfuscation and denials of accountability characteristic of white supremacist rhetoric; for instance, "defense attorneys and two high-profile defendants who are representing themselves argued none of the plaintiffs had proven the defendants had organized racial violence" (Elamroussi). Once again, "both sides" resurfaced. During the trial, white nationalist Richard Spencer invoked Trump's comment as an attempt to deflect blame from himself. As journalist Aya Elamroussi reports:

> In a tense moment between Spencer and the judge, Spencer recalled then-President Donald Trump's infamous statement about the rally: "There were good people on both sides." But Moon told him that quote was never entered into evidence. Spencer said he agreed with the sentiment, ignoring the judge's orders. "There were some bad people on both sides," Spencer said, referring to antifa.

In this context, "both sides" itself did not stand up in a court as a valid defense. However, it continues to circulate in political discourse.

Though Trump's "both sides" remark equating white supremacist violence with antiracist protesting may not initially seem to have much in common with liberal appeals to civility, this chapter has traced the common rhetorical scaffolding that actually unites these threads and allows for the widespread appeal of "both sides" strategies. Activist challenges to "both sides" reclaim control over time to insist on the importance of history and the need to make changes now in order to build a future accountable to the needs of those currently most marginalized. They also make use of naming and contextualizing in order to call for the accountability that "both sides" deliberately dodges. Further, activists know that civility claims are used as weapons against those fighting white supremacy, and they refuse to capitulate to civility rhetoric when discussing "both sides." In doing so, activist rhetors enact an unapologetic stance that will not accept the premises behind "both sides" claims or waste any time on these claims. This strategy is in contrast to those of liberalism, which often endorses rhetoric like "crossing the aisle" or unifying the "sides" when it comes to political debates, further time-wasting strategies. Though they may be labeled uncivil for doing so, activists responding to Unite the Right offer a model for insisting that there is no compromising with white supremacy.

The rhetorical scaffolding of "both sides" reveals a complex interweaving of contemporary right-wing and old liberal American ideas, all twisted into a disinformation trap and hidden within a deceptively simple-seeming trope. Rather than seeking to argue with "both sides" using its own logic of abstraction, which only serves to waste time, rhetoricians should look to the time-reclamation strategies of activists who root their counterclaims in specific histories and material conditions. This may also prompt rhetoric scholars to reconsider our field's historical privileging of certain forms of argumentation. For instance, some variation of "both sides" can be found in tenets of Rogerian argument, as well as classical rhetorics such as stasis theory and dissoi logoi. Based on such models, students in the US are commonly taught to look at both sides of an issue to understand where the "sides" are coming from, with the goal of reaching compromise or negotiation (Roberts-Miller). Such models seem almost laughable in the time of post-truth politics, especially in digital spaces, where conspiracy theories are more likely to flourish than any model of civil discussion. However, this chapter has shown how "civil discussion" itself has never been a neutral political concept, and it has demonstrated how the act of refusing to waste time provides another resource for challenging disinformation claims—one that does not rely on civil discourse and at times actively challenges it.

CHAPTER 4

Whose Insurrection?

Rhetorical Gaslighting after January 6 and the Uses and Limits of Testimonial Acts

"Gaslighting" refers to a specific kind of manipulation: deceiving someone by making them doubt their perception of reality. Though the term itself began as a colloquialism, originating with a 1938 film in which a husband terrorizes his wife, it is recognized in psychology as a strategy that abusers use to make victims question their powers of reasoning and trust in what is real. Though anyone can gaslight, it is associated with gendered violence rooted in heteropatriarchal oppression, and it also has racialized connotations in terms of who is believed and who is discredited. Beyond individual cases of abuse, gaslighting has come to represent a widespread political ethos grounded in bids for control of people's perceptions of reality. In this chapter, I examine gaslighting as a post-truth rhetorical strategy and analyze activist counter-strategies grounded in testimonial and witnessing.

In a 2016 *Teen Vogue* article, author Lauren Duca went viral with the headline argument "Donald Trump Is Gaslighting America." Duca argues that gaslighting is a productive way to understand Trump's political strategies and to challenge them:

> To gaslight is to psychologically manipulate a person to the point where they question their own sanity, and that's precisely what Trump is doing to this country. He gained traction in the election by swearing off the lies of politicians while constantly contradicting himself, often without bothering

> to conceal the conflicts within his own sound bites. He lied to us over and over again, then took all accusations of his falsehoods and spun them into evidence of bias. At the hands of Trump, facts have become interchangeable with opinions, blinding us into arguing amongst ourselves as our very reality is called into question.

Including multiple examples of Trump manipulating truth and distorting reality, then insisting to audiences that it is *their* perception that is wrong, Duca warns readers to stay vigilant about checking his claims and challenging his lies. Written at the beginning of the first Trump presidency, Duca's article proved even more prescient over time. Gaslighting's association with Trump became further sedimented through numerous articles across the political spectrum (Hemmer; Eltis; Sarkis; Azarian) and by conservative commentator and former Ted Cruz staffer Amanda Carpenter in her 2018 book *Gaslighting America: Why We Love It When Trump Lies to Us.*

This chapter focuses on one example of gaslighting at the very end of the first Trump presidency: the January 6, 2021, insurrection on the US Capitol. The obfuscations, denials, and distortions of that day's events can best be understood through the lens of rhetorical gaslighting, or persuasive strategies that attempt to make audiences doubt their own grasp on reality and their perceptions, with the goal of publicly discrediting activist rhetors (Graves and Spencer, "Against Knowing" and "Rethinking"). Even when individuals may remain firm in their convictions about what happened, rhetorical gaslighting operates on a broader scale by sowing seeds of doubt in public discourse and questioning the validity of some individuals' accounts of events. The audience for public gaslighting is thus not the original narrator, but those witnessing the narration.

In an online environment of obfuscation, distortion, and overwhelm, it becomes difficult for individuals to persuade others to believe their perceptions and experiences, however firm their own grasp on reality is and however solid their evidence may be. Rhetorical gaslighting is effective as a persuasive strategy because it works to make facts and evidence irrelevant—exactly what gaslighting also does as an individual abuse tactic. Theorizing gaslighting also emphasizes the embodied and affective components of post-truth rhetorical strategies. In public gaslighting, the gaslighter's intention is to provoke an affective response and to trigger an emotionally taxing experience for the original narrator, and to encourage doubt and outrage in witnesses, which may shut down further engagement. In order to fight this public gaslighting, activists use strategies grounded in testimonial in order to reclaim epistemic authority and to heal from the affective components of being gaslit, which also requires an audience willing to act as witnesses. However, to be more broadly effective, this reclamation and healing also needs to be situated in a broader collective witnessing: reckoning with the violence of white supremacy and intersecting oppressions.

Rhetorical Gaslighting as Epistemic Injustice

Epistemic injustice works by denying someone's capacity to make knowledge-based claims. As Miranda Fricker defines it, epistemic injustice is a "wrong done to someone specifically in their capacity as a knower" (1). For example, in a legal context, as Patricia Hill Collins explains, "epistemic oppression suppresses the epistemic agency of some members of the group while elevating that of others, thus producing privileged and derogated categories of knowers" ("Intersectionality" 120). This suppression works subtly and progressively on subordinated groups as a method of "eroding their epistemic authority" (Hill Collins, "Intersectionality" 119). Gaslighting is one strategy for suppressing epistemic agency, as it is based on the goal of forcing doubt—either persuading someone to doubt their own epistemic authority or encouraging others to do so. Not just a dynamic between individuals, gaslighting is a structural element of heteropatriarchal white supremacy, a "set of standards of cognition that encompass an agreement by dominant agents to misinterpret the world" (Berenstain 735). Structural gaslighting individualizes that which is actually systemic, a manipulation tactic that is a mainstay of American politics. For example, individuals experiencing oppression are often blamed for their own "poor choices," which conceals "how the mechanisms of power function to asymmetrically distribute harms" (Berenstain 734). By blaming individuals, those in power can dodge accountability for the decisions that have led to certain groups of people being harmed. As Alison Bailey argues, "Complex systems of domination require structural gaslighting, among other things, to keep their infrastructures in good working order" (668). Gaslighting is not an isolated strategy used by certain bad actors but is built into the structure of American institutions themselves.

As both an abuse tactic, at the individual level, and as a broader political strategy, gaslighting is a bid for epistemic control. The epistemic is intricately tied to rhetoric in its questions about who has authority to make knowledge claims and from what positions, which are complicated by oppressive power relations (Godbee). Gaslighting clearly illuminates "the relationship between 'reality' and 'knowledge' as mediated by rhetoric," as Clint G. Graves and Leland G. Spencer explain, drawing from Celeste Condit's structural-material model that understands "truth" to be rhetorically constructed rather than existing in some imagined prediscursive objective reality, but that also does not advocate for pure relativism (Graves and Spencer, "Rethinking" 52). As Graves and Spencer detail, such a model "enable[s] evaluation of knowledge claims along a continuum of 'truthfulness'" in relation to evidence, "including rigorously collected empirical observation or individuals' and groups' lived, corporeal/sensorial experience of the world" (53). The latter—individuals' and groups' lived experience—is especially important for marginalized knowledges, and what is most likely to be targeted for doubt by those in power through their use of gaslighting.

Like other disinformation strategies that involve decontextualization, gaslighting works in insidious ways to divorce individual experiences from larger systems and histories—one of the most effective ways to discredit activist rhetors, because the context necessary for evaluating their truth claims is erased. Graves and Spencer argue that "rhetoric mediates [the] link between social power and gaslighting dynamics, enabling gaslighters to manifest their power through multiple appeal structures that undermine a gaslightee's sense of reality" (54). Especially in digital contexts characterized by rapid circulation and the creation of noise and overwhelm as a political strategy, gaslighters are not always attempting to undermine an individual gaslightee's sense of reality, but rather trying to persuade a larger witnessing audience that an individual or group of marginalized rhetors are not credible. The goal is to amass a large enough audience to perform distrust of an activist rhetor speaking from a marginalized position, interfering in the circulation of their position and denying them witnesses.

Testimonial forms of discourse, both in the legal system and in broader public contexts, are used when there is a question of truth or injustice, and they imply "obligations of witnessing" (Ahmed and Stacey 1–2). Testimonial exchange, defined by Fricker as "the sort of discursive exchange in which knowledge can be imparted from speaker to hearer," is heavily influenced by power dynamics (16). Fricker argues that in a distinct form of epistemic injustice termed "testimonial injustice," a speaker is unable to be fully heard due to the hearers' prejudices. This "prejudicial dysfunction in testimonial practice" can manifest in either a "credibility excess" or a "credibility deficit" for the speaker (17). Many marginalized speakers enter testimonial exchange with a credibility deficit as judged by the hearers. Jennifer Hornsby writes that successful communication requires "being able not only to voice meaningful thoughts but also to be heard" (134), but the conditions required for being heard are controlled by those in power. As Kristie Dotson also explains, "The extent to which entire populations of people can be denied this kind of linguistic reciprocation as a matter of course institutes epistemic violence" (238). As a tool of heteropatriarchal white supremacy, gaslighting denies oppressed groups the ability to be heard in testimonial exchange, no matter how much or how insistently they speak. After all, "the need to demand recognition from the dominant culture or group is a symptom of the pathology of oppression" (K. Oliver 78). Structural gaslighting sustains long-standing but invisibilized barriers that prevent oppressed groups from being heard, framing their concerns as fringe, unreasonable, or dangerous.

Against epistemic injustice, feminist scholars have countered with theories of standpoint epistemology, foregrounding the authority of subordinated groups to construct knowledge about their experiences of subordination and to critique power based on this knowledge. Feminist standpoint epistemology treats identity not as an automatic guarantee of individual authority, but as a collective achievement of what Sandra Harding terms an "oppositional and shared consciousness in oppressed groups" (3). Queer epistemologies also make strategic use of critical and playful negotiations of identity in relation to culture, fluid and adaptable standpoints from which one may challenge dominant power (Hall). For example, in his theory of disidentification, José Esteban Muñoz explores how people positioned outside the racial and sexual mainstream use performance to refuse both identifying with dominant culture and identifying completely outside it. Disidentification is a "survival strategy that works within and outside the public sphere simultaneously," as those "whose identities are formed in response to the cultural logics of heteronormativity, white supremacy, and misogyny" can also transform elements of dominant culture for their own purposes (Muñoz, *Disidentifications* 5). In his work, Muñoz focuses on queer of color performances that circulate in subcultural spaces. While it is possible to take up the theory of disidentification in other contexts, including its potential use by subjects with greater access to power (Muñoz, *Disidentifications* 5), it is necessary to mark these differences. For instance, in her work exploring how white subjects may strategically disidentify with normative whiteness in service of solidarity with people of color, Stephanie Hartzell uses the term "performative disidentification" to signal a focus not on staged performances for an audience but on "everyday discursive attempts at resisting full interpellation into dominant norms of particular subject positions" (68). Performative disidentification allows for a rethinking of standpoint in relation to testimonial, in which those who simultaneously occupy marginalized and privileged positions may take up components of expected testimonial genres to signal subversive aims.

Working against epistemic injustice in the form of gaslighting, especially structural gaslighting, is a difficult process for activist rhetors seeking to critique power from a disempowered position, as well as for those seeking to leverage what power they may have to advocate for change. They cannot counter every false claim or every attempt at public gaslighting, especially not on social media, where direct responses to disinformation often allow the disinformation to spread further because platforms are designed to read any uptake as valuable "engagement." In some cases, the most strategic option is disengagement for self or community protection. Silence itself can sometimes be a powerful rhetorical strategy for the oppressed (Smilges). However, disengagement is not always possible or desired, as it can also represent succumbing to "rhetorical exhaustion," in which case a disinformation campaign has been successful (Bradshaw). Activist rhetors are frequently motivated to fight against public gaslighting in order to express solidarity with each other and to maintain and grow an audience of witnesses who might trust their positions, against the gaslighters' own base of witnesses willing to support distorted claims. In doing so, they not only use but also subvert genres of testimonial.

The following sections detail the workings of public gaslighting as a disinformation strategy and explore how it can be countered, in the specific context of the US Capitol insurrection on January 6, 2021. I first analyze how gaslighting operated during the insurrection and its aftermath, then explore specific examples of counter-gaslighting strategies that use dynamics of testimonial and witnessing in different ways.

Gaslighting during and after the Capitol Insurrection

In "Donald Trump Is Gaslighting Us on the January 6 Riot," CNN editor Chris Cillizza begins with Trump's statement about that day: "Our hearts and minds are with the people being persecuted so unfairly relating to the January 6th protest concerning the Rigged Presidential Election. . . . In addition to everything else, it has proven conclusively that we are a two-tiered system of justice. In the end, however, JUSTICE WILL PREVAIL!" As Cillizza argues, "This is a classic bit of gaslighting by Trump. He's trying to make you believe that the way you remember the January 6 insurrection at the US Capitol isn't, actually, how it played out. In Trump's conception, these were peaceful protesters gathered to draw attention to the fact that the 2020 election was stolen." Trump's portrayal of "peaceful protesters" also makes use of the strategies detailed in chapter 2 that define "violence" in terms of specific instances of physical destruction only, rather than as structural violence. In this formulation, white supremacist protesters can be framed as "peaceful" for reasons such as some members of the group choosing not to engage in property damage, while racial justice activists can be framed as "violent" for responding defensively to police officers' excessive force. These gaslighting strategies were echoed and circulated by many fellow Republicans, most of whom did not speak against Trump's comments or his earlier role in inciting the insurrection.

The House of Representatives impeached Trump for the constitutional offense of "incitement of insurrection" based on the events of January 6 (United States Congress, House). The pretrial brief details how Trump refused to accept the election results for months leading up to the insurrection: "He spent months asserting, without evidence, that he won in a 'landslide' and that the election was 'stolen'" (Raskin et al. 2), using his online and offline presence to assert this view continuously, especially through Twitter, his favored platform. As with other cases, Trump created a feedback loop of false claims using social media and public appearances, appealing to a wide variety of audiences, from mainstream Republicans to groups such as QAnon. Trump's use of social media to spark the insurrection eventually led to his ban from Twitter and Facebook.

However strong the evidence that Trump lost the election, his online and offline strategies were effective in their relentlessness. A persistent refusal to accept reality can itself become a reality, especially when those with power endorse it. In such a communicative environment, factual arguments are ineffective because the terms for discussion are no longer grounded in a factual reality. In his work on rhetorical exhaustion, Bradshaw invokes gaslighting as one practice implicated in the political work of wearing down audiences (4). As an abuse tactic, gaslighting is designed to make someone doubt their reality, or even if they hold on to their conviction in the truth, they are unable to act based on that conviction because the gaslighter persistently shuts them down. Public gaslighting goes a step further by recruiting witnesses to the cause of doubting those who speak from a disempowered position. In this public performance of denying some people's perceptions in favor of others', one goal is recruiting audiences to share in the gaslighter's alternative reality and contribute to an environment of exhaustion, as disempowered rhetors insisting on their realities now have to contend with a large and forceful mass who are persistently circulating denials. Individuals may continue to trust their own reality, but their narrations of this reality may be dismissed in public discourse. Public performances of gaslighting also help to sediment group identities and shared realities—for example, Trump supporters' denials of alternate first-person testimonials about the insurrection.

In the months after the 2020 election, Trump used rhetorical gaslighting in social media and public appearances to lay the groundwork for what would become the insurrection. The House pretrial brief recounts his actions and attitude on the day itself:

> With his options running out, President Trump announced a "Save America Rally" on January 6. He promised it would be "wild." By the day of the rally, President Trump had spent months using his bully pulpit to insist that the Joint Session of Congress was the final act of a vast plot to destroy America. As a result—and as had been widely reported—the crowd was armed, angry, and dangerous. Before President Trump took the stage, his lawyer called for "trial by combat." His son warned Republican legislators against finalizing the election results: "We're coming for you." Finally, President Trump appeared behind a podium bearing the presidential seal. Surveying the tense crowd before him, President Trump whipped it into a frenzy, exhorting followers to "fight like hell [or] you're not going to have a country anymore." Then he aimed them straight at the Capitol, declaring: "You'll never take back our country with weakness. You have to show strength, and you have to be strong." (Raskin et al. 2)

Trump was able to mobilize followers to great effect on January 6 because of the shared reality he and they had already created—that the election was "stolen." He used terms connoting violence, war, and heteropatriarchal masculine strength (avoiding "weakness," "fight[ing] like hell [or] you're not going to have a country anymore"). Typical of Trumpian rhetoric, this was paired with a mobilization of white nostalgia through the language of "taking back" America and restoring it to a time in the past before the alleged "theft." His use of terms like "theft," "stealing," "taking back," and "saving" slides across multiple meanings. He makes specific claims about the "election victory stolen by emboldened radical-left Democrats" and the "fake news media," and works more broadly to constitute his audience as an *us* to whom America belongs ("Our country has been under siege for a long time. Far longer than this four-year period"), in opposition to an invading *them* ("They also want to indoctrinate your children in school by teaching them things that aren't so. They want to indoctrinate your children. It's all part of the comprehensive assault on our democracy") (Naylor). Detailing the response of the mob to Trump's exhortations, the pretrial brief continues:

> Incited by President Trump, his mob attacked the Capitol. This assault unfolded live on television before a horrified nation. But President Trump did not take swift action to stop the violence. Instead, while Vice President

> Pence and Congress fled, and while Capitol Police officers battled insurrectionists, President Trump was reportedly "delighted" by the mayhem he had unleashed, because it was preventing Congress from affirming his election loss. (Raskin et al. 2)

In the impeachment trial, the charge of "incitement of insurrection" required evidence that Trump intended to incite violence and was successful in doing so, hence the focus on his speech and social media posts before the attack on the Capitol and his lack of effort to stop it and "delight" during and afterward. Ultimately, the Senate judged him not guilty as charged in the Article of Impeachment by a vote of 57 to 43, ten votes short of the two-thirds majority required by the Constitution for impeachment. Structural gaslighting is a productive framework for understanding this outcome, as those with political power control the terms for what counts as valid and substantial enough evidence to support a claim.

Trump's legal team and supporters argued that the accusation of "incitement to insurrection" could not be proven because of a lack of evidence that his words about the election results *caused* the violence at the Capitol. Under this logic, the only way Trump could be impeached for this charge would be if he had, on record, directly instructed his audience to organize an insurrection on that specific day and time—which he would obviously be motivated *not* to do in order to dodge culpability. Further, because rhetoric is never a matter of simple cause and effect, the absence of a direct and empirically provable line of causation does not mean that a rhetor's words had no influence on a later outcome. However, because influence is difficult to prove in a legal setting, people in positions of power can often dodge accountability for their words by denying their own rhetoricity—framing their statements as mere words rather than rhetorical actions with the ability to persuade an audience. They can also use their "credibility excess" (Fricker; Medina) granted by a position of power to place disproportionate emphasis on textual evidence that might support their innocence, rather than what might support their guilt. For example, Trump's defense lawyers used one line in his speech, "I know that everyone here will soon be marching over to the Capitol building to peacefully and patriotically make your voices heard," as evidence that he did not intend to incite violence (Naylor), deemphasizing many other parts of the speech where he used the rhetoric of fighting and war. Meanwhile, those in disempowered positions in the legal system often face the opposite phenomenon: Their casual utterances are assumed to have a much greater and more nefarious intentionality, parts of their speech that could support their guilt are weighted more heavily than other parts that could support their innocence, and much lower standards for evidence of cause and effect are applied (Picalini).[1]

Overall, the House pretrial brief is also telling in its framing of the insurrection, Trump's role, and who and what were threatened. The trial brief frames the insurrectionists as dangerous because of instances of physical violence and threats against police officers and politicians, and because of their violation of the hallowed spaces of American government, weaving nostalgic nationalist rhetoric about the sanctity of American institutions with examples of insurrectionists' violent acts:

> In a grievous betrayal of his Oath of Office, President Trump incited a violent mob to attack the United States Capitol during the Joint Session, thus impeding Congress's confirmation of Joseph R. Biden, Jr. as the winner of the presidential election. As it stormed the Capitol, the mob yelled out "President Trump Sent Us," "Hang Mike Pence," and "Traitor Traitor Traitor." The insurrectionists assaulted police officers with weapons and chemical agents. They seized control of the Senate chamber floor, the Office of the Speaker of the House, and major sections of the Capitol complex. Members and their staffs were trapped and terrorized. Many officials (including the Vice President himself) barely escaped the rioters. The line of succession to the Presidency was endangered. Our seat of government was violated, vandalized, and desecrated. Congress's counting of electoral votes was delayed until nightfall and not completed until 4 AM. Hundreds of people were injured in the assault. Five people—including a Capitol Police officer—died. (Raskin et al. 1)

What is not foregrounded is that the insurrectionists were motivated not only by Trump, but by white supremacy. Many made this obvious by carrying or wearing imagery like the Confederate flag and a wide variety of other symbols associated with white supremacist groups (Washington Post Staff). However, the pretrial brief only includes one brief mention of "white nationalism," using Trump's instruction during the previous fall's presidential debate for the white nationalist group the Proud Boys to "stand back and stand by" as one piece of evidence among others that he is "comfortable urging, approving, and even celebrating violence" (14). The House Select Committee paid little attention to the racialized dynamics of the Capitol insurrection, focusing instead on proving Trump's intent to incite violence and framing the conflict

1. See, for example, the numerous Black activists in Ferguson, Missouri, charged for "inciting a riot" on the evidence of one or a small number of social media posts with potentially but not provably "violent" language (Rivas).

as politically partisan in nature (Republicans contesting the victory of a Democratic presidential candidate), rather than foregrounding the role of white racial resentment in the insurrection and in Trump's messaging (Davis and Wilson 84–85).

The committee's focus on proving Trump's culpability for causing violence with his rhetoric, as well as the committee's choice to denounce the insurrection because it threatened the spaces of the political establishment, reveals the structural inability of the American political and legal system to reckon deeply with white supremacy. After all, these institutions are themselves built upon white supremacist history, their founding condition. More recent reforms, such as civil rights legislation, have provided vital avenues for certain oppressed people to fight some of the circumstances of their oppression and to access previously denied opportunities. However, the January 6 insurrection, the House committee, and Trump's second impeachment trial reveal the limitations, even with reforms, of systems that were not designed with the protection of people racialized as Black and Brown in mind.

Within these systems, Trump can only be charged for intentional and provable incitement of physical violence against specific politicians, Capitol police officers, and buildings that are sacred symbols of America. He cannot be held accountable in the American legal system for the everyday violence of white supremacy that he perpetuates. This reveals the structural gaslighting at the core of the legal system: Those oppressed by the daily systemic violence of white supremacy have no mechanism to seek recourse, and further, are invalidated for even seeking that recourse. However, those who maintain white supremacy have plenty of legal avenues to be heard and to escape culpability.

Building upon this analysis, the following sections focus on examples of public discourse in the insurrection's aftermath, how gaslighting was used, and how people responded to and subverted gaslighting for activist goals. I consider the uses and limitations of disidentification through personal testimonial to counter public gaslighting through analysis of a video by politician Alexandria Ocasio-Cortez. Then, I juxtapose the history of Black insurrection in the US with the antiviolence rhetoric used by liberals after the January 6 insurrection, revealing the necessity of a larger-scale public witnessing of white supremacy in order to counter structural gaslighting.

Resisting Gaslighting by Performing Testimonial

On January 12, 2021, and then February 1, 2021, Alexandria Ocasio-Cortez, the Democratic representative for New York's Fourteenth Congressional District, told her story of the Capitol insurrection in two ninety-minute videos using Instagram Live, a live-streaming video feature of the image-centric platform owned by Meta. In the first video, she gave her account of the events of January 6 (Guardian News), then received swift backlash from social media users claiming that she was lying about where she was during the insurrection, though she was not (Swenson). In the second video, Ocasio-Cortez responds to those attempting public gaslighting in order to discredit her version of events, and she also makes the narrative more personal by revealing her history of sexual assault ("What Happened"). After finishing the second live stream, Ocasio-Cortez also uploaded the video to her public YouTube page to be viewed and circulated by additional audiences. Ocasio-Cortez's video is influenced both by her marginalization as a young woman of color in public office and by her relative proximity to social power as a US Congress member, a position in which she has often used personal narrative as part of a political strategy designed to achieve wide circulation in a time when social media and politics have become deeply intertwined.

Ocasio-Cortez, the youngest woman to serve in the US Congress, became known early in her first campaign for using social media skillfully to build and sustain support. In addition to posts across platforms including Instagram and Twitter, Ocasio-Cortez has favored live streams, often going live to her followers while cooking in her home and speaking about a political issue. Live streams offer more unfiltered and unedited forms of social media engagement than more highly edited posts. In the case of Ocasio-Cortez, her streams are often unusually long examples of the often more compressed genre, heightening the effect of inviting viewers into her space for a long discussion. Of course, in the case of any public figure, a live stream is a performance created for an audience and not a window into their life. A live-stream performance involves a construction of intimacy heightened beyond other forms of social media interaction, as the speaker is talking synchronously to viewers rather than making a post and receiving only temporally distanced reactions. Those in the audience can react by posting live comments that appear during the stream or clicking a heart to respond to something a speaker said.

Because of these features, live streams are an apt medium for the genre of testimonial, which seeks to constitute an audience to bear witness to the speaker's reality as represented through their testimonial. Ocasio-Cortez, while the target of public gaslighting by critics, was able to resist this gaslighting through her base of supporters, whom she mobilized through testimonial to act as witnesses for her account of the insurrection (Morris). Further, especially through her use of strategic disidentification with nationalist rhetoric, she is able to offer an alternate stance to the Democratic mainstream while also protecting herself from more extreme backlash. Witnesses were motivated to take up the language she provided for understanding connections between personal trauma and political events, resisting structural gaslighting strategies that aim to disconnect the two.

In her second live stream about the Capitol attacks, Ocasio-Cortez faces her phone camera, dressed casually in a turtleneck sweater with a backdrop of a plain wall. She invites viewers to understand disinformation about the insurrection through the framework of abuse, sharing her experience as part of a larger context. She begins by saying that her experience is only one among many, including those more marginalized. She then establishes the exigence for sharing her story at this moment: the widespread calls by conservatives for people to "move on" from the insurrection, an example of public gaslighting attempting to downplay the importance of the event. Ocasio-Cortez states:

> The reason why I think it's important to share is because so many of the people who helped perpetrate and take responsibility for what happened in the Capitol are trying to tell us all to move on, to forget what happened, they're trying to tell us that it wasn't a big deal, they're trying to tell us to move on, without any accountability, without any truth-telling, without actually confronting the extreme damage, physical harm, loss of life, trauma that was inflicted on not just me as a person, not just other people as individuals, but all of us as a collective, and on many other people. We cannot move on without accountability. We cannot heal without accountability. And so all of these people who want to tell us to move on are doing so at their own convenience. ("What Happened")

Here at the beginning of her live stream, Ocasio-Cortez establishes several interconnected themes: public gaslighting ("move on," "forget what happened," "it wasn't a big deal"), trauma, truth-telling, and accountability, which she returns to throughout her video. She continues by transitioning into a personal moment, saying, "To friends and loved ones close to me, I want to apologize to them in advance, sorry if my voice is shaking, but if you are learning things about me in the course of this live that you didn't know before, and it's not a thing about hiding or anything like that, but sometimes you just can't tell the same story over and over." Here, she invites viewers to become witnesses—both those who know her who may be watching and the larger public audience are led into a moment of intimacy that is also a moment of strategic public vulnerability. Rather than the imposed vulnerability of public gaslighting, strategic vulnerability is a rhetor's choice and can be powerful in testimonial when audiences agree to bear witness. This foundation allows her to continue making her next point connecting trauma to the insurrection and the gaslighting afterward, which she narrates while starting to cry:

> These folks who tell us to move on, that it's not a big deal, that we should forget what's happened, even telling us to apologize, these are the same tactics of abusers. And I'm a survivor of sexual assault. And I haven't told many people that in my life. But when we go through trauma, trauma compounds on each other, and so whether you had a neglectful parent, or you had someone who was verbally abusive to you, whether you are a survivor of abuse, whether you experienced any sort of trauma in your life, small to large, these episodes can compound on one another. There's now something really big happening to you and then you deal with it and move on and when something else happens to you, you deal with that and then you move on. All of our experiences make us who we are. And that's also to say that most people live with trauma. That doesn't even diminish any of the trauma that any one of us many have been through. But it is to say there is a community of so many people who can understand. (Ocasio-Cortez, "What Happened")

By situating her experience in a larger context and invoking a community, Ocasio-Cortez establishes that she is not alone and that others are not alone in experiences of trauma, asking for witnesses by invoking shared experiences, wherein the act of bearing witness is "a rhetorical space of intersubjectivity" (Hesford 105). She constitutes a "we" based on a shared experiential and epistemic stance of "living with trauma." This is in contrast to gaslighting strategies, which work in part by isolating the victim, denying them witnesses in order to make them feel that they are alone in their own perception of reality. Instead of this isolation, Ocasio-Cortez continues to emphasize community throughout her video. She then returns directly to the insurrection:

> They're trying to say you're making too big a deal over it. Or my favorite, this past week Ted Cruz and now Representative Chip Roy, and oh by the way, some of the other representatives who actually encouraged people to threaten members of Congress or tweeted out the location of the Speaker, are now telling me to apologize for saying and speaking truth to what happened. These are the tactics of abusers. And so when I see this happen how I feel and how I felt was, "not again." . . . As a survivor I struggle with the idea of being believed. And what's odd is that I am in a job where people are constantly calling me untruthful or that I'm exaggerating, so there's a real irony in that. But the reason why I think it's important for us to hold this to account is because we know that if we do not hold people accountable, what

> they are asking for when they say, "Can we just move on?" is "Can we just forget this happened so that I can do it again without recourse." (Ocasio-Cortez, "What Happened")

Ocasio-Cortez touches on many aspects of gaslighting and abuse here: the pressure that gaslighters use to punish people who speak truth, such as calling for her to apologize; "the idea of being believed," or the way in which repeated experiences of going unheard can cause someone to enter into testimonial exchanges expecting an audience of disbelievers, which can be retriggered by gaslighting and which abusers use in their favor; and the importance of accountability. By turning toward accountability, Ocasio-Cortez takes this dynamic of gaslighting into a broader public. Rather than "can we just forget," Ocasio-Cortez calls for insistent collective memory. Entering her story into public memory is one example of this, and the size of her audience means extensive witnessing. This call for accountability also invites others to share their own experience and evidence as a broader strategy for public witnessing (which the House committee later utilized in investigating the insurrection).

In the rest of her live stream, Ocasio-Cortez shares her testimonial of what happened on January 6, starting by recounting her observations that there was minimal security around the Capitol, especially considering the threats that she and others had heard, and that there was an environment of hostility and escalation in the area as she noticed people from out of town watching her. On the day itself, she was in her office and began to hear banging on her office door; she hid while someone shouted, "Where is she?," fearing for her life as she believed someone was coming to attack her. The person was a Capitol police officer, but she explains that something did not add up, as he had "no partner, was not yelling 'Capitol Police,' but then it didn't feel right, because he was looking at me with a tremendous amount of anger and hostility." Later, she reflects on her thought process during this time, when she felt endangered but also questioned whether her perception of danger was accurate, and she emphasizes the role of witnesses who were there and affirmed her intuition. The police officer told her and her staffer to go to another building but did not specify the room or anything else about the exact location, but she and her staffer ran to the general area, while hearing yelling and people seemingly trying to break into the building. She ended up hiding in Representative Katie Porter's office for several hours, and then joining up with Representative Ayanna Pressley, another member of a young cohort of women of color Democratic House representatives. Ocasio-Cortez emphasizes the role of community witnessing in processing trauma, recounting how Pressley listened to and validated Ocasio-Cortez's experience:

> When I told the story to Representative Pressley she told me right away that what you experienced was traumatizing and you need to take care of yourself. It was like having her as a friend and a sister hear what I was saying and tell me that, mentally, it forced me to pump my brakes and be like oh, oh. So I think it was so important and I think for so many people out there if you have experienced any sort of trauma, just the fact of recognizing that and admitting it is already a huge step, especially in a world where people are constantly trying to tell you that you didn't experience what you experienced or that you're lying, those are additional traumas on top of what you already experienced. ("What Happened")

Again, relational activist knowledge and practices are vital when facing a hostile environment. Ocasio-Cortez continues this theme by extending this moment of community recognition into a broader dynamic of witnessing, emphasizing throughout the rest of her video that abusers use isolation as a strategy to disconnect a victim from community, but that shared solidarity and witnessing are vital for processing trauma—on an individual and a systemic level.

Some have read Ocasio-Cortez's videos about the Capitol attack as evidence of a problematic pattern of women of color performing trauma for public consumption. For example, Yasmin Nair criticizes Ocasio-Cortez for placing her personal traumas in relation to the events of January 6 as a political strategy and for circulating an individual narrative rather than a structural critique. In Nair's interpretation, especially the second video's emotionality is an example of Ocasio-Cortez using a story of trauma "to shift the needle of sympathy towards her" and to "forestall any possibility of ever questioning" her. Further, Nair argues that Ocasio-Cortez "stitches her personal narrative onto a nationalist one" by narrating her personal trauma alongside language about the Capitol attacks such as "the citadel of democracy" or "our country." For Nair, this weaving of personal trauma with nationalist imagery forecloses the possibility of deeper engagement with the violent history of the US. As she claims, "It is a particular irony of the times we live in that a woman of colour helps to suspend any ongoing awareness of the deathliness of American history by retelling her personal trauma," and in the process of making her trauma visible, Ocasio-Cortez "makes certain things invisible, including the brutality of America, before and after Trump." In this formulation, Ocasio-Cortez's choice to frame her video about the Capitol attacks in relation to personal trauma plays into the harmful expectations placed upon women of color politicians to perform sad stories in order to qualify as people worth listening to, which leads to the repetition of individual trauma narratives but no larger change to the systems that cause trauma on a broader scale.

I am certainly amenable to Nair's critique of the ways in which people in disempowered positions are expected to perform their trauma in public, and I agree with her larger points about the commodification of trauma narratives. However, I offer an alternate reading of Ocasio-Cortez's strategy in relation to the epistemic dynamics of gaslighting—one that does not seek to glorify Ocasio-Cortez but to more closely examine her rhetorical strategies as a politician in public office with a large following, and as a leftist young woman of color under high scrutiny. Ocasio-Cortez is conscious of her need to sustain "likeability" for political success; as Nair points out, this is necessary for her as "a woman, a woman of colour, and a millennial" in politics. Her trauma narrative is told in a way that aims to engender sympathy for her, which may translate to ongoing or new political support. However, I argue that she is also doing something more complicated in her second video, especially in her engagement with nationalist rhetoric.

Ocasio-Cortez includes nods to nationalist language that are, as Nair says, "standard issue for any politician," similar language to what would also be used in the House impeachment trial brief, which represented the insurrectionists as violators of the sacred spaces of American democracy. However, where Ocasio-Cortez breaks with such sentiment is in her portrayal of Capitol police. Documents such as the pretrial brief would later largely present the Capitol police as the victims of insurrectionists' violence (Raskin et al. 22) or as "defenders" who "put their own lives at risk" and acted "shrewdly and heroically" to protect the Capitol (23). While this may be true of some, the House pretrial brief ignores the possibility that the ranks of Capitol police may have included some sympathetic to the cause of the insurrection, or at least that they did not take the threat seriously (Froomkin). Ocasio-Cortez does not directly accuse police of anything in this video, without evidence that would meet the standards necessary to sustain such a critique. However, she is critical of the institution of policing and vocal in her support of efforts to defund police (Dixon; Moreno). In her video, she smuggles a critique of Capitol police into her personal trauma narrative and in the process disidentifies with the nationalist rhetoric of the Democratic mainstream after the insurrection.

Ocasio-Cortez is in a double bind as a woman of color with a leftist activist background who has entered political office—she must find ways to advocate for the progressive causes her constituents have elected her to support, while navigating heightened scrutiny within the hostile environment of the American political establishment (Del Valle). Especially in an environment of rapidly circulating and escalating disinformation, she must carefully calculate what she is able to risk saying directly and what would cause a degree of hyperbolic backlash that is not worth the risk in service of longer goals. Instead, she invites her audience to connect the dots themselves and to speculate on the Capitol police force's role when she points out her surprise at the lack of security around the Capitol and then details the "anger and hostility" of the officer she encountered, whose behavior contributed to her fearing for her life. She locates the trauma trigger in this very moment, narrating the role of this officer at length. She uses a disidentification strategy when she nods briefly to one kind of nationalist rhetoric (brief mentions of "the citadel of democracy," "our country") and later refuses another: solidarity with and praise of the Capitol police. In this way, she is able to signal that she does not fully buy into the rhetoric of American institutions as sacred and worth protecting. Though she may have to play this political game at times, she hints that she does not accept the rules of the game. She creates and circulates a testimonial in the way expected of a woman of color in American politics (a tearful narrative of trauma), but she also subverts this common public genre to draw attention to the role of police in the violence of the insurrection. In doing so, she offers witnesses another way to talk about the insurrection that breaks with the Democratic mainstream and its reliance on nationalist and pro-police rhetoric.

Further, in my interpretation, her personal trauma narrative does not invisibilize the brutality of America; instead, it provides audiences with forms of logic and language to connect personal traumas with the systemic violence of American history, in the process actually illuminating some of that violence. For example, her trauma narrative is one of heteropatriarchal violence, both in the act of sexual assault and in the gaslighting dynamics that deny sexual assault survivors the ability to be heard and witnessed. This reveals the implicit connection she is making between the events of January 6 and the personal abuse testimonial: Both are rooted in systems of heteropatriarchal violence, which is part of the violence at the core of America, though not the full story. Her critique of police—potentially easy to miss in the context of her tearful trauma narrative, but nonetheless present points to a larger network of claims she has made in other public contexts against police brutality. She is thus asking audiences not only to believe her story of trauma, but to make that connection and see the broader structure of violence at play. The rhetorical strategies of her video are designed not only to elicit sympathy for her, though as a politician that is always part of her aim; they also invite uptake and circulation, which may lead to more activist work than what she can accomplish in her position alone. She provides an example that others may take up and apply elsewhere to connect individual examples of trauma with larger structures of heteropatriarchal violence, and to make critical connections between these examples and political events.

Ocasio-Cortez's rhetorical work in this context can be further complexified by expanding beyond an analysis of the video as a static artifact and considering how she takes advantage of digital circulation to deepen her message. After her second video, opponents again attempted public gaslighting. Fox News host and right-wing commentator Tucker Carlson mocked her testimony on his show *Tucker Carlson Tonight,* specifically her fears of sexual violence, saying "this is crazy" and that she should "get a therapist" rather than going public with her story. The accusation of "crazy" is a public performance for Carlson's audience, inviting them to participate in gaslighting. He uses common gaslighting strategies that have specifically been used to discredit and force doubt in people who have experienced sexual assault: dismissal and laughter. By attempting to frame Ocasio-Cortez's narrative as "crazy," he uses an ableist trope to dismiss her authority over her own experience. Further, Carlson laughs about it, another especially cruel form of gaslighting in which someone's capacity as a knower is not only denied but openly mocked, indicating to his audience the attitude he wants them to take—viewing her claims as ridiculous and not even worth contemplation.

This dismissal and laughter are deeply familiar to anyone who has experienced abuse. In a social media response, Ocasio-Cortez defuses Carlson's accusations by linking them to these histories of discrediting sexual assault survivors: "I couldn't care less about what this talking inferiority complex has to say, but I do feel for the women and survivors in his life who now see they wouldn't be believed or safe with him. Many survivors of assault don't tell family, friends, etc bc of how they see others treated" (Ocasio-Cortez, "I couldn't care"). She partly engages Carlson on his own terms of insult—"talking inferiority complex"—showing that she also does not take him seriously as a knower. She then shifts the terms back onto those who are harmed by rhetorics of dismissal and laughter ("women and survivors"), positioning herself as someone with the epistemic authority to speak about the experience of assault, and dismisses him right back, showing she "couldn't care less" about his opinion and framing him as someone unworthy of trust. "I do feel for" also enacts a specific tone here. She does not know if there are any survivors in Carlson's life, but by constructing these hypothetical survivors, she creates a proxy audience for her followers to identify with. Ocasio-Cortez positions the discussion as not just about her, but about this larger potential group of silenced onlookers—those who "don't tell" because "of how they see others treated."

These dynamics of watching and seeing, or witnessing, are essential components of testimonial exchange in public online spaces. This is not a debate between Carlson and Ocasio-Cortez, but a matter of both of them designing performances for their audiences. In Carlson's performance, he attempts rhetorical gaslighting, and in Ocasio-Cortez's, she demonstrates one way to refuse it. Ocasio-Cortez's testimonial performance, both in her live-stream videos and through their circulation, is characteristic of minoritized subjects seeking engagement with the political mainstream, especially by invoking some of the codes of dominant culture while subverting others.

Black Insurrection and the Limits of Testimonial

While Ocasio-Cortez's testimonial offers audiences a way to understand the mechanisms of heteropatriarchal violence in the Capitol attacks and hints at histories of racialized violence in its critique of police, it should be paired with other forms of engagement with the meanings of the January 6 insurrection, especially to understand its violence as white supremacist in origin. The history of Black insurrection, specifically, illustrates the stark limitations of nationalist rhetoric and the flaws in liberal democracy's rhetoric of violence as threat. There are also limits to the usefulness of enacting disidentification-based testimonial strategies in relation to these rhetorics. As Muñoz explains, "Disidentification is *not always* an adequate strategy of resistance or survival for all minority subjects. At times, resistance needs to be pronounced and direct; on other occasions, queers of color and other minority subjects need to follow a conformist path if they hope to survive a hostile public sphere" (*Disidentifications* 5). In the case of many examples of Black insurrection, "pronounced and direct" resistance is the only remaining option available to survive white supremacist violence. As Hartzell explains in her analysis of racially privileged subjects' use of disidentification with normative whiteness, it is also necessary to acknowledge the limits of using the codes of power to speak against that power (75). For non-Black people to bear witness to Black insurrection, other rhetorical resources are needed.

After the January 6 insurrection, many politicians and public figures used the rhetoric of peaceful protest, contrasted with violent insurrection, and civil discourse in their attempts to control the narrative of the insurrection. For example, when House Speaker Kevin McCarthy granted Tucker Carlson access to 41,000 hours of video from Capitol Police security cameras on the day of the insurrection, and Carlson aired footage on Fox News that was edited to portray the event as a "peaceful protest" (Kane et al.), Republicans who wished to distance themselves from Trump critiqued Carlson's editing because it did not show evidence of violence. Such politicians used language similar to that of the House trial brief to portray Trump and his supporters as violent and dangerous, and to portray themselves as calm and reasonable in contrast. In this version of reality, the problem with Trump and the insurrection is violence itself, regardless of context. The implicit definition of "violence" as a universal moral negative participates in a form of structural gaslighting that purposefully neglects to consider the history and context of the violence (in this case, white supremacist violence). By drawing attention to the physical violence of the insurrection and siding against Carlson or Trump, some Republicans can attempt to court support by claiming the moral high ground, distanced from the overtly violent white supremacy of specific groups like the Proud Boys, while still subtly working to enact policies that uphold the violence of covert white supremacy.

Further, some politicians combined this understanding of violence with the liberal rhetoric of civil discourse, such as Ted Cruz (R-Texas), who used "both sides" language to refer to Carlson's edits (recalling Trump's "both sides" remarks about Charlottesville, whether intentionally or not). Cruz stated, "I don't doubt from the video that players on multiple sides can take portions of video and tell the story they want to tell. . . . There were some people who engaged in acts of violence—and if you engaged in acts of violence, you should be prosecuted and go to jail—and there were many other people who engaged in peaceful protest" (Kane et al.). Several Republicans also frame the violence of the insurrection as a violation of nationalism. Mitt Romney (R-Utah) stated, "I think it's a very dangerous thing to do to suggest that attacking the Capitol of the United States is in any way acceptable and is anything other than a serious crime against democracy and against our country" (Kane et al.), framing the problem as an attack on a symbol of American patriotism, defined as a moral negative in and of itself, regardless of the motivation for the attack.

It is important to correctly name what happened on January 6, 2021, as a violent insurrection and not a "peaceful protest"; however, what is missing is the vital context that it was a white supremacist violent insurrection, which both Republican and Democratic politicians did not name. This erasure is a more subtle form of public gaslighting than what Trump and his most vocal supporters do when they attempt to rewrite the events of January 6. Those Republicans wishing to appear more moderate or civil than Trump, as well as Democrats who denounce the insurrection solely on the terms of its violence, are still engaging in gaslighting when they do not name the white supremacist nature of the insurrection and frame the problem as the act of insurrection itself, divorced from context.

By establishing the equation of insurrection = violence = bad, politicians lay rhetorical groundwork for denouncing *any* insurrectionary acts, grouping an insurrection to uphold white supremacy and the history of Black insurrection in the same category. This is another subtle way in which liberalism works to halt racial justice. As writer Kandist Mallett observes, after the January 6 insurrection:

> The primary narrative that has emerged is one of overwhelming nationalism, not unlike what transpired after September 11. Trump is cast as treasonous while Democrats and a handful of opportunistic Republicans clear a path to reclaim the greatness of the country after four years during which resistance to the federal government was a fashionable position. We must consider what this sweeping condemnation of "insurrection"—and turn toward unquestioning patriotism—might mean for Black people, for whom insurrectionary acts and rebellion have been part of our pursuit of true freedom for more than 400 years.

Denunciations of the January 6 insurrection through a liberal civility and nationalistic framework may challenge Trump and allow other politicians to claim a moral high ground by framing themselves as loyal in contrast to his acts of treason, but they obscure the white supremacist origins of the January 6 insurrection. Further, the equation of insurrection = violence = bad sets rhetorical groundwork for also condemning those protesting racial justice using insurrectionary acts. The comparison has already been made many times between the treatment of the January 6 insurrectionists and the many Black Lives Matter protests across the US that have been met with extreme police force. In these cases, BLM activists defending themselves from police violence are represented in media as those who started the violence, while the police are represented as those seeking to restore order and peace. However, the truth is the other way around, as police often start the violence by arriving to protests in riot gear, tear-gassing protesters, and shooting rubber bullets into the crowd.

Under white supremacy, those racialized as Black and people of color are framed as those whom the nation (racialized as white) needs to be defended *from*. As political philosopher Sabeen Ahmed argues in her analysis of the January 6 insurrection, sustaining the fiction of "a civilized, modern, and progressive Western identity" in service of continued domination requires "imbuing Otherness—nonwhiteness and solidarity with nonwhiteness—with threat and in turn legitimizing defense as a preemptive justification for the use of force, within state borders or outside of them" ("Coup"). It is not enough to denounce Trump or the insurrectionists as violent or uncivil; it is also necessary to ask what that violence aims to sustain or disrupt. Mallett continues:

> There has been very little engagement with this substance in the mainstream response to the violence at the Capitol. What has followed instead has been blanket condemnations of insurrection, a patriotic posture—shared by Democrats and Republicans—that holds the American state as a stable force for good. In his address to the nation responding to the Trump loyalists' attack, President-elect Joe Biden said that America "is about honor. Decency, respect, tolerance—that's who we are, that's who we've always been."

Biden's remarks here are classic liberalism, upholding honor, decency, respect, and tolerance as essential American values and framing threats to these things as unpatriotic and worth condemnation. Again, the white supremacy of the insurrection is erased in favor of "blanket condemnations" of the uncivil behavior of the insurrectionists. It is easy to flip these condemnations onto Black protesters who are also regularly framed as uncivil and unpatriotic. As Mallett observes, "Black history exposes another version of America, one far different from the one Biden describes. . . . A hollow turn toward nationalism in this moment not only erases the history of radical Black rebellion—it endangers its future," as the same rhetoric used to denounce the January 6 insurrectionists may quickly be turned on Black activists, with history and context collapsed.

In many examples of radical Black rebellion, violence is what happens when there is not just an imbalance of power in testimonial exchange that grants more credibility to certain rhetors, but a nonrecognition so complete that there is no possibility for recourse through rhetoric alone. In this context, the motivations and goals for insurrectionary action are extremely different from those of the January 6 attack. Politicians, both Republican and Democrat, were quick to name that event as an insurrection and condemn it for its violence, but not to name it as white supremacist despite clear evidence that it was. The act of bearing public witness to white supremacist violence threatens the existing social order because it also requires bearing witness to the history and possibility of Black insurrection. It is important to challenge public gaslighting in both its more overt manifestations and its more subtle structural machinations, not only telling the truth—that what happened on January 6 was a violent insurrection, in contrast to those trying to downplay the event—but also to situate it in its full context of American white supremacist violence and resistance to that violence.

CHAPTER 5

Anti-Trans Disinformation and t4t Care through Joy and Spite

Between 2015 and 2024, anti-transgender legislation surged from a rarity to a mainstay of right-wing American politics. According to the Trans Legislation Tracker (an independent research organization), in 2015, only twenty-one anti-trans bills were considered across the nation; in 2024, there were 692. Trans people, especially children but also adults, are targeted through such bills in a variety of categories: access to medical care, education, sports, public accommodations, accurate identification, and free expression, among others. Legislators have proposed and enacted bills that would prohibit teachers from using students' chosen names and pronouns or force them to "out" children to parents, as well as restricting teachers' own freedom to be "out" in the classroom; criminalize performances such as drag shows (often with vague language that would actually criminalize a trans person doing anything in public); make it illegal for a trans person to use the bathroom aligned with their gender; eliminate the ability for someone to change a gender marker on their identification or make it more difficult to change gender markers and names; prohibit trans athletes from competing; and criminalize gender-affirming care, strip public funding from such care, make it so difficult to access that most people would not be able to, or use fear tactics to prevent it, such as by threatening the medical licenses of doctors who provide gender-affirming care or characterizing a parent's support for a child receiving such care as "child abuse" and threatening that parent's custody over their child (ACLU). Florida has been a national leader in such legislation, spearheaded by governor Ron DeSantis, and Texas, Tennessee, and Missouri have also enacted especially restrictive laws, but many more states are involved. According to trans activist Erin Reed, who regularly updates an Anti-Trans Legislative Risk Map on her website, the majority of US states are currently unsafe for trans people, with more labeled likely to become high-risk in the future.

This wave of anti-trans legislation did not come out of nowhere but is the result of a coordinated political strategy. As journalist Madison Pauly reports in a *Mother Jones* feature showing leaked emails from various Republicans and other members of the religious right, planning anti-trans legislation that especially targets children is a favored strategy for these groups to gain political power. The spike in anti-trans bills has been planned by this network for years (Pauly). These networks mobilize rhetoric of "protecting the children," especially by targeting gender-affirming care and using disinformation strategies to reframe it as child abuse, mutilation, or unproven and untested medicine. This rhetoric also makes use of nostalgia through both implicit and explicit claims about childhood innocence (racialized as white and gendered as cis). For example, Abigail Shrier's 2020 book *Irreversible Damage: The Transgender Craze Seducing Our Daughters* argues that teens assigned female at birth who experiment with a trans or nonbinary identification are influenced to do so by social media personalities, educators, and peers, and frames this influence as a frightening threat. Shrier's argument relies on a discredited and retracted study by Lisa Littman about the concept of "rapid-onset gender dysphoria" among adolescents.[1] The cover image for *Irreversible Damage* could not be any more telling about the gendered and racialized fears behind its argument: A young white girl in the style of 1950s children's books is shown with a hole cut out where her reproductive organs would be. This image of nostalgic white mid-century childhood beckons potential readers concerned about the "transgender craze" with a rallying call that essentially equates to "make our children cis again."

As Pauly summarizes, gender-affirming care is evidence-supported and viewed as having positive outcomes within the medical community, especially

1. Littman's study on "rapid-onset gender dysphoria" was extremely methodologically flawed. Littman's evidence came from a survey of parents recruited from specific websites and blogs with deep anti-trans biases. Littman presented the opinions of these parents as evidence for a phenomenon she terms "rapid-onset gender dysphoria," without interrogating these biases and without conducting any research with the children themselves who are said to be experiencing this "condition."

in light of statistics on high suicide rates among transgender youth who are not able to receive this care. "Gender-affirming care" here also refers to a wide range of practices provided for people in different age groups. For young children, this care usually refers to support for forms of "social transition," such as trying a different name or pronouns or experimenting with clothing. For adolescents, this may also involve puberty blockers, which give the adolescent time to consider their desires before going through the irreversible changes of puberty. For older teens, hormone replacement therapy may be introduced. In almost all cases, surgery—especially genital surgery—is only an option for legal adults. However, in anti-trans rhetorics, there is no amount of evidence that is considered enough to support any form of gender-affirming care (including that for young children, which amounts mostly to allowing the child to change clothes).

Broad anti-trans rhetorics (such as the association of childhood with white, gender-normative innocence; the understanding of gender as binary and fixed, or if not quite fixed, still restricted; and the framing of trans people as inherently untrustworthy) give rise to specific pieces of disinformation about trans people (such as claims that trans children taking puberty blockers or hormones are causing "irreversible damage" to themselves, neglecting the fact that one's "natural" puberty is also irreversible). Highly coordinated political networks are often able to advance their agendas through the use of anti-trans rhetoric that focuses on children and their supposed innocence and corruptibility. As in many past examples of antiqueer rhetoric, the children invoked here are metaphorical children implicitly racialized as white who, in being corrupted by an alleged trans threat, metonymically stand in for the threat that transness poses to the normative (white, heteropatriarchal) state. Meanwhile, real children's lives are endangered and the freedoms of adults are also restricted in service of protecting imaginary children. Further, in what V. Jo Hsu terms the "affective drift" of race, gender, and sexuality within anti-trans rhetorics, policies seeking to restrict gender-affirming care are also a political tool for advancing larger agendas with negative impacts not only on trans people, but broadly on people of color, disabled people, and cisgender women as well. For example, antiabortion rhetoric equates cisgender womanhood with heteronormative reproduction using the same logics of gender normativity present in anti-trans rhetoric, and women of color are barred from participation in sports due to their bodies' perceived deviation from the metrics of white femininity (Hsu 63).

There are several disinformation strategies involved in these legislative attacks, but what I will focus on here is one specific disinformation strategy:

setting an unreachable standard for evidence. In detailing this strategy, I attend to the specific legislative context when it is used most often (bans or restrictions on gender-affirming care). Within the logic of much of this legislation, there would *never* be enough evidence to support an individual's claim that they are transgender because there is no way to prove absolute certainty. There is an assumption that people, especially children, have a core cisgendered self that is then corrupted by the threat of alternately gendered desire, introduced by an outside force (such as teachers, the media, or other children and adults). This assumed-cis self does not require evidence to support; no one ever asks why someone has chosen to *remain* the gender they were assigned at birth, because it is not framed as a choice but rather the default. However, deviation from this default is met with the demand for evidence to prove the reason for the deviation. In some legislation that allows for gender-affirming care to be provided in certain narrow contexts, the burden of evidence that one is "really trans" is extremely high. In the case of legislation aiming to restrict all gender-affirming care and eliminate trans people from public life, the assumption is that there is no valid evidence for alternately gendered desire and thus the desire is targeted for eradication.

In this legislative context, pro-LGBTQ liberal rhetorics use the frameworks provided by the legal system to make claims based on individual rights and self-knowledge in order to fight the harm that will be done by anti-trans laws. However, in doing so, they must play into the hand of anti-trans rhetorics that insist on evidence to support one's claim of transness and resultant desire for gender-affirming care (such as evidence that one's core self *is trans*, thus deserving of legal rights and protections based on this category). This legal strategy is sometimes useful to protect some trans people from the risk posed by anti-trans legislation. However, it also has its limitations, particularly in terms of entrenching an individualist narrative that is at odds with trans experiences and that keeps state power intact. Trans people of color, especially those without class privilege, as well as white trans people who oppose the normative state, have limited routes to resist within liberal trans rights discourse, meaning other strategies are also necessary.

To illustrate the history of these dynamics further, the following section analyzes precedents for the current anti-trans rhetoric of "protecting the child." I then turn toward an exploration of trans phenomenologies and liberal rights frameworks as in conflict, necessitating rhetorics of trans rest and recovery—or t4t rhetorics—when engaging with these dominant frameworks. The rest of the chapter analyzes two examples of such t4t rhetorics, rooted in complementary emotions theorized from trans experiences: joy and spite.

The Anti-Trans Rhetoric of "Protecting the Child"

Attacking queer people under the rubric of "protecting the child" is nothing new. As Lee Edelman critiques in *No Future,* antiqueerness relies on an imagined child as a rhetorical figure that is "innocently" straight and gender normative, and queerness is that which brings "children and childhood to an end" (293). In service of the rhetorical figure of the innocent child, restrictions are placed on "the lives, the speech, and the freedoms of adults, especially queer adults" (Edelman 293). Edelman is opposed to the culture of "reproductive futurism" that, in valuing an imagined future child over real people in the present, he argues will always endanger queer people. He also critiques an assimilationist strand of LGBTQ politics that accepts the terms of reproductive futurism, such as by advocating for inclusion in the institution of marriage and the nuclear family, arguing that doing so shuts down other possibilities for queer life that would be animated by an embrace instead of "no future," or queerness as the death of the existing social order.

As Jose Esteban Muñoz's response to Edelman emphasizes, the figure of the child is a racialized figure. "Innocence" is coded as an implicitly white default, while Black and Brown populations are racialized and othered. While agreeing with the need to critique the many ways in which American politics mobilize the figure of the child to justify violence against queer people, and also rejecting assimilation, Muñoz is also critical of Edelman's no-future stance, arguing that queer and trans people of color especially cannot afford to give up on the future. Rather than fully rejecting Edelman's argument, Muñoz deepens queer studies' understanding of the figure of the child by taking a queer of color approach, arguing that "it is important not to hand over futurity to normative white reproductive futurity," which requires "call[ing] on a utopian political imagination that will enable us to glimpse another time and place: a 'not-yet' where queer youths of color actually get to grow up" (*Cruising Utopia* 95–96). The life chances of queer youths of color will not be improved by white reproductive futurity or by a rejection of futurity altogether; instead, an alternate imaginary is required to consider what would constitute this "not-yet": what would or would not be present in a time and place without white supremacist, heteropatriarchal oppression.

Building on a queer of color approach, Jules Gill-Peterson explores anti-trans disinformation and moral panics focused on children in her book *Histories of the Transgender Child.* Against conceptions of trans childhood as something new—either in the form of right-wing panics about how many trans kids there seem to be these days, or in the form of liberal enthusiasm about a new vanguard of gender-creative children—Gill-Peterson traces longer histories of trans childhood and ties these histories to racialized dynamics of medicalization. Grounding her argument in a trans of color critique of medicine, Gill-Peterson explains that in addition to the figure of the default-cis, innocent, implicitly racialized white child mobilized in anti-trans rhetoric, "the dominant figure of the trans child" in the US public sphere also "underwrites . . . a potent 'racial innocence' that empties trans childhood of its content, including race, rendering it conceptually white while simultaneously libeling the existence of black trans and trans of color childhood" (2). This is why, in contemporary liberal trans advocacy in the legal system, the "trans child" made to prove their need for gender-affirming care is usually an image of a white child, while Black and trans of color childhood is absent from the public sphere. Through exploring and unpacking these histories, Gill-Peterson also calls for a need to "imagine different futures for trans children that do not instrumentalize their living bodies and dismiss their self-knowledge" (5). In this formulation, the self-knowledge of trans children is not the unimpeachable certainty of self supported by the weight of evidence that is demanded within mainstream trans discourse, but something more creative and more rooted in trans of color lifeworlds, rather than the need to meet the standards set by white, heteropatriarchal power.

Trans people now, including youths, often find themselves struggling to live at the nexus of these political and medical histories, compelled to translate desire into identity and to marshal evidence in support of that identity claim in order to access desired resources. In seeking to challenge legislative restrictions on care, trans activists need to navigate a legal system that does not accommodate trans experiences. The failures of a liberal legal framework for understanding trans experiences creates a need for trans people to work within these systems while also developing alternative rhetorics focused on community care and recovery from hostile spaces.

Medicalization, Liberal Rights Frameworks, and Trans Phenomenology in Conflict

Throughout the history of trans medicalization, trans people have had to make appeals on the terms of gatekeepers without trans experience, including meeting a burden of proof set on the terms of white heteropatriarchal power. Doubt of trans people's desires and motivations for transition, as well as a framing of trans people as untrustworthy, is structured into the history of trans medicine itself. As historian Beans Velocci details, mid-twentieth-century gender clinics in the US, led by Harry Benjamin, began with a specific burden of proof at their core: In order to access desired medical resources such as hormones and surgeries within the medical system, trans people must provide evidence to support their claim of transness, treated as a discrete individual identity that one does or does not possess. Desire alone, such as for physical changes brought about by hormone replacement therapy, has historically not been considered enough of a reason if this desire is not tied to an identity claim. For instance, within this dominant logic, one's desire for the physical effects of medical treatments like hormone replacement therapy proceeds from a sense of identity that was present *before* the desire (e.g., one's existing sense of "being a woman" or "being a man" leads one to wish for physical features that are associated with womanhood or manhood to reflect this internal gender identity). If one cannot prove the identity behind the desire, one is framed as untrustworthy, *self*-deluded first and then motivated to delude others (Velocci 464).[2] This claims-and-evidence understanding of trans identity also works to entrench gendered and racialized stereotypes; for instance, as trans theorist Sandy Stone explains, in being asked to prove one's womanhood for a heteropatriarchal audience, one is compelled to cite the conventions of white heteronormative womanhood in the hope of being believed (5). Those who cannot or will not do so are then cast outside the realm of legibility.

Further, as C. Riley Snorton details in *Black on Both Sides: A Racial History of Trans Identity*, the contemporary conception of transness as a medicalized category is also historically connected to white supremacist discourses that framed Black people's bodies as more mutably gendered than those of white people. Gill-Peterson also traces the ways in which racialized ideas of plasticity have influenced trans medicalization. She traces a historical process throughout the twentieth century through which some gender-diverse young white people came to be incorporated into a newly medicalized identity category, "transgender," in a way framed as empowering, while many youths of color who defied gendered expectations were differently medicalized through institutionalization and incarceration. These histories point to contemporary trans activism's uneasy relationship with medicalization, but in legislative contexts, an enthusiastic embrace of medicalization is often expected in order to challenge laws that would restrict care.

Today, a wider variety of pathways exist for gender-affirming care that go beyond the Benjamin model, including those that use the framework of informed consent (Chiang and Bachmann; Coleman et al.). However, transness is still medicalized and pathologized, and trans people seeking insurance

2. See also shuster.

coverage for gender-affirming care in most cases must first receive a diagnosis of gender dysphoria from a mental health professional, as specified in the DSM-5. The assumption of trans people's untrustworthiness, beginning with self-delusion and persisting into the delusion of others and tied to an undue burden of evidence, is still built into political debates about gender-affirming care. This is why politicians and others in power are so easily able to mobilize what Mikey Elster calls the rhetoric of "insidious concern," veiling anti-trans sentiment under the guise of protecting trans people from doing harm to themselves as well as others (409). Much of this concern is not only about a fear of transition but a larger fear of detransition, where reidentifying with one's gender assigned at birth (after accessing hormones or surgeries for the purpose of transition) is framed not as a neutral change in one's desire but as evidence that one was not really trans all along (Paul). In a context when "trans people and/or children stand in for a conception of the population rooted in cis, heterosexual, and white assumptions" (Elster 409), any desire to break with these assumptions is rendered suspect.

These standards of evidence place trans people attempting to make arguments against anti-trans rhetorics in the public sphere in a double bind. Like other marginalized populations, trans people enter the legislative sphere with a "credibility deficit" (Fricker 17), in this case tied to the medical histories that constituted transness itself as an identity category, so they must first attempt to be seen as rhetorical agents with the authority to speak rather than as objects of distrust or concern. In testimonial exchange, trans activists in legislative spaces must often narrativize trans experiences in a way made palatable for dominant audiences in order to be recognized at all—a process that may sometimes result in legal victories but at the cost of trans exhaustion and the erosion of trans lifeworlds, especially if there is no trans-centered space to recover.

In challenging legislative attacks, trans advocates must make arguments through a dominant liberal framework of individual rights. In this framework, people gain access to legal protections through membership in specific bounded classes constructed as unified identities. Arguments for trans rights in this context turn on several truisms that most trans people experience as untrue or at least complicated, but that are simplified in public discourse for an often hostile and usually at best uninformed audience without trans experience: that one has intimate knowledge of their own gendered self, and that self is innate and stable; that a desire to transition (often understood as a unidirectional and one-time process) stems from an identity that can be proven and traced back over time in a coherent and linear way; and that trans people should be protected because they have no choice *but* to be trans (similar to "born this way" gay rights narratives). Overall, legal constructions of trans identity reify a sense of gender as a characteristic of a core self, claims of which must be supported by evidence, against the much more complex and evolving lived experience of many trans people (Perkins et al.). Narratives in favor of gender-affirming care made within a narrow liberal legal rights framework are expedient and may reflect certain trans people's experiences, but they are not usually made on trans people's terms, and are ill equipped to describe the variety of trans lifeworlds, especially those farthest outside of a white, heteropatriarchal, medicalized norm.

This framework is also problematic in the context of a neoliberal sphere defined by privatization, rampant capitalism, and a single-axis political model. As trans legal scholar Dean Spade explains, the mainstream LGBT rights movement has become detached from its radical queer roots through an agenda based on "preserving and promoting the class and race privilege of a small number of elite gay and lesbian professionals while marginalizing or overtly excluding the needs and experiences of people of color, immigrants, people with disabilities, indigenous people, trans people, and poor people" (34). Spade cautions that contemporary trans rights discourse may be heading in this same direction—protecting a small number of trans people who are racialized as white and/or with class privilege and neglecting the needs of a broader population. Legal reforms that mostly benefit white and class-privileged trans people do not usually address the struggles of trans people of color and poor trans people, which are rooted in "economic marginalization, vulnerability to imprisonment, and other forms of state violence" that such reforms do not address (Spade 36–37).

Trans experiences, conceived in a more liberatory way beyond a medicalized model, are in conflict with a liberal legal rights framework because they challenge liberal conceptions of the self as individualistic, bounded, and knowable. For example, in Gayle Salamon's work on trans phenomenology, she "seeks to challenge the notion that the materiality of the body is something to which we have unmediated access, something of which we can have epistemological certainty" (1) directly against the historical construction of epistemological certainty about one's gender as a prerequisite for accessing gender-affirming care. Rather, Salamon "contend[s] that such epistemological uncertainty can have great use, both ethically and politically, in the lives of the non-normatively gendered" (1). Also taking a phenomenological approach to the constitution of gender identity, trans law and bioethics scholar Florence Ashley argues if "gender identity reflects a dynamic equilibrium rather than a static endpoint," then this also allows for a reconciliation of "how different people offer seemingly incompatible accounts of their gender identity without questioning the authenticity or validity of their accounts" (1054). One's trans body and sense of oneself as gendered or not in particular ways come into being through interactions with the world, possibly changing over time. In this model, one's gender is not necessarily an internal and coherent sense of self but an experiential and unfolding phenomenon, in which people can provide a variety of accounts for what gender feels like to them in order to explore, rather than being compelled to fit their experience within a claims-and-evidence structure for trans identity.

Gender does not have to have a straightforward trajectory or a telos, and can instead exist as a perpetual craft project, played with in affirming community. In its opening up of gender experimentation to anyone with the desire to try, this understanding of transness is more threatening to the white, patriarchal status quo than the more gatekept medicalized and legal models that separate "cis" and "trans" into opposite categories with the goal of preventing too much crossover from the former to the latter.[3] A priori epistemological certainty, not a phenomenological state of curiosity, is the dominant framework for gender transition within the medical and legal systems. In the alternate framework provided by trans phenomenology, "transition" might be understood not as steps one takes to align one's body with an a priori sense of a gendered self, but rather experiences that one tries in order to explore whether one form of embodiment feels better than another. This is truer to most trans people's experiences, but illegible within some medical and most legal frameworks, where desire alone is considered insufficient evidence.

However, trans activists must still make claims through the framework of medicalization and legal rights in order to fight bans on the care that they and their communities desire and to attempt to access protections. Facing a credibility deficit in testimonial exchange, trans rhetors claim authority based on the standpoint of their embodied knowledge. However, queerness raises an important challenge for standpoint epistemology. Queer frameworks de-prioritize identity as "a point of departure for shared consciousness" and instead favor modes of "affective knowing" (Hall 164), such as trans phenomenology. At the same time, queer activists may use identity as a standpoint when necessary for political expediency (Hall 164). Trans people may speak very differently to a dominant audience and to a trans audience—all while trans people talking to other trans people is still considered rare in public space, in favor of an expectation to perform, educate, and explain for an assumed-cis

3. For example, in *Irreversible Damage,* Shrier acknowledges that some people might be *actually trans,* but this is a "tiny sliver of the population" (qtd. in Hsu 62). One assumption behind the professed need to protect AFAB children from "rapid onset gender dysphoria" is that it would be a bad thing for a greater percentage of the population to be trans.

interlocutor. Chase Strangio, a trans ACLU lawyer and activist, explains this double bind well in an Instagram post:

> I navigate the different rules depending on the context—court, legislatures, media.
>
> I try to ensure that my presence, my body, my history, my smile is ever present refuting not only the lies of our opponents, but of the very questions.
>
> As we piece together our next steps, I am struck by what has always been missing in these spaces: our ability to name, know and love ourselves.
>
> In many anti-trans contexts, the state contrives a fake victim (the cis person in the bathroom, on the sports field). But here they would have you believe we are the victims of our own existence. They argue that we need to be saved from ourselves and so many have gone along with that claim and premise.
>
> Well, enough.
>
> In the false and violent binaries of our legal structures we might be posited as victims, as voiceless, as pawns. But we have always dreamed of ourselves outside of law and it is there that we will continue to exist in defiance and disruption of the lies and questions put forth in defense of our subjugation and of the system that allows them to be put forth and asked.

As Strangio emphasizes, the framework through which trans people must make claims in order to gain legal recognition always depends on a false conception of trans people. This may be a conception of trans people as inherently aberrant or as predatory and threatening, or it may be the seemingly more gentle but also damaging liberal framework that relies on making individualistic claims rooted in evidence of one's stable sense of a gendered self. The power of Strangio's rhetorical move here—"we have always dreamed of ourselves outside of law"—points to the ways in which trans people sustain each other and build richer shared imaginaries against and outside of a hostile political environment.

A t4t Approach

In light of this need for trans people to affirm each other and build not only arguments *against* dominant power, but *for* trans lifeworlds and experiences, trans studies scholars have theorized "t4t" (trans-for-trans) as a generative framework. Originally started as a Craigslist term for trans people seeking sexual or romantic partners who are also trans, "t4t" is now used widely in trans spaces as a more general term for trans people caring for other trans people and for creating trans spaces that can serve as enclaves within a gender-normative society. In the introduction to a special issue on t4t in *Transgender Studies Quarterly*, Cameron Awkward-Rich and Hil Malatino explain that rather than being an idealized portrayal of community, t4t as a coalitional ethos can be fraught, characterized by some of the same struggles to be in relation with each other that affect marginalized groups in general but with an especially trans valence. For example, "when taken as an uncritical utopian horizon or an a priori ethical form, t4t can cover over—and so reinforce—white racial dominance" (Awkward-Rich and Malatino 3). However, t4t as a concept can offer a generative place from which to theorize trans relationalities and world-making practices, especially as waystations at which trans people may pause when exhausted from fighting anti-trans attacks, resting in a contingent trans-created space to gain the strength to continue. Awkward-Rich and Malatino write, "t4t 'for real'—in an ideal or even 'better' iteration—would require the end of the world but might, as a concept for the meanwhile, provide (for some of us, sometimes) places of rest, generative conflict, a bit of pleasure, scenes to run away from with a better sense of why we are running" (5). They are careful to frame t4t—in its contingent, everyday form, even if not the "t4t 'for real'" that would require a different world—as "a concept for the meanwhile" that is not a solution for "the multivalent crises of the present," but a necessary reprieve.

In the rest of this chapter, I analyze two t4t moments that, while not a remedy for rampant anti-trans political disinformation in this contemporary context, mobilize a refusal to engage on the terms of the dominant in favor of reprieve, rest, and pleasure for trans people, rooted in a sense (however imperfect and potentially temporary) of "mutual (if always partial) knownness" (Awkward-Rich and Malatino 5) that trans people are commonly denied. This need to experience rest and pleasure is often not prioritized in conversations about resisting disinformation, but it is a vital way that members of marginalized groups sustain themselves and their communities. I include two not opposed but complementary examples of trans youth activists mobilizing different emotions—joy and spite—in the context of recent anti-trans legislation in the US.

Refusal through Trans Joy

This section analyzes an instance in which an activist brought a t4t ethos into legislative testimony, accomplishing a dual purpose of insisting on the validity of trans ways of being in front of a cis audience while also performing a t4t ethos to a trans audience, and hinting at ways in which these two purposes may be bridged in some cases in trans people's public activism. This activist, a white nonbinary trans person, uses the framework of trans joy as a way to refuse to engage on the legislature's terms (which ask implicitly for a futile performance of trans pain).

Florida has enacted some of the harshest bans on trans health care, as part of a political agenda rooted in preserving the white heteronormative nuclear family that also targets schools, sports, and other areas, and is connected to policies limiting or eliminating education about racism in the US. In February 2023, a hearing took place in Tallahassee, where the Board of Osteopathic Medicine voted to bar transgender youth from receiving gender-affirming treatment including puberty blockers and hormone replacement therapy (HRT). In contexts like this, trans activists and allies participate in testimonial exchange with the goal of providing evidence to prove the validity of trans experiences, to make these experiences seem more concrete and personal for audiences without trans experience, and to argue for the safety, efficacy, and necessity of gender-affirming care.

In Tallahassee, twenty-five-year-old Lindsey Spero, a nonbinary youth worker and community activist in St. Petersburg, refused to engage on these terms and instead decided to use their time at the podium to inject their weekly testosterone dose. In their testimonial, recorded and later shared widely online (I draw here from the full testimonial posted by the TikTok account @openlynews [Openly]), Spero stands at the podium wearing a casual outfit and a trans flag tied around their neck and draped behind him like a cape. They introduce themself and say that they have been subjected to conversion therapy "treatments" in the past, which a woman who spoke before him had advocated for, and they stated that they could "guarantee that her child is going to grow up hating her," earning sounds of agreement from the crowd. He goes on to say, "I'm sure you've heard many stories like mine already," acknowledging the "trans siblings" who have "put their hearts on full display and vulnerably pleaded with you to listen to our stories and perspectives" in these public testimonials, and references the American Academy of Pediatrics, who had already spoken out against Florida's actions. Spero continues:

> I could stand here and tell you about all the times I've attempted to end my life because I didn't have access to gender-affirming care, but I know—I know you don't care. I see you sneering at us while we come here and talk to you. Instead I'm going to take the rest of my time to demonstrate the sacred and weekly ritual of my shot in front of you in this body. My medication is

> life saving. I will use HRT for the rest of my life. Your denial of my need for this medication doesn't make my existence as a trans person any less real. (Openly)

Spero then adds, turning back toward the watching audience, "I will be giving myself my subcutaneous shot in my stomach. If you have a needle phobia please look away." After this gesture of care, they turn back to the podium, raise their shirt, and inject 0.5 ml of testosterone into their stomach. At the end of his time, he raises a fist at the podium, shouts, "Trans liberation today, tomorrow, forever," and then steps down.

In later interviews about this act, Spero explains why they chose to use their time this way rather than giving a traditional testimonial. In an interview with *The Independent,* they state:

> I came to the conclusion that I could give them all the logic and reason in the world. . . . I could offer that Board of Medicine every sympathetic story, every tear-jerking response, I can put my heart on full display, I can call them out for their lack of understanding. None of these tactics seem to have been effective or changed their perspectives in any way. . . . It just seemed like a powerful way to show them that we would be willing to do more than just stand at that podium and talk. . . . We are going to have to take action, even when it's hard and even when it's scary. (Dodds)

Here, Spero emphasizes how "logic and reason" do not work when an audience with power has already decided to be hostile and to reject any evidence that a disempowered rhetor might provide—in this case, the board operating within a reality created by Republican lobbying that frames gender-affirming care, especially for youth, as wrong, abhorrent, disgusting, and scientifically uncredible. Trans people and those who support them are tasked with an impossible burden of evidence and set up to fail. This does not mean that trans activists and allies should stop asserting their own realities and insisting on the validity of other forms of evidence—but as Spero points out here, that is not enough. The board has already decided to vote the way it did, and nothing was going to change their mind. In light of this, Spero decided to do something that was both an act of defiance against these political actors *and* a gesture of trans care to watching audiences. They explain the dual audience for their performance in the same interview:

> I wanted the Board to see and be forced to bear witness, because I could tell they are the kind of people that would be uncomfortable with something like

> that. . . . But even more, I did want it to be something that would encourage our trans siblings. . . . An injection can be a really intimidating routine thing to have to participate in, and it's even more intimidating to know how important it is and still have people essentially gaslighting you over the necessity of your medication, despite you overcoming all the barriers to be able to get it. This was one big old "fuck you" to all of that, and a declaration of the necessity and the sacredness of this medication for myself and my body. (Dodds)

This is an act of t4t care smuggled into a public political performance in the form of testimonial. Injecting HRT is a common trans ritual that is often done in a community context. While individuals may administer their medication in private, many also post about it online, such as in social media images or videos capturing the ritual of administering testosterone or estrogen. It is common for trans people to assist each other with HRT, such as by physically helping someone inject or by providing hormones to people who can't access them, who have had delays filling a prescription, or who are on long gender clinic waiting lists and struggling with dysphoria in the meanwhile. Access to HRT is gatekept through the medicalization of transness, but there are also rich histories of trans people creating alternate routes to "DIY transition" (Gill-Peterson). Spero taps into these long histories and visual tropes of trans community care by administering their shot during public testimonial.

In another interview, he also addresses disinformation about what gender-affirming care actually looks like: "It's crazy how many people have never seen it before" (Kalish). They move "gender-affirming care" outside the realm of abstracted debate and into a specific physical act. In doing so, he points to a common disinformation tactic used by those seeking to restrict or eliminate access to such care: mystifying or demonizing it to create a public image that, in its sense of abstract threat, is more frightening than the concrete reality. For example, anti-trans politicians use terms like "mutilation" to equate gender-affirming care with surgery on minors, despite the fact that the vast majority of trans youth do not receive surgery, and the only young people likely to receive genital surgeries are intersex children subjected to surgeries that are medically unnecessary but used to align their bodies with a cisgender norm—in which case the surgery is framed as "corrective," not an act of "mutilation" (Karkazis 255). They spread disinformation about hormone therapy as unnatural and untested, using terms like "experimental" and persuading audiences to believe that young people are coerced into receiving such treatment, even though these treatments have long been used safely in both transgender *and* cisgender populations (Schall and Moses). As Spero indicates, the reality of

HRT when used for gender-affirming care—the medication itself, such as a vial of injectable T or a bottle of Androgel or a bottle of estradiol tablets, or the act of administering this medication—is much less dramatic than what disinformation actors make it out to be and may even be familiar to some cisgender people since the same medications are also used for purposes other than gender transition. The resistantly joyful tone of Spero's performance stands in contrast with the negative, fearmongering tone of anti-trans rhetorics.

Further, the simple physicality of Spero's injection is also not framed in terms of an identity claim. Spero does not say that they need the medication *because* of identity. They characterize their testosterone injection as "lifesaving" and point to "the necessity and the sacredness of this medication for myself and my body," but this is not tied to any claims about a preexisting gendered sense of self. Instead, the need for the medication is rhetorically tied to a sense of the ineffable. Spero uses the language of the "sacred" and of "ritual" to refer to administering testosterone daily, gesturing toward a trans phenomenological conception of the physical body as creatively and relationally made. These word choices refuse the identity-based claims-and-evidence testimonial structure that trans people are expected to perform in medical and legal spaces. In making these choices, Spero also refuses to stand as a palatable image of white transgender youth.

These multiple forms of refusal, paired with Spero's emphasis on community, makes this a t4t subversion of testimonial. While cisgender audiences may benefit from Spero's performance, such as by seeing HRT being administered or being able to stand in solidarity, Spero's performance is primarily one of t4t joy. They use this common, affirming trans ritual to gesture to other trans people, also implying that they will find a way to access care regardless of what the board rules that day. Spero's performance is a powerful statement that, while those who support anti-trans legislation want trans people to feel isolated and alone, it is possible to find community and affirmation even in an environment as hostile as this hearing.

Refusal through Trans Spite

As a counterexample to Spero's performance of trans joy, rooted in refusal but with a positive affect, I now turn to a different rhetorical action by another young trans person, which also enacts refusal in the context of legislative attacks, but instead through trans spite.

This example appears in a digital zine created by TransLash, a news organization and multimedia platform with the tagline "We tell trans stories to save trans lives." Founded and led by Imara Jones, a Black trans journalist, TransLash produces podcasts, films, personal essays, and journalism by trans and gender-nonconforming people. The *TransLash Zine* is an ongoing print and digital publication created in collaboration with POC (People of Color) Zine Project, featuring writing and artwork by trans creators with each edition organized around a central theme. Volume 6, titled *Anti-Trans Hate Machine,* was published in April 2023 as part of the platform's larger #AntiTransHateMachine campaign, which also included a season of the podcast titled "The Anti-Trans Hate Machine: A Plot against Equality." What TransLash terms "the anti-trans hate machine" is the contemporary disinformation campaign against trans children and adults, represented by escalating legislative attacks. This section analyzes one essay in this edition of the zine, "The Burden of Trans Grief: Finding Solace through Spite" by Anonymous, who describes herself as "a 20 year old trans woman from the southern US." Though I do not know her motivation for not attaching her name to the essay, the author's anonymity does interesting rhetorical work that refuses the current cultural hypervisibility of trans women. Throughout the essay, Anonymous enacts refusal in several other ways, culminating in an argument about the value of trans spite.

In this essay, Anonymous details interconnected assaults on her autonomy, enacted at home by her parents and on the national scale by politicians seeking to enact anti-trans policies. She begins the essay with grief and suffering:

> Grief is a reaction to loss, and in that regard, it puzzles me that the mere act of claiming my autonomy causes such a feeling in others. In the eyes of our family and friends, the prospect of someone they know transitioning can often be the same as them dying. Maybe it is for this reason that our screams, cries, and pleas for help are ignored or met with indifference—our living bodies are put on display in an open but soundproof casket, anything that happens to us after no longer mattering. Dead bodies decompose, and so it should follow that living trans bodies do as well. To cis society, the mandate of our suffering needs not be stated. Instead, it is assumed to be a natural consequence of our transition, for we have already submitted ourselves to death through the desecration of our sex. (37)

Here, two dominant frameworks for understanding transness are invoked: the grief that a trans person is supposedly causing her family and friends when she transitions, and the assumption that suffering is a "natural consequence" for trans people. Anonymous uses the horrifying imagery of "an open but soundproof casket" to convey how these frameworks work together to deny trans autonomy, since cis grief and trans suffering are both figured here on cis people's terms. Rather than paying attention to the character of suffering the trans person experiences when being prevented from transition ("our screams, cries, and pleas for help are ignored or met with indifference"), the trans person's suffering is put on visual display to be observed and interpreted by watching eyes, but prevented from being heard. Again, no amount of evidence will ever be judged "enough" by those in power. For the trans woman here, evidence is rendered especially suspect when communicated in her own voice—a cautionary tale about the suffering invited or *deserved* by "the desecration of our sex."

After opening with this arresting imagery, Anonymous details through personal narrative how her parents continued to restrict and narrow her life, leading to forced detransition, institutionalization, suicidal ideation, and dissociation (37). She explains how she continued to try to appeal to her parents to recognize her and her trans community, but how this was a futile effort:

> My begging them to open their eyes, ears, and heart, recognize not only my humanity but that of my friends only inspired further contempt against me, against the evil ghost that they were convinced had stolen their son from them. To them, none of my words could possibly be my own, for I was an easily manipulatable child, incapable of making any decisions for myself. The only plausible explanation for my desire to transition was that I must have been overtaken by a spirit or social con. I killed their son and was their son, and thus became the simultaneous object of both their grief and hatred. (38)

Similarly to Spero, Anonymous encounters only futility and exhaustion when attempting to explain her desire to transition to her parents. The "son" is framed with their logic as a core cis self that the intruder-as-trans-woman-self is corrupting. She is dismissed as both killed and killer, figured as inert, an "object of grief" who can only be narrativized by others, not herself. Rather than continuing to attempt to be heard on her parents' terms, Anonymous turns toward refusal, which also serves as the turning point of the essay. She writes: "My refusal to accept their beliefs and bend to their will meant I was doomed to become the black sheep of our family. I hope by doing so, I have begun to break the sickening cycle of harrowing dysfunction, senseless hatred, and irrational fear" (38). Refusal comes with a cost—becoming the "black sheep" or being ostracized, nonrecognized by the family—but in this "break," she opens space to begin doing something else outside the terms set by the family.

This is where Anonymous turns toward the systemic, situating what happened to her in a broader context of trans youth experiencing conversion therapy and ostracization from family, harmful media portrayals of trans people, and the recent legislative attacks on transition care and on the teaching of gender- and sexuality-related content in schools. Interestingly, Anonymous points to how politicians use the rhetoric of "truth" and "facts" to justify these attacks:

> These conservatives believe themselves to be free from bias, their opinions informed by only the most objective of evidence. They position themselves in sharp contrast to hystericism, to progressivism, mocking any pro-social positions as utopian. One of their catchphrases, "Facts don't care about your feelings" has become something of a meme for them, a masturbatory celebration of their supposed commitment to "hard truth." However, those who utter this phrase are, ironically, also subjugated by their own intense feelings towards us, fueled by disgust and fear. They rely on highly emotional, manufactured narratives of our lives that serve to support their bigotry. (39)

In a clever rhetorical move, Anonymous undermines politicians' claims of "facts" and "truth" by revealing the "manufactured narratives" of trans lives that underlie their constructions of what they consider "truth." When trans stories are told on the terms of hostile anti-trans politicians, and a standard of evidence is set that is designed to set trans people up to fail to "prove" their transness, of course these stories will be distorted into a framework of "hystericism," which the politicians can then use to position themselves as opposed to this emotion through their allegedly superior reasoning. This process only works because the broader society, attached to white heteropatriarchal assumptions, largely accepts these terms for telling trans stories (as Anonymous's opening example of trans bodies in an "open but soundproof casket" viscerally shows). Anonymous writes that "our grief, our stories, are ignored; we are much too unreliable narrators" because of the widespread portrayal of trans people as delusional, resulting from an impossible standard for evidence.

This is where Anonymous turns to spite as a source of power. She writes:

> I am of the opinion that if we are denied even the most universal of emotions, grief, love, belongingness, maybe we ought to turn to spite. After several failed suicide attempts, I began to find solace in this feeling. Spite is often seen as a negative emotion, but I reject this; I believe it has been a powerful motivator for me. My desire to spite our corrupt society, to spite

> everyone who has ever made me feel like my existence is wrong and unwelcome has done much to keep me alive in the moments I felt closest to my coffin. (35)

Here, rather than another futile attempt to appeal to the dominant to have her humanity as a trans person recognized, Anonymous embraces abjection (being "denied even the most universal of emotions") and finds power there. On the terms of the dominant, spite is "negative," framed in opposition to positive affects such as love and belongingness. However, for Anonymous spite is "a powerful motivator" on the terms of the oppressed, even a life-giving force. She continues:

> When I felt like nothing mattered, like my life was meaningless as I had been told so many times both implicitly and explicitly, I had spite. Spite was there. Spite and anger over the injustices thrown at me, at my trans siblings, and every other wicked oppression in the world have been a constant, unrelenting force that energizes me, bringing me life and purpose. As such, I had no other option than to declare that I would make every effort to become the best person I can, claiming my liberation and happiness despite societal pleas that I end my own life and cede my narrative. (35)

Spite is now not only a motivator to fight injustice and oppression, but something associated with life itself—what I want to frame here as a t4t life. Spite is what finally allows Anonymous to refuse to "cede [her] narrative," which means telling her story and those of her "trans siblings" on their own terms, not on the terms of the dominant audiences that want to gather as spectators around the "soundproof casket" and then interpret their own inability to hear the trans person's voice as a fault originating with the trans person. Only in claiming a trans affect of spite can Anonymous find this life-giving narrative force.

The two examples I have analyzed in this chapter—Spero's trans joy and Anonymous's trans spite—are not opposites, but complement each other as different but related counter-disinformation strategies both rooted in trans phenomenologies. They begin with refusal to engage on the terms provided—whether that is performing pain on the legislative floor or pleading with one's family to recognize the validity of one's desires. When audiences are already as hostile as those in this example, trans rhetorical agency is framed as impossible from the start and trans pain is considered the logical outcome of attempting to change one's gender assignment, rather than the result of systemic anti-transness. Activists persist in this difficult environment in doing the necessary work of attempting to change the opinions of those in power. However, as these examples show, it is also powerful for some trans people to refuse and to do something else—something that may be deemed a failure because it does not change legislative outcomes, but that accomplishes other vital work to sustain trans life from a t4t stance.

In a disinformation environment, activists do not only engage in public-facing work to respond to and correct false claims and damaging portrayals. They also create performances and spaces that gesture to the value of community epistemologies and care, an essential way to rest and recover from a violent disinformation climate. These strategies—here framed as t4t in the context of widespread anti-trans disinformation—can themselves be understood as vital counter-disinformation strategies, part of a larger ecosystem that activists use to create and insist on truths capacious enough to account for their unfolding lived experiences.

CONCLUSION

When Trump was once again elected as president in November 2024, I was surprised—despite having spent the previous six years writing a book about the ways in which his ascent was unsurprising when historicized in the systems of oppression programmed into American liberal democracy and considered in the context of the global rise of the far right. I also felt a scrambling desire to stop and reverse time, to go back to before this election happened, to a time when *I* felt safer. The intensity of my surprise and backward longing, even after writing this book, demonstrates the power of white liberal nostalgia. This fleeting comfort comes with a price: To feel comforted by white nostalgia, one must abandon solidarity.

White people like me often find it easy to give up solidarity with people who, in being oppressed, never had the option of this fleeting comfort—and we might not even know that is what we are doing. We are largely terrible at community, taught to locate connection within the narrow parameters of the nuclear family and to view friendships as forms of entertainment more than webs of care, encouraged to live in segregated neighborhoods, walled off from perceived outside threats. An even larger problem is a tendency especially for middle- and upper-class white liberals to view solidarity as a slog, a form of discipline we must subject ourselves to rather than a natural desire to connect with and enjoy the presence of other people. After 2016, another cottage industry emerged, selling white people books and worksheets and seminars to help us look deep within ourselves and root out the racism lurking there (often with cheery self-help taglines to appeal to an audience familiar with therapy-speak and relentless self-interrogation). White people across the US committed to "doing the work," to becoming "antiracist," to overcoming our "white fragility."[1] The obsessive inward focus of whiteness, even when meant to challenge white supremacy, comes with a potently damaging side effect—forgetting that social change can be fun, neglecting moments of emergent joy and connection. The condition of whiteness is perhaps better described as loneliness. But we don't have to accept that loneliness as a natural condition of our lives, and that involves shifting our mindset toward connection—part of, as adrienne maree brown details, the necessity of "learning to make justice and liberation the most pleasurable experiences we can have on this planet" (*Pleasure Activism* 8).

Part of this connective work involves knowing what we are all up against, together, and finding small and specific ways to survive and resist—including ways that prioritize imagination, relation, joy, humor, and rest. This book has excavated the rhetorical scaffolding of several contemporary disinformation trends connected to the phenomenon termed "post-truth politics," referring to an allegedly diminished connection between political claims and truth that I have argued is in fact not new, but a long-standing feature of systems of oppression. In doing so, I have provided a conceptual tool kit for rhetoric scholars to use to analyze and challenge political rhetorics of disinformation in a way that is grounded in the community epistemologies of intersectional activist traditions. I have focused in particular on forms of activism that actively resist, run counter to, or play with liberal rhetorics of civil discourse, such as narrative activism, relational knowledge, acts of refusal to waste time, and forms of testimonial both subtly and overtly subversive, in order to shed light on several lesser-discussed strategies that people targeted by disinformation use for immediate and longer-term survival and resistance.

Chapter 1 developed the book's intersectional frame and arguments by analyzing the counter-disinformation efforts of Black Lives Matter activists, from a queer and racial justice lens. The chapter begins by situating disinformation about BLM in a long history of people in power in the US using racist villainization and dog whistles related to "violence" to threaten Black activists, which are taken up not only in the rhetoric of the right wing but also in liberal rhetorics. The chapter highlights narrative activism as one specific imaginative strategy that BLM activists use. In particular, I chose to foreground narrative activism as a method that activists use to build an intersectional coalitional

1. See Saad; Kendi; DiAngelo.

imaginary, and I argued that this imaginary is an essential part of an activist foundation for resisting disinformation attacks. A coalitional imaginary can also be very difficult to negotiate, but narrative and other creative forms can help activists with different positionalities to place their experiences in dialogue for the purpose of imagining together.

Chapter 2 built upon the previous chapter by further theorizing relational knowledge as a counter-disinformation strategy, using examples from BLM and the Women's March to detail how a strong base of relational knowledge built slowly over time allows activists to respond quickly to disinformation in the moment, and conversely, how a weak foundation of relational knowledge can make movements more vulnerable to disinformation. The chapter began with a key issue in the 2016 presidential election, the disinformation attack coordinated between the Trump campaign and the Russian Internet Research Agency, to demonstrate the centrality of multipronged disinformation attacks to politics today. This disinformation campaign relied not only on spreading overt falsehoods or fact-checkable lies, but also on multiple complex rhetorical performances that were designed to encourage confusion, disorder, and exhaustion. In this chapter, I also analyzed the rhetorical framing of Black Americans as victims of such disinformation attacks, and I troubled this framing by highlighting the rhetorical innovation of Black activists in using relational knowledge to challenge disinformation on the ground. The second half of the chapter complicated relational knowledge through the case of the Women's March on Washington and its aftermath, with a focus on the difficulty of building and sustaining intersectional coalitions and how this is further exacerbated in a disinformation environment. I turned to disinformation campaigns targeting Women's March organizers after the march itself, analyzing how disinformation agents used similar strategies to those that targeted BLM in chapter 1. However, in this chapter, I explore how the coalition's fragile and limited stock of relational knowledge made it less resilient to such attacks.

In chapter 3, I turned to the Unite the Right rally in Charlottesville, Virginia, and its political aftermath. Chapter 3 focused on one rhetorical strategy that is not limited to Trump, but was further popularized by him in the response to Charlottesville, which I termed the "both sides" strategy. Fundamentally, "both sides" is a time-wasting strategy, so I situate the disinformation in this act of wasting time through "both sides" claims. This chapter, at the heart of the book, shows how "both sides" is not only a right-wing disinformation strategy, but it relies on the ideals of liberalism in order to gain its power. "Both sides" as an implicit core tenet of American liberal democracy emphasizes ideals of "free speech" divorced from context and frames all "sides" as deserving equal space and attention within civil discourse. In practice, this civil discourse allows for the further circulation of white supremacist and heteropatriarchal rhetorics, while threats to these systems of power are often framed as "uncivil." Thus, the chapter also explored the role of civility rhetoric in "both sides" and how the logic of "civil discourse" wastes time. I highlighted how Charlottesville activists challenged "both sides" rhetoric through the act of refusing to waste time, using quick moves such as naming and recontextualization.

Chapter 4 unpacked the phenomenon of rhetorical gaslighting as another disinformation strategy by analyzing some of the aftermath of the white supremacist insurrection at the US Capitol in January 2021. The chapter framed rhetorical gaslighting as a public disinformation strategy rooted in testimonial injustice as a specific form of epistemic injustice. The chapter's consideration of testimonial built on previous chapters' discussion of narrative activism through a focus on a specific narrative genre that originated in the legal system but has come to be used in public culture more broadly. After analyzing dynamics of gaslighting in political rhetoric about the insurrection, including Trump's speech and the House impeachment trial brief, I conducted an extended reading of one example of testimonial by analyzing New York Representative Alexandria Ocasio-Cortez's video testimonial about her traumatic experience during and after the insurrection. I unpacked how Ocasio-Cortez used testimonial to resist public gaslighting and to constitute an audience of witnesses. I explored the ways in which she used testimonial both to capitulate to dominant expectations by nodding toward the rhetoric of nationalism as used by other Democratic politicians after the insurrection, and to enact subtle resistance that broke with the Democratic mainstream through a critique of police. I framed this both/and strategy in terms of performative disidentification. To add further complexity, the end of the chapter turned toward the limits of testimonial—including disidentificatory testimonial—in the context of Black insurrection. I provided more examples of how the term "insurrection" has been used after this event, how the white supremacist motivations for the insurrection are often erased in favor of condemning the violence of insurrection in and of itself, and point to the problems that this poses for understanding Black insurrection.

Chapter 5 extended the project's queer threads by framing the escalation of anti-trans legislation based on disinformation in longer histories. I located the disinformation strategy here as the act of setting an exclusionary standard for evidence that is designed to invalidate trans experiences, historicizing this strategy in both medical and legal constructions of transness that are also racialized. In contrast, I explored trans phenomenology as an alternate framework grounded in desire more than identity, which is truer to trans experiences but rendered illegible within a liberal legal rights framework. Trans activists seeking legal protections under this framework are put in an exhausting double bind that may allow them to fight harmful legislation in the short term but that also erodes trans lifeworlds in the long term. I turned toward t4t (trans-for-trans) strategies for creating spaces of rest, recovery, and community care in a disinformation environment. I analyzed how two trans youth activists performed different acts of t4t care and solidarity rooted in trans joy and spite.

Across these chapters, I have analyzed several activist rhetorical strategies that I framed as counter-disinformation strategies that do not fully rely on, or that refuse, the terms of liberal civil discourse. Cutting across individual examples and contexts, several rhetorical strategies emerged as especially important: building and sustaining relational knowledge; insisting on naming, contextualization, and historicization; and attending to dynamics of testimonial and witnessing as well as their subversion. Importantly, these are all rooted in activists' community epistemologies and movement traditions.

In the wake of Russian disinformation targeting Black Lives Matter, activists used localized relational knowledge to determine social media accounts that were fake and that may have been attempting to co-opt local organizing, creating events for fake protests, in order to further an environment of "rhetorical exhaustion" (Bradshaw) that makes it difficult for activism to flourish. In doing so, BLM activists cared for each other and their local communities, demonstrating the limits of disinformation campaigns with the goal of exhaustion when up against the deep historical and contemporary knowledge of local activists working in relation with others. Women's March organizers—a fragile coalition with many cross-positionality difficulties—struggled to enact and sustain relational knowledge, which was exacerbated by disinformation attacks. Because they represented not an already formed local coalition with history and longevity, but a new group attempting to come together on a national scale (and facing heightened scrutiny because of this), the coalition was especially vulnerable to disinformation. Both of these examples, from different angles, demonstrate the importance of activist relational knowledge in a disinformation climate. This importance is further emphasized by other examples, including Charlottesville activists' knowledge of local politics and history, new House representatives' reliance on each other during the Capitol insurrection, and trans activists' invocations of community and care in light of increasing legislative attacks.

Across chapters, I also analyzed several instances of activists using naming, contextualization, and historicization as counter-disinformation strategies, often devoting their public airtime to these strategies specifically. In doing so, they work quickly to get their truths on record—in the news, on TV, in documentaries—and in doing so also resist civility discourse. For example, Charlottesville activists used writing and public media appearances to name white supremacy and antiracism as the "sides" in play during and after the Unite the Right rally, refusing the false equivalency of "both sides" that relies on an absence of context and history. They also brought context and history back to public discussions of the rally by being sure to describe how white supremacy as a system had long been structuring power differentials in Charlottesville and how the rally further perpetuated these dynamics, and they tied their points to long histories of racism in the US by invoking the anti-Blackness at the roots of the nation. Relatedly, in the chapter on the Capitol insurrection, I explored how one writer used similar strategies to name, contextualize, and historicize the history of Black insurrection in the US, in contrast with both Republicans' and Democrats' refusal to name the January 6 insurrection as white supremacist.

Notably, this ability to name, contextualize, and historicize—often within a temporally constrained context—requires relational knowledge, as previously explored; activists with strong relations to local movements as well as movement histories are more likely to be able to harness the moments made available to them to steer the discussion toward opportunities to name power dynamics like white supremacy and to bring context and history back to the conversation. In addition to being public performances for any audiences observing who may learn from this context and history when it would otherwise be erased, these moves also represent additional acts of activist care. In naming power and reiterating context and history, activists affirm each other's knowledge and experiences, fighting public gaslighting and contributing to the work of sustaining relational knowledge, including localized connections but also a felt sense of movement history.

Across chapters, I also analyzed how activists use narrative and testimonial genres as counter-disinformation strategies. For example, Black Lives Matter activists frequently engage in narrative activism to frame their experiences as a form of authority, in a disinformation environment that seeks to discredit them. I explored how two BLM cofounders, Patrisse Khan-Cullors and Alicia Garza, use narrative activism through the memoir genre. They refuse to engage with disinformation on its own terms, instead shifting the focus back onto their own experiential truths, such as in the case of Khan-Cullors not directly arguing with the claim that BLM activists are "terrorists" but instead narrating her experience as an affirmation of Black life and drawing attention to the real terror of white supremacy. In this chapter, I also explored how BLM activists in the *Black Futures Month* series use imagination as an activist rhetorical strategy, one that serves not only to narrate present realities but also to contribute to activist imaginaries—an important form of coalition-building, as in the act of imagining possible futures, activists must determine whom these future imaginings are meant to serve, who is centered and who is rendered marginal, whose needs are foregrounded and who is left out. This imagining is a counter-disinformation strategy because it works against the ways in which disinformation actors also use imagination but for oppressive purposes, such as by restricting dominant imaginaries through a white lens and in the process persuading audiences that other options are impossible or unthinkable.

Narrative was also present across other chapters in the specific form of testimonial genres. After the Capitol insurrection, Alexandria Ocasio-Cortez used the genre of personal testimonial in her Instagram Live video narrating her experience of that day, how it intersected with her trauma history, and how others in her community played an important role in processing the experience, emphasizing the importance of testimonial and witnessing as rhetorical strategies for fighting gaslighting both personal and public. In addition, trans activists have used narrative and testimonial frequently in public hearings across the country about proposed anti-trans legislation. They use these hearings for a variety of purposes, including relating personal stories of accessing or struggling to access gender-affirming care to emphasize the necessity of this care. I focused on how trans activists subvert the genre of testimonial, such as Lindsey Spero using their time to do their testosterone shot rather than sharing a more traditional narrative. These examples illustrate how narrative and testimonial, as activist rhetorical strategies, are complex, nuanced, and evolving, especially in a disinformation context.

While I have analyzed and amplified the above activist rhetorical strategies, crossing racial justice and queer movement contexts, this work has several limitations in terms of scope and time available, but I hope my work here can serve as a starting point for others to build upon. In any intersectional project, one must choose what to foreground and what to background, while acknowledging that all oppressions are interconnected. I have chosen "antiracist" and "queer" as my main operative terms in order to be able to do specific work analyzing how oppressive rhetorics work at the specific intersection of white supremacy and heteropatriarchy, centering anti-Blackness as that which white supremacy requires to function, and to choose activist works that intervene in these particular dynamics. While acknowledging that white supremacy and heteropatriarchy also require colonialism, capitalism, ableism, xenophobia, and other forms of oppression to sustain themselves, and that these are all intimately connected and also connected to the historical and contemporary abjection of Black and Brown people worldwide, it was not possible to devote analytical space to all of these specific interconnected threads and also maintain specificity—and finish the project. Further, in foregrounding anti-Blackness as an analytic, the complex positionalities of non-Black people of color are backgrounded in this project, and in this work's focus on domestic American politics, it does not delve deeply into the interconnectedness of worldwide struggles for liberation against empire. My focus may mean that other rich sites of analysis have been bracketed or excluded from this work, but this does not mean I do not think they are also vital to our ongoing fight for intersectional liberation. This points to a need for future work by scholars and activists with a variety of focuses, as well as opportunities to come together to analyze and intervene in interconnected problems.

As one major example, while the COVID-19 pandemic has been important context for several moments in this book, I have not devoted extensive space to COVID disinformation and chose not to devote a chapter or case study to the pandemic itself. I started this project long before the pandemic, and as it has unfolded, I found myself not ready to write about it and in fact realized it to be a site of unprocessed experience that would not be best dealt with in this space. However, COVID is obviously a key element of our contemporary political moment, intersecting with every form of oppression, and it will continue to shape politics and activism for a long time. For work on COVID, I recommend reading and following the lead of scholars working in disability studies, including Sami Schalk, Leah Lakshmi Piepzna-Samarasinha, and Alice Wong. In rhetoric and writing studies, sarah madoka currie has shared many resources for trauma-informed writing pedagogy. For a thorough analysis of antivaccine rhetoric and antivax disinformation, I recommend Heidi Yoston Lawrence's *Vaccine Rhetorics*. For evidence-driven research into what role the arts can play in the public health sphere, including but not limited to COVID, I recommend the work of Tasha L. Golden. These are only a few examples from multiple fields.

In addition, while digital rhetoric has been a context for many of the examples in the book, I was not able to engage in analysis of all the digital infrastructures at play in each example, such as the design and profit structures of individual digital platforms. Other scholars have done important work analyzing how elements of platform design such as algorithms shape rhetorical action (see Beck; Benjamin; Ingraham; Noble). Future work on the rhetoric of disinformation and activist responses may pay even more attention to the material infrastructures behind such rhetoric's circulation, such as by analyzing the corporate interests that structure social media engagement. In this work, I have treated digital spaces more as the air we breathe or the water we swim in—important and ever-present, as there is no contemporary rhetorical action I can think of that does not involve digital mediation at least in some part. The air we move through, like the digital spaces that politics move through, is of course material, and its condition shapes every aspect of our lives (as I wrote many parts of this book during COVID quarantine in 2020 and 2021, afraid of the air outside before vaccines, and finished the draft of the full manuscript between bouts of wildfire-stained air quality in upstate New York in 2023, experiencing ever-heightened awareness that the air is far from a neutral medium). Similarly, the digital is an essential part of our contemporary rhetorical condition.

Throughout this book, I have focused in particular on one specific kind of digital disinformation: the politically motivated induction of what Jonathan Bradshaw terms "rhetorical exhaustion." Rhetorical exhaustion works through accumulation and amplification, or the strategy of circulating a large volume of material in order to create confusion and overwhelm for audiences. The goal is not only persuasion, but to get people to shut down and disengage, which serves those in power. Importantly, rhetorical exhaustion cannot be countered using liberal rhetorics of civil discourse. Engaging in debate about the factual inaccuracy of a piece of disinformation, for instance, will often only allow the disinformation to spread further, feeding into the strategy of accumulation. Rhetorical exhaustion thus reveals some of the limitations of liberal approaches to challenging disinformation. In contrast, activist rhetorics tied to community epistemologies, such as a Black feminist temporality or t4t care, are often more effective in fighting rhetorical exhaustion. Further, I have sought to draw attention to the fact that, despite the current cultural focus on forms of disinformation as a new digital phenomenon, these are old strategies rooted in American white supremacy and heteropatriarchy.

I have chosen to focus on public activist writing, visual art, and other forms of media available online, as well as other publicly available materials such as documentary footage, news coverage, and social media content. This has allowed me to look at widely circulating contemporary political and activist rhetorics. With any methodological decision, there are also limitations, and by focusing on public works, I relied on methods of textual and visual analysis rather than person-based or engaged research. It would be productive for future work building upon this to explore how the ideas in this book—such as how activists care for each other in a post-truth context—play out in local, in-person spaces such as community organizations and grassroots activist groups. Because I only analyzed public materials, I was not able to access information such as the behind-the-scenes conversations that may have taken place, which are often especially revealing of activist dynamics. Future work using methods like interviews or ethnography would better be able to analyze these dynamics and deepen the picture. Such work may be especially enriched through a community-engaged framework where scholars collaborate with activist groups to work on projects decided upon by these groups.

As I have written this book, violence—epistemic and concrete—has continued to escalate in America. Amidst ever-present racial injustice, the ongoing COVID-19 pandemic, climate change, increasing anti-trans and antiqueer policy decisions, and incessant economic divides and precarity wrought by capitalism and colonialism, it can be difficult to see a way forward. In what is termed the "post-truth" condition, rhetoricians may find ourselves alternately baffled or despondent about what resources we may have to navigate a broken world. However, as I have argued throughout this work, it is vital to name what has broken the world—white supremacy and all its connected tools, including heteropatriarchy, colonialism, ableism, and other interconnected forms of oppression. Perhaps the most damaging facet of the post-truth rhetorical condition is how violent actors are easily able to obfuscate their own commitments and detach their actions in public view from longer histories. Knowing these histories and insisting on naming the systems behind post-truth is essential for survival.

When asking how rhetorical studies may resist the escalating threats posed by disinformation, scholars should listen to people who already have long histories and deep rhetorical traditions for resisting the lie of white supremacy, including multiply marginalized changemakers working in many activist contexts, from the public-facing to the fugitive (and, especially in cases of fugitivity, we should take particular care to listen when told to stay quiet). Situating such activist practices as survival and resistance strategies against escalating fascism may reinvigorate our field and provide strategies for working against disinformation strategies like restricting imagination, scapegoating, villainization, decontextualization, gaslighting, and others. These are all part of our contemporary rhetorical moment, but they do not have to define it—instead, we may be defined by the choices we make, on both large and small scales, to refuse compliance with both fascist oppression and the liberal rhetorics that enable it, to practice care, and to grow solidarity.

ACKNOWLEDGMENTS

Since much of this book is about invisibilized histories, infrastructures, and relations, I hope to use these acknowledgments to make visible the many support structures and relationships that have enabled my research and writing, and without which this book would not have been possible.

I am grateful that this project found its perfect home in the Intersectional Rhetorics series at The Ohio State University Press, where my focus on marginalized knowledges and rhetorical traditions has been taken seriously from the start. All my thanks to Karma R. Chávez and Tara Cyphers for understanding my vision and for your careful and thorough editorial guidance, and to the two peer reviewers who closely read the draft proposal and manuscript; provided necessary feedback about refining the book's argument, analysis, and structure; and pointed me toward bodies of scholarship and history that deepened the project in multiple ways. Thank you as well to all the production staff for your work in shepherding this project to publication.

Thank you to the University at Albany, SUNY for providing an intellectual home for my work and for the institutional support that allowed me to complete this project, including a research leave awarded through the Dr. Nuala McGann Drescher Leave Program and funding through the Faculty Research Award Program (FRAP-B). I am also grateful for my union, United University Professions (UUP), and have benefited from multiple UUP Individual

Development Awards to cover travel costs to give conference presentations related to the subject matter of this book.

I could not have asked for a more supportive department than the English department at UAlbany. Particular, ebullient thanks to Laura Wilder for your mentoring, both in smaller day-to-day acts of care and larger gestures of generosity (including reading a draft manuscript on a fast turnaround and providing feedback that got me unstuck at a panicked moment when I really needed it). Many thanks to Eric Keenaghan, Kir Kuiken, Erica Fretwell, and Helene Scheck for your mentorship and support of my work, and to Bianca Hedges, Jaime Moore, and Karen Williams for the administrative and advising support that keeps the department running and enables this work. I am very lucky to have a cherished group of friends in this department who have done so much for me, from answering anxious texts to gathering for vent sessions and celebrations: in addition to those mentioned above, Vesna Kuiken, Ineke Murakami, and Wendy Roberts. For additional mentoring and support in the department and for modeling ways to enact union values, thank you to Bret Benjamin and Paul Stasi.

I am grateful for several opportunities that allowed me to develop the foundational ideas for this project. My interest in activist counter-disinformation strategies began at the University of Alabama English Department's 2019 Biennial Symposium on Digital Rhetoric/Digital Media in the Post-Truth Age, directed by Amber Buck and Cindy Tekobbe. Thank you to Amber and Cindy for including me as a participant; to the University of Alabama for the funding that covered travel and lodging, enabling me and other participants to attend; and to all the other scholars whom I had the privilege of learning from during this event. Thank you to *Enculturation* for publishing my article that emerged from this symposium, "'Who Are Your People?': Black Lives Matter Activists' Use of Relational Knowledge to Counter Disinformation Campaigns," which I expanded upon in chapter 2 of this book. This project was also strengthened by my participation in the 2019 Rhetoric Society of America Summer Institute seminar on African American rhetoric led by Tamika L. Carey and Elaine Richardson. My process of writing this book and seeking publication benefited greatly from the structure and mentoring provided by Stephanie Kerschbaum's first-book writing groups, and thanks to my group members Jenny Lambe, Sharon Mitchler, Sarah Singer, and Ben Stanley. For first teaching me about the areas of study that I would later take up in this book, I also thank my graduate school mentors: from my time at the University of Louisville, Karen Kopelson, Mary P. Sheridan, Dànielle Nicole DeVoss, Kiki Petrosino, Bruce Horner, and Bronwyn Williams, and from Emerson College, John Trimbur, Jabari Asim, and Jerald Walker. Additional thanks to my undergraduate professors at the University of Rhode Island, especially Mary Cappello, Peter Covino, and Talvikki Ansel, for being the first people to see this first-gen student having a place in academia.

I would also like to thank all the students who had a role in this project, and from whom I have learned so much. Thank you to Farhana Islam for your research assistance in spring 2021. Thanks are also due to the doctoral students who have worked as TAs in my courses, especially in my undergraduate Queer Theory course. Thank you to Robert Williams-Taylor for the conversations about Afropessimism, which have deepened my thinking about the limitations of liberal rhetorics of civility. Thanks also to Sof Voet for your work on queer and trans autotheory, which has nuanced my approach to queer/trans genres of life writing and testimonial. I am also grateful to the thesis students I have supervised and to the students in my courses for thinking with me about many topics related to this book, especially my Digital Rhetoric and Rhetoric of Science and Technology graduate seminars and my undergraduate Queer Theory and Rhetoric of Moral Panics courses.

Many friends in Albany have supported me in countless material and immaterial ways as I worked on this project. Thank you to Erin Baker, Sarah Domoff, and Angie Wootton for the writing time, pool time, and brunch time, and extra thanks to Angie for the lake house days that pushed me toward the finish line. Thanks to Loretta McNamee, Emily Shrum, Heather Sheridan, and Jill Einhort-Hitt for spaces to play; to Betty Lin, Francisco Vieyra, and Drake Niepoetter for the pre-COVID-vaccine writing parties in public parks, patios, garages, and backyards; and to Alex Valm for bingo of various kinds and for listening to me panic about this book at various Albany establishments. Thank you to Shannon Draucker for commiseration and encouragement, and to Rebecca Colesworthy for your combined editor's and writer's perspectives—the two of you are the best things I found on Twitter (RIP). To Key K. Bird and Randolph Bird, thank you for the tea and cheese afternoons and for Friday Buddies. I would also like to thank the many local mental and physical health professionals without whose care I would not have been able to write this.

Other beloved friends and family are separated by geographical distance but no less present in these pages. Shannon DeScioli, I'm so glad we recognized each other as fellow French Canadian vegetarian writers of weird essays way back in 2011, and I'm grateful for your best friendship every day. Megan Faver Hartline, it was hard to write a long project without you there to push me like in our UofL days, but thank you for always being a trusted first reader. Thank you to Jennifer Crystal for intuitively knowing when to text with a joke, a vent, or info about a clearance sale. To my Rhode Island friends, Nicole

Cote, Kandace Richmond, and Holly Richmond, thank you for being as close as an only child gets to growing up with sisters. I am lucky to have grown up in a home that modeled found family and the importance of gathering, and thank you especially to Elaine Skurka, Kathy Mackin, E and Anne Beauregard, Suzanne Richmond, and Jane Schweinsburg for always cheering me on.

My parents, Judy and Carl Tetreault, deserve a whole acknowledgments section for creating a home for me to imagine and grow while making sure I always had comfort to return to. You are two of the most intellectually curious people I know and I'm the luckiest to be your kid. It says a lot about my life and career that my first time in a voting booth was as a baby during the final months of the Reagan administration—thanks, Mom, and thanks for encouraging my fire while also standing by with the extinguisher in case of emergency. Dad, thank you for our shared twisted sense of humor and love of the absurd, and for showing me that it's possible to learn anywhere and create from anything.

My wife, Emily Thomas, deserves nothing less than an ode (and the world's largest cake, and at least a million dollars) for putting up with me during the long and often painstaking process of researching and writing this book. Thank you for sticking it out, laughing at my Serious Reading Face, and along with Elroy and Fitzwilliam, reminding me to stop doomscrolling and rejoin the world.

WORKS CITED

Abraham, Matthew. "Steven Salaita's Rhetorical Refusal: Taking to Twitter as a Form of Political Resistance and Protest." *Unruly Rhetorics: Protest, Persuasion, and Publics*, edited by Jonathan Alexander et al., U of Pittsburgh P, 2018, pp. 72–87.

ACLU. "Mapping Attacks on LGBTQ Rights in U.S. State Legislatures." 7 July 2023, https://www.aclu.org/legislative-attacks-on-lgbtq-rights.

Acosta, Jim, and Daniella Diaz. "Read the White House's Talking Points on Trump's News Conference." *CNN*, 16 Aug. 2017, https://www.cnn.com/2017/08/16/politics/charlottesville-white-house-surrogates-talking-points/index.html.

Ahmed, Sabeen. "A Coup by Any Other Name: Reflections on Democracy, Defense, and White Supremacy." *APA Online*, 20 Jan. 2021, https://blog.apaonline.org/2021/01/20/a-coup-by-any-other-name-reflections-on-democracy-defense-and-white-supremacy/.

Ahmed, Sabeen. "Provocations on the Liberal Onto-Epistemology of Fascism." *Philosophy Today*, vol. 67, no. 1, 2023, pp. 1–19.

Ahmed, Sara. *Living a Feminist Life*. Duke UP, 2017. Kindle edition.

Ahmed, Sara, and Jackie Stacey. "Testimonial Cultures: An Introduction." *Cultural Values*, vol. 5, no. 1, 2001, pp. 1–6.

Alexander, Jonathan, and Jacqueline Rhodes. "Queer Rhetoric and the Pleasures of the Archive." *Enculturation: A Journal of Rhetoric, Writing, and Culture*, 2012, https://enculturation.net/queer-rhetoric-and-the-pleasures-of-the-archive.

Alexander, Jonathan, et al., editors. *Unruly Rhetorics: Protest, Persuasion, and Publics*. U of Pittsburgh P, 2018.

American University. "The Project on Civic Dialogue." https://www.american.edu/spa/civic-dialogue/. Accessed 25 June 2024.

Anonymous. "The Burden of Trans Grief: Finding Solace through Spite." *Translash Zine,* vol. 6. 19 Apr. 2023, pp. 37–45, https://issuu.com/translash/docs/translash-zine-volume-6-antitranshatemachine-2023.

Arif, Ahmer, et al. "Acting the Part: Examining Information Operations within #BlackLivesMatter Discourse." *Proceedings of the ACM on Human-Computer Interaction,* vol. 2, no. 20, 2018, pp. 1–27.

Ashley, Florence. "What Is It Like to Have a Gender Identity?" *Mind,* vol. 132, no. 528, 2023, pp. 1053–73, https://doi.org/10.1093/mind/fzac071.

Atwater, Deborah F. *African American Women's Rhetoric: The Search for Dignity, Personhood, and Honor.* Lexington Books, 2009.

Awkward-Rich, Cameron, and Hil Malatino. "Meanwhile, t4t." *Transgender Studies Quarterly,* vol. 9, no. 1, 2022, pp. 1–8, https://doi.org/10.1215/23289252-9475467.

Azarian, Bobby. "Trump Is Gaslighting America Again—Here's How to Fight It." *Psychology Today,* 31 Aug. 2018, https://www.psychologytoday.com/us/blog/mind-in-the-machine/201808/trump-is-gaslighting-america-again-here-s-how-fight-it.

Baez, Kristiana L., and Ersula Ore. "The Moral Imperative of Race for Rhetorical Studies: On Civility and Walking-in-White in Academe." *Communication and Critical/Cultural Studies,* vol. 15, no. 4, 2018, pp. 331–36.

Bailey, Alison. "On Gaslighting and Epistemic Injustice: Editor's Introduction." *Hypatia,* vol. 35, 2020, pp. 667–73.

Bailey, Moya Z. *Misogynoir Transformed: Black Women's Digital Resistance.* New York UP, 2021.

Baker, Al, et al. "Beyond the Chokehold: The Path to Eric Garner's Death." *The New York Times,* 13 June 2015, https://www.nytimes.com/2015/06/14/nyregion/eric-garner-police-chokehold-staten-island.html.

Baker, Catherine. "Want to Know Where Trump's 'Blame on Both Sides' Rhetoric Could Lead? Look to Yugoslavia." *Prospect,* 17 Aug. 2017, https://www.prospectmagazine.co.uk/politics/want-to-know-where-trumps-blame-on-both-sides-rhetoric-could-lead-look-to-yugoslavia.

Baker, Ella. "The Black Woman in the Civil Rights Struggle—1969." Archives of Women's Political Communication, Iowa State University, https://awpc.cattcenter.iastate.edu/2019/08/09/the-black-woman-in-the-civil-rights-struggle-1969/. Accessed 19 Nov. 2021.

Baker-Bell, April. *Linguistic Justice: Black Language, Literacy, Identity, and Pedagogy.* Routledge, 2020.

Baldwin, James. "On Being White . . . and Other Lies." *Antiracism Digital Library,* https://sacred.omeka.net/items/show/238. Accessed 27 June 2024.

Banks, Adam J. *Digital Griots: African-American Rhetoric in a Multimedia Age.* Southern Illinois UP, 2011.

Banks, William P., et al., editors. *Re/Orienting Writing Studies: Queer Methods, Queer Projects.* Utah State UP, 2019.

Barrett, Ted. "McConnell Blames Political Rhetoric on 'Both Sides' in Wake of Violence." *CNN,* 29 Oct. 2018, https://www.cnn.com/2018/10/29/politics/mitch-mcconnell-both-sides-bombs-shooting/index.html.

Barry, Ellen. "How Russian Trolls Helped Keep the Women's March Out of Lock Step." *The New York Times,* 18 Sept. 2022, https://www.nytimes.com/2022/09/18/us/womens-march-russia-trump.html.

Barthel, Michael, et al. "Many Americans Believe Fake News Is Sowing Confusion." *Pew Research Center,* 15 Dec. 2016, https://www.pewresearch.org/journalism/2016/12/15/many-americans-believe-fake-news-is-sowing-confusion/.

Bazelon, Emily. "If Prisons Don't Work, What Will?" *The New York Times*, 5 Apr. 2019.

Beck, Estee. "A Theory of Persuasive Computer Algorithms for Rhetorical Code Studies." *Enculturation: A Journal of Rhetoric, Writing, and Culture*, 2016, https://enculturation.net/a-theory-of-persuasive-computer-algorithms.

Beck, Estee, et al. "Writing in an Age of Surveillance, Privacy, and Net Neutrality." *Kairos: A Journal of Rhetoric, Technology, and Pedagogy*, vol. 20, no. 2, 2016, https://kairos.technorhetoric.net/20.2/topoi/beck-et-al/index.html.

Beckett, Lois, et al. "The Real 'Shy Trump' Vote—How 53% of White Women Pushed Him to Victory. *The Guardian*, 10 Nov. 2016, https://www.theguardian.com/us-news/2016/nov/10/white-women-donald-trump-victory.

Bender, Michael C., and Michael Gold. "Trump's Dire Words Raise New Fears about His Authoritarian Bent." *The New York Times*, 20 Nov. 2023, https://www.nytimes.com/2023/11/20/us/politics/trump-rhetoric-fascism.html.

Benjamin, Ruha. *Race after Technology: Abolitionist Tools for the New Jim Code*. Polity, 2019.

Berenstain, Nora. "White Feminist Gaslighting." *Hypatia*, vol. 35, 2020, pp. 733–58.

Bessette, Jean. "Queer Rhetoric in Situ." *Rhetoric Review*, vol. 35, no. 2, 2016, pp. 148–64.

Bey, Marquis. *Black Trans Feminism*. Duke UP, 2022.

Bey, Marquis. *Them Goon Rules: Fugitive Essays on Radical Black Feminism*. The U of Arizona P, 2019.

Biko, Cherno. "Black Trans Lives Matter, Too." *The Huffington Post*, 4 Feb. 2016, https://www.huffingtonpost.com/cherno-biko/black-translives-matter-_b_9157514.html.

Black Lives Matter. "About." 9 Apr. 2018, https://blacklivesmatter.com/about/.

Black Lives Matter. "Black Lives Matter Global Network Responds to Senate Intelligence Committee Reports." 18 Dec. 2018, https://blacklivesmatter.com/pressroom/black-lives-matter-global-network-responds-to-senate-intelligence-committee-reports/.

Bonilla-Silva, Eduardo. *Racism without Racists: Color-Blind Racism and the Persistence of Racial Inequality in America*. Rowman & Littlefield, 2017.

Bradshaw, Jonathan L. "Rhetorical Exhaustion and the Ethics of Amplification." *Computers and Composition*, vol. 56, June 2020, pp. 1–14.

Bradshaw, Samantha, and Amélie Henle. "The Gender Dimensions of Foreign Influence Operations." *International Journal of Communication*, vol. 15, 2021, pp. 4596–618.

Brock, André, Jr. *Distributed Blackness: African American Cybercultures*. New York UP, 2020.

Browdy, Ronisha. "Patrisse Khan-Cullors's *And When They Call You a Terrorist: A Black Lives Matter Memoir*: Storytelling as Black Feminist Counter-Attack on Mis-Labelling of Black Identity." *Prose Studies*, vol. 40, nos. 1–2, 2018, pp. 15–39.

brown, adrienne maree. *Emergent Strategy: Shaping Change, Changing Worlds*. AK Press, 2017.

brown, adrienne maree. *Pleasure Activism: The Politics of Feeling Good*. AK Press, 2019.

brown, adrienne maree, and Walidah Imarisha, editors. *Octavia's Brood: Science Fiction Stories from Social Justice Movements*. AK Press, 2015.

Brown, Heber, III. "I'm just hearing that you're not from Baltimore. . . ." *Facebook*, 15 Apr. 2016, https://www.facebook.com/photo.php?fbid=10154097683603610&set=a.423996223609&type=3&theater.

Browne, Simone. *Dark Matters: On the Surveillance of Blackness*. Duke UP, 2015.

Butler, Judith. *Gender Trouble: Feminism and the Subversion of Identity*. Routledge, 2006.

Cadwalladr, Carole, and Emma Graham-Harrison. "Revealed: 50 Million Facebook Profiles Harvested for Cambridge Analytica in Major Data Breach." *The Guardian,* 17 Mar. 2018, https://www.theguardian.com/news/2018/mar/17/cambridge-analytica-facebook-influence-us-election.

Carey, Tamika L. "Necessary Adjustments: Black Women's Rhetorical Impatience." *Rhetoric Review,* vol. 39, no. 3, 2020, pp. 269–86.

Carey, Tamika L. *Rhetorical Healing: The Reeducation of Contemporary Black Womanhood.* SUNY Press, 2016.

Carpenter, Amanda. *Gaslighting America: Why We Love It When Trump Lies to Us.* Broadside Books, 2018.

Carrington, André. *Speculative Blackness: The Future of Race in Science Fiction.* U of Minnesota P, 2016.

Carruthers, Charlene A. *Unapologetic: A Black, Queer, and Feminist Mandate for Radical Movements.* Beacon Press, 2018.

Cauterucci, Christina. "How the Women's March Might Have Played Out Differently." *Slate,* 21 Jan. 2022, https://slate.com/news-and-politics/2022/01/womens-march-five-year-anniversary.html.

Césaire, Aimé. *Discourse on Colonialism.* Monthly Review Press, 1999.

Chadwick, Kayla. "I Don't Know How to Explain to You That You Should Care about Other People." *Huffpost,* 26 June 2017, https://www.huffpost.com/entry/i-dont-know-how-to-explain-to-you-that-you-should_b_59519811e4b0f078efd98440.

Chaput, Catherine. "Rhetorical Circulation in Late Capitalism: Neoliberalism and the Overdetermination of Affective Energy." *Philosophy & Rhetoric,* vol. 43, no. 1, 2010, pp. 1–25.

Chávez, Karma R. *Queer Migration Politics: Activist Rhetoric and Coalitional Possibilities.* U of Illinois P, 2013.

Chiang, Taylor, and Gloria A. Bachmann. "The Informed Consent Model Is Adequate for Gender-Affirming Treatment: Issues Related with Mental Health Assessment in the United States." *The Journal of Sexual Medicine,* vol. 20, no. 5, 2023, pp. 584–87.

Cillizza, Chris. "Donald Trump Is Gaslighting Us on the January 6 Riot." *CNN,* 17 Sept. 2021, https://www.cnn.com/2021/09/17/politics/donald-trump-september-18-january-6/index.html.

Cillizza, Chris. "How the Heck Can Voters Think Donald Trump Is More Honest Than Hillary Clinton?" *The Washington Post,* 2 Nov. 2016, https://www.washingtonpost.com/news/the-fix/wp/2016/11/02/donald-trump-hasnt-told-the-truth-repeatedly-in-this-campaign-voters-still-think-he-is-more-honest-than-hillary-clinton/.

Cloud, Dana L. *Reality Bites: Rhetoric and the Circulation of Truth Claims in U.S. Political Culture.* The Ohio State UP, 2018.

Coburn, Claire, et al. "Newsroom Objectivity in the Age of Black Lives Matter." Center for Media Engagement, University of Texas at Austin, 20 Jan. 2021, https://mediaengagement.org/research/newsroom-objectivity-in-the-age-of-black-lives-matter/.

Cohen, Cathy. *Democracy Remixed: Black Youth and the Future of American Politics.* Oxford UP, 2010.

Cohen, Cathy. "Punks, Bulldaggers, and Welfare Queens: The Radical Potential of Queer Politics?" *GLQ,* vol. 3, no. 4, 1997, pp. 437–65.

Coleman, E., et al. "Standards of Care for the Health of Transgender and Gender Diverse People, Version 8." *International Journal of Transgender Health,* vol. 23, sup. 1, 2022, pp. S1–S259.

Condit, Celeste. *Angry Public Rhetorics: Global Relations and Emotion in the Wake of 9/11.* U of Michigan P, 2018.

Conger, Kate, and Ryan Mac. *Character Limit: How Elon Musk Destroyed Twitter.* Penguin, 2024.

Cooper, Brittney C. "The Racial Politics of Time." *TED,* Oct. 2016, https://www.ted.com/talks/brittney_cooper_the_racial_politics_of_time?language=en.

Corley, Cheryl. "Black Lives Matter Fights Disinformation to Keep the Movement Strong." *NPR,* 25 May 2021, https://www.npr.org/2021/05/25/999841030/black-lives-matter-fights-disinformation-to-keep-the-movement-strong.

Crawford, Kate. *Atlas of AI: Power, Politics, and the Planetary Costs of Artificial Intelligence.* Yale UP, 2022.

Crick, Nathan, editor. *The Rhetoric of Fascism.* U of Alabama P, 2022.

C-SPAN. "First 2020 Presidential Debate between Donald Trump and Joe Biden." *YouTube,* 29 Sept. 2020, https://www.youtube.com/watch?v=wW1lY5jFNcQ.

Cultural Rhetorics Theory Lab. "Our Story Begins Here: Constellating Cultural Rhetorics." *Enculturation: A Journal of Writing, Rhetoric, and Culture,* 25 Oct. 2014, https://enculturation.net/our-story-begins-here.

Daniels, Jessie. *White Lies: Race, Class, Gender, and Sexuality in White Supremacist Discourse.* Routledge, 1997.

Davis, Angela Y. "Political Prisoners, Prisons, and Black Liberation." *The Anarchist Library,* 1971, https://theanarchistlibrary.org/mirror/a/ay/angela-y-davis-political-prisoners-prisons-and-black-liberation.lt.pdf.

Davis, Angela Y., et al. *Abolition. Feminism. Now.* Haymarket, 2022.

Davis, Darren W., and David C. Wilson. "'Stop the Steal': Racial Resentment, Affective Partisanship, and Investigating the January 6th Insurrection." *The ANNALS of the American Academy of Political and Social Science,* vol. 708, no. 1, pp. 83–101.

Del Hierro, Victor, et al. "We Are Here: Negotiating Difference and Alliance in Spaces of Cultural Rhetorics." *Enculturation,* vol. 21, 2016.

Del Valle, Gaby. "The Alexandria Ocasio-Cortez You Don't Know." *The New York Times,* 4 May 2024, https://www.nytimes.com/2024/05/04/opinion/alexandria-ocasio-cortez.html.

DiAngelo, Robin. "White Fragility." *International Journal of Critical Pedagogy,* vol. 3, no. 3, 2011, pp. 54–70.

Dickinson, Tim. "'Bloodbath,' 'Vermin,' 'Unified Reich': A Guide to Trump's Fascist Rhetoric." *Rolling Stone,* 24 Sept. 2024, https://www.rollingstone.com/politics/politics-features/trump-fascist-talk-bloodbath-vermin-dictator-1234992957/.

DiResta, Renee, et al. *The Tactics and Tropes of the Internet Research Agency.* New Knowledge, 2019.

Dixon, Emily. "Alexandria Ocasio-Cortez Was Asked about Defunding the Police and Her Answer Went Viral." *Marie Claire,* 12 June 2020, https://www.marieclaire.com/politics/a32849383/alexandria-ocasio-cortez-defund-the-police/.

"Documenting Hate: Charlottesville." *Frontline,* produced by Richard Rowley et al., season 2018, episode 13, PBS, 7 Aug. 2018, https://www.pbs.org/wgbh/frontline/film/documenting-hate-charlottesville/.

Dodds, Io. "'One Big F*** You': Why This Trans Protester Injected Himself with Testosterone in Front of Florida Officials." *The Independent,* 15 Feb. 2023, https://www.independent.co.uk/news/world/americas/us-politics/lindsey-spero-florida-trans-healthcare-ban-b2282627.html.

Dotson, Kristie. "Tracking Epistemic Violence, Tracking Practices of Silencing." *Hypatia,* vol. 26, no. 2, pp. 236–57.

Duca, Lauren. "Donald Trump Is Gaslighting America." *Teen Vogue,* 10 Dec. 2016, https://www.teenvogue.com/story/donald-trump-is-gaslighting-america.

Duggan, Lisa. "The New Homonormativity: The Sexual Politics of Neoliberalism." *Materializing Democracy: Toward a Revitalized Cultural Politics,* edited by Russ Castronovo and Dana D. Nelson, Duke UP, 2002, pp. 175–94.

Edelman, Lee. *No Future: Queer Theory and the Death Drive.* Duke UP, 2004.

Edwards, Dustin. "On Circulatory Encounters: The Case for Tactical Rhetorics." *Enculturation: A Journal of Rhetoric, Writing, and Culture,* 4 Oct. 2017, http://enculturation.net/circulatory_encounters.

Elamroussi, Aya. "Jury Begins Deliberations in Charlottesville Unite the Right Civil Trial." *CNN,* 19 Nov. 2021, https://www.cnn.com/2021/11/19/us/charlottesville-unite-the-right-civil-trial-jury-deliberation/index.html.

Elliott, Debbie. "'Hear Me By Any Means Necessary': Charlottesville Is Forced to Redefine Civility." *NPR,* 20 Mar. 2019, https://www.npr.org/2019/03/20/704902802/hear-me-by-any-means-necessary-charlottesville-is-forced-to-redefine-civility.

Elster, Mikey. "Insidious Concern: Trans Panic and the Limits of Care." *TSQ: Transgender Studies Quarterly,* vol. 9, no. 3, 2022, pp. 407–24.

Eltis, Alfie. "Trump, and the History of Political Gaslighting." *Varsity,* 2 Oct. 2020, https://www.varsity.co.uk/opinion/19909.

Fernandes, Sujatha. *Curated Stories: The Uses and Misuses of Storytelling.* Oxford UP, 2017.

Finnegan, Michael. "Scope of Trump's Falsehoods Unprecedented for a Modern Presidential Candidate." *Los Angeles Times,* 25 Sept. 2016, https://www.latimes.com/politics/la-na-pol-trump-false-statements-20160925-snap-story.html.

Flores, Lisa A. "Between Abundance and Marginalization: The Imperative of Racial Rhetorical Criticism." *Review of Communication,* vol. 16, no. 1, 2016, pp. 2–24.

Foss, Sonja K., and Cindy L. Griffin. "Beyond Persuasion: A Proposal for an Invitational Rhetoric." *Communication Monographs,* vol. 62, 1995, pp. 2–18.

Fricker, Miranda. *Epistemic Injustice: Power and the Ethics of Knowing.* Oxford UP, 2007.

Froomkin, Dan. "The Story No One Wants to Touch: Why the Capitol Police enabled 1/6." *Press Watch,* 24 Jan. 2023, https://presswatchers.org/2023/01/the-story-no-one-wants-to-touch-why-the-capitol-police-enabled-1-6/.

Frum, David. "The Seven Broken Guardrails of Democracy." *The Atlantic,* 31 May 2016, https://www.theatlantic.com/politics/archive/2016/05/the-seven-broken-guardrails-of-democracy/484829/.

Fuller, Kadeem. "Uncaged Black Futures Now." *The Huffington Post,* 11 Feb. 2017, https://www.huffingtonpost.com/entry/uncaged-black-futures-now_us_589f8293e4b0ab2d2b15a74a.

Garza, Alicia. *The Purpose of Power: How We Come Together When We Fall Apart.* One World, 2020.

Gelms, Bridget, and Dustin Edwards. "A Technofeminist Approach to Platform Rhetorics." *Computers & Composition Online,* 2019, http://cconlinejournal.org/techfem_si/02_Gelms_Edwards/.

Gill-Peterson, Jules. *Histories of the Transgender Child.* University of Minnesota Press, 2018.

Gilyard, Keith, and Adam Banks. *On African-American Rhetoric.* Routledge, 2018.

Glaser, April. "Russian Trolls Were Obsessed with Black Lives Matter." *Slate*, 11 May 2018, https://slate.com/technology/2018/05/russian-trolls-are-obsessed-with-black-lives-matter.html. Accessed 26 Feb. 2019.

Godbee, Beth. "Writing Up: How Assertions of Epistemic Rights Counter Epistemic Injustice." *College English*, vol. 79, no. 6, pp. 593–618.

Golstein, Alyosha, and Simón Ventura Trujillo, editors. *For Anti-Fascist Futures: Against the Violence of Imperial Crisis*. Common Notions, 2022.

Graves, Clint G., and Leland G. Spencer. "Against Knowing: The Rhetorical Structure of Epistemic Violence." *Southern Communication Journal*, vol. 87, no. 5, 2022, pp. 403–17.

Graves, Clint G., and Leland G. Spencer. "Rethinking the Rhetorical Epistemics of Gaslighting." *Communication Theory*, vol. 32, no. 1, 2022, pp. 48–67.

Gray, Richard. "Lies, Propaganda and Fake News: A Challenge for Our Age." *BBC*, 1 Mar. 2017, https://www.bbc.com/future/article/20170301-lies-propaganda-and-fake-news-a-grand-challenge-of-our-age.

Gries, Laurie. *Still Life with Rhetoric: A New Materialist Approach for Visual Rhetorics*. Utah State UP, 2015.

Guardian News. "'I Thought I Was Going to Die': AOC Describes Washington Capitol Attack." *YouTube*, 13 Jan. 2021, https://www.youtube.com/watch?v=AkrM6IKhvA4.

Hall, Kim Q. "Queer Epistemology and Epistemic Injustice." *The Routledge Handbook of Epistemic Injustice*, edited by Ian James Kidd et al., Routledge, 2017, pp. 158–66.

Harding, Sandra D., editor. *The Feminist Standpoint Theory Reader: Intellectual and Political Controversies*. Routledge, 2004.

Harriot, Michael. "Donald Trump Just Blamed the White Supremacist Hunger Games on 'Many Sides.' Here's What He Meant." *The Root*, 12 Aug. 2017, https://www.theroot.com/donald-trump-just-blamed-the-white-supremacist-hunger-g-1797785951.

Hartman, Saidiya. *Scenes of Subjection: Terror, Slavery, and Self-Making in Nineteenth-Century America*. Oxford, 1997.

Hartzell, Stephanie L. "An (In)visible Universe of Grief: Performative Disidentifications with White Motherhood in the We Are Not Trayvon Martin Blog." *Journal of International and Intercultural Communication*, vol. 10, no. 1, 2017, pp. 62–79.

Harvard University. "Civil Discourse." https://www.fas.harvard.edu/initiatives/civil-discourse/. Accessed 25 June 2024.

Hemmer, Nicole. "Trump Is Gaslighting America." *US News and World Report*, 15 Mar. 2016, https://www.usnews.com/opinion/blogs/nicole-hemmer/articles/2016-03-15/donald-trump-is-conning-america-with-his-lies.

Hesford, Wendy S. "Documenting Violations: Rhetorical Witnessing and the Spectacle of Distant Suffering." *Biography*, vol. 21, no. 1, 2004, pp. 104–44.

Hill Collins, Patricia. *Black Feminist Thought: Knowledge, Consciousness, and the Politics of Empowerment*. Routledge, 2000.

Hill Collins, Patricia. "Intersectionality and Epistemic Injustice." *The Routledge Handbook of Epistemic Injustice*, edited by Ian James Kidd et al., Routledge, 2017, pp. 115–24.

Hope, Jeanelle K., and Bill V. Mullen. *The Black Antifascist Tradition: Fighting Back from Anti-Lynching to Abolition*. Haymarket, 2024.

Hornsby, Jennifer. "Disempowered Speech." *Philosophical Topics*, vol. 23, no. 2, pp. 127–47.

Howard, Philip N., et al. *The IRA, Social Media and Political Polarization in the United States, 2012–2018*. U of Oxford, 2019.

Hsu, V. Jo. "Irreducible Damage: The Affective Drift of Race, Gender, and Disability in Anti-Trans Rhetorics." *Rhetoric Society Quarterly,* vol. 52, no. 1, 2022, pp. 62–77.

Hunter, Lourdes Ashley. "Every Breath a Black Trans Woman Takes Is an Act of Revolution." *The Huffington Post,* 6 Feb. 2015, https://www.huffingtonpost.com/lourdes-ashley-hunter/every-breath-a-black-tran_b_6631124.html.

Ingraham, Chris. "Toward an Algorithmic Rhetoric." *Digital Rhetoric and Global Literacies: Communication Modes and Digital Practices in the Networked World,* edited by Gustav Verhulsdonck and Marohang Limbu, IGI Global, 2013, pp. 62–79.

Jackson, George L. *Blood in My Eye.* Black Classic Press, 1990.

Jackson, Sandra, and Julie Moody Freeman. *The Black Imagination, Science Fiction and the Speculative.* Routledge, 2011.

Jacobs, Ben, and Oliver Laughland. "Charlottesville: Trump Reverts to Blaming Both Sides Including 'Violent Alt-Left.'" *The Guardian,* 16 Aug. 2017, https://www.theguardian.com/us-news/2017/aug/15/donald-trump-press-conference-far-right-defends-charlottesville.

Johnson, Jenna, and Mike Wagner. "Trump Condemns Charlottesville Violence but Doesn't Single Out White Nationalists." *The Washington Post,* 12 Aug. 2017, https://www.washingtonpost.com/politics/trump-condemns-charlottesville-violence-but-doesnt-single-out-white-nationalists/2017/08/12/933a86d6-7fa3-11e7-9d08-b79f191668ed_story.html.

Kaba, Mariame. *We Do This 'Til We Free Us: Abolitionist Organizing and Transforming Justice.* Haymarket, 2021.

Kalish, Liz. "A 25-Year-Old Trans Activist Injected Testosterone in Front of the Florida Board of Medicine to Protest a Ban on Gender-Affirming Care for Minors." *BuzzFeed News,* 13 Feb. 2023, https://www.buzzfeednews.com/article/lilkalish/trans-activist-injects-testosterone-florida-medicine-meeting.

Kane, Paul, et al. "'Just a Lie': Senate Republicans Blast Tucker Carlson's Jan. 6 Narrative." *The Washington Post,* 7 Mar. 2023.

Karkazis, Katrina. *Fixing Sex: Intersex, Medical Authority, and Lived Experience.* Duke UP, 2008.

Kelley, Robin D. G. *Freedom Dreams: The Black Radical Imagination.* Beacon Press, 2003.

Kelley, Robin D. G. "A Poetics of Anticolonialism." *Colonialism.* Monthly Review Press, 1999.

Kendi, Ibram X. *How to Be an Antiracist.* One World, 2019.

Khan-Cullors, Patrisse, and asha bandele. *When They Call You a Terrorist: A Black Lives Matter Memoir.* St. Martin's, 2018.

Lartey, James. "Race and Russian Interference: Senate Reports Detail Age-Old Tactic." *The Guardian,* 24 Dec. 2018, https://www.theguardian.com/world/2018/dec/24/race-russian-election-interference-senate-reports.

Law, Martin, and Lisa M. Corrigan. "On White-Speak and Gatekeeping: or, What Good Are the Greeks?" *Communication and Critical/Cultural Studies,* vol. 15, no. 4, 2018, pp. 326–30.

Lehmann, Chris. "The 'Is Donald Trump a Fascist?' Debate Has Been Ended—by Donald Trump." *The Nation,* 14 Nov. 2023, https://www.thenation.com/article/politics/donald-trump-fascist-vermin/.

Leingang, Rachel. "Another Week, Another Trump Flirtation with Fascism." *The Guardian,* 22 May 2024, https://www.theguardian.com/global/article/2024/may/22/another-week-another-trump-flirtation-with-fascism.

Lemieux, Jamilah. "Why I'm Skipping the Women's March on Washington." *Colorlines,* 17 Jan. 2017, https://www.colorlines.com/articles/why-im-skipping-womens-march-washington-opinion.

Levin, Sam. "Did Russia Fake Black Activism on Facebook to Sow Division in the US?" *The Guardian,* 30 Sept. 2017, https://www.theguardian.com/technology/2017/sep/30/blacktivist-facebook-account-russia-us-election.

Licona, Adela C., and Karma R. Chávez. "Relational Literacies and Their Coalitional Possibilities." *Peitho,* vol. 18, no. 1, 2015, pp. 96–107.

Licona, Adela C., and Stephen T. Russell. "Transdisciplinary and Community Literacies: Shifting Discourses and Practices through New Paradigms of Public Scholarship and Action-Oriented Research." *Community Literacy Journal,* vol. 8, no. 1, 2013, pp. 1–7.

Littman, Lisa. "RETRACTED ARTICLE: Rapid Onset Gender Dysphoria: Parent Reports on 1655 Possible Cases." *Archives of Sexual Behavior,* vol. 52, 2023, pp. 1031–43.

Lopez, German. "Freddie Gray Died in Baltimore Police Custody. The Justice System Will Punish No One for It." *Vox,* 27 July 2016, https://www.vox.com/2016/7/27/12296670/freddie-gray-baltimore-police-trial.

López, Ian Haney. *Dog Whistle Politics: How Coded Racial Appeals Have Reinvented Racism and Wrecked the Middle Class.* Oxford UP, 2015.

Lozano-Reich, Nina M., and Dana L. Cloud. "The Uncivil Tongue: Invitational Rhetoric and the Problem of Inequality." *Western Journal of Communication,* vol. 73, no. 2, 2009, pp. 220–26.

Luscombe, Richard. "Florida Bill Would Allow Students to Record Professors to Show Political Bias." *The Guardian,* 25 Apr. 2021, https://www.theguardian.com/us-news/2021/apr/25/florida-bill-record-professors-universities.

Mallett, Kandist. "The Response to the Capitol Riot Is Whitewashing the History of Black Insurrection." *The New Republic,* 18 Jan. 2021, https://newrepublic.com/article/160962/living-tradition-black-insurrection.

Manne, Kate. "I Have Been So Numb." *More to Hate,* 27 Aug. 2024, https://katemanne.substack.com/p/i-have-been-so-numb.

Marantz, Andrew. "Why We Can't Stop Arguing about Whether Trump Is a Fascist." *The New Yorker,* 27 Mar. 2024, https://www.newyorker.com/books/under-review/why-we-cant-stop-arguing-about-whether-trump-is-a-fascist.

Martin, Londie T., and Adela C. Licona. "Remix as Unruly Play and Participatory Method for Im/Possible Queer World-Making." *Unruly Rhetorics: Protest, Persuasion, and Politics,* edited by Jonathan Alexander et al., U of Pittsburgh P, 2018, pp. 244–60.

Martinez, Aja Y. "Critical Race Theory: Its Origins, History, and Importance to the Discourses and Rhetorics of Race." *Frame,* vol. 27, no. 2, 2014, pp. 9–27.

Marwick, Alice, et al. "Critical Disinformation Studies: A Syllabus." Center for Information, Technology, and Public Life, University of North Carolina at Chapel Hill, 2021, https://citap.unc.edu/critical-disinfo.

Matthews, Shanelle. "Black Imagination, A Vital Way Forward." *The Huffington Post,* 1 Feb. 2017, https://www.huffingtonpost.com/entry/black-imagination-vital-wayforward_us_5891dc4fe4b0522c7d3e1467.

McKee, Heidi A. "Policy Matters Now and in the Future: Net Neutrality, Corporate Data Mining, and Government Surveillance." *Computers and Composition,* vol. 28, no. 4, 2011, pp. 276–91.

McKerrow, Raymie. "Coloring Outside the Lines." *Southern Communication Journal,* vol. 67, no. 3, 2002, pp. 290–94.

McNamara, Russ. "Is Donald Trump a Fascist? A Fascism Scholar Says He Certainly Sounds Like One." *WDET Detroit Public Radio,* 23 Feb. 2024, https://wdet.org/2024/02/23/is-donald-trump-a-fascist-a-fascism-scholar-says-he-certainly-sounds-like-one/.

McSweeney, Leah, and Jacob Siegel. "Is the Women's March Melting Down?" *Tablet,* 10 Dec. 2018, https://www.tabletmag.com/sections/news/articles/is-the-womens-march-melting-down.

Medina, José. "The Relevance of Credibility Excess in a Proportional View of Epistemic Injustice: Differential Epistemic Authority and the Social Imaginary." *Social Epistemology,* vol. 25, no. 1, 2011, pp. 15–35.

Mejia, Robert, et al. "White Lies: A Racial History of the (Post) Truth." *Communication and Critical/Cultural Studies,* vol. 15, no. 2, 2018, pp. 109–26.

Mercieca, Jennifer. *Demagogue for President: The Rhetorical Genius of Donald Trump.* Texas A&M UP, 2020.

Miller, Robert J. "Nazi Germany's Race Laws, the United States, and American Indians." *St. John's Law Review,* vol. 94, no. 3., 2020, pp. 751–817.

Mills, Charles. *Black Rights / White Wrongs: The Critique of Racial Liberalism.* Oxford University Press, 2017.

Montgomery, David. "Sandra Bland, It Turns Out, Filmed Traffic Stop Confrontation Herself." *The New York Times,* 7 May 2019, https://www.nytimes.com/2019/05/07/us/sandra-bland-video-brian-encinia.html.

Moreno, J. Edward. "Ocasio-Cortez Dismisses Proposed $1B Cut: 'Defunding Police Means Defunding Police.'" *The Hill,* 30 June 2020, https://thehill.com/homenews/house/505307-ocasio-cortez-dismisses-proposed-1b-cut-defunding-police-means-defunding/.

Morris, Seren. "Alexandria Ocasio-Cortez's Instagram Video about Capitol Riots Receives Praise, Support." *Newsweek,* 2 Feb. 2021, https://www.newsweek.com/alexandria-ocasio-cortez-instagram-video-capitol-riots-praise-support-1566031.

Morrison, Aaron. "AP Exclusive: Black Lives Matter Opens Up about Its Finances." *AP News,* 23 Feb. 2021, https://apnews.com/article/black-lives-matter-90-million-finances-8a80cad199f54c0c4b9e74283d27366f.

Mullen, Bill V., and Christopher Vials, editors. *The US Antifascism Reader.* Verso, 2020.

Muñoz, José Esteban. *Cruising Utopia: The Then and There of Queer Futurity.* New York UP, 2019.

Muñoz, José Esteban. *Disidentifications: Queers of Color and the Performance of Politics.* U of Minnesota P, 1999.

Nair, Yasmin. "AOC and the Weaponisation of Trauma." *yasminnair.com,* 27 Feb. 2021, https://yasminnair.com/aoc-and-the-weaponisation-of-trauma/.

Naylor, Brian. "Read Trump's Jan. 6 Speech, A Key Part of Impeachment Trial." *NPR,* 10 Feb. 2021, https://www.npr.org/2021/02/10/966396848/read-trumps-jan-6-speech-a-key-part-of-impeachment-trial.

Nelson, Alondra. "Introduction: Future Texts." *Social Text,* vol. 20, no. 2, 2002, pp. 1–15.

New Day. "Panelist to Sanders: 'Shut Up' in Fiery Debate." *CNN,* 14 Aug. 2017, https://www.cnn.com/videos/us/2017/08/14/heated-debate-sanders-cuccinelli-shut-up-sot-newday.cnn.

Noble, Safiya Umoja. *Algorithms of Oppression.* New York UP, 2018.

North, Anna. "The Women's March Changed the American Left. Now Anti-Semitism Allegations Threaten the Group's Future." *Vox,* 21 Dec. 2018, https://www.vox.com/identities/2018/12/21/18145176/feminism-womens-march-2018-2019-farrakhan-intersectionality.

NPR / PBS NewsHour / Marist Poll. "Civility in America." Marist University. 19 Dec. 2018.

Obie, Brooke. "Woman in Viral Photo from Women's March to White Female Allies: 'Listen to a Black Woman.'" *The Root,* 23 Jan. 2017, http://www.theroot.com/woman-in-viral-photo-from-women-s-march-to-white-female-1791524613.

Ocasio-Cortez, Alexandria [@AOC]. "I couldn't care less about what this talking inferiority complex has to say. . . ." *Twitter,* 13 Aug. 2021, https://twitter.com/AOC/status/1426311395323297795.

Ocasio-Cortez, Alexandria. "What Happened at the Capitol Instagram Live." *YouTube,* 2 Feb. 2021, https://www.youtube.com/watch?v=fWNWoNaImQA.

The Ohio State University. "Civil Discourse for Citizenship." https://cehv.osu.edu/civil-discourse-citizenship. Accessed 25 June 2024.

Oliver, Brittany. "Why I Do Not Support the Women's March on Washington." Brittany T. Oliver's blog [discontinued], 16 Nov. 2016, https://web.archive.org/web/20170224073925/http://www.brittanytoliver.com/blog/2016/11/16/why-i-do-not-support-the-one-million-women-march-on-washington.

Oliver, Kelly. "Witnessing and Testimony." *Parallax,* vol. 10, no. 1, 2004, pp. 79–88.

Omi, Michael, and Howard Winant. *Racial Formation in the United States: From the 1960s to the 1990s.* Routledge, 1994.

Ono, Kent A., and John M. Sloop. "The Critique of Vernacular Discourse." *Communication Monographs,* vol. 62, 1995, pp. 19–46.

Openly | LGBTQ+ News [@openlynews]. "Full Unedited Video: A Transgender Activist Injected Himself HRT before the Florida Board of Medicine" *TikTok,* 11 Feb. 2023, https://www.tiktok.com/@openlynews/video/7198878821767040261.

Oppel, Richard A., Jr., et al. "What to Know about Breonna Taylor's Death." *The New York Times,* 9 Mar. 2023, https://www.nytimes.com/article/breonna-taylor-police.html.

Ore, Ersula. *Lynching: Violence, Rhetoric, and American Identity.* UP of Mississippi, 2019.

O'Sullivan, Donie. "Her Son Was Killed—Then Came the Russian Trolls." *CNN,* 29 June 2018, https://www.cnn.com/2018/06/26/us/russian-trolls-exploit-philando-castiles-death/index.html.

Pariser, Eli. *The Filter Bubble: How the New Personalized Web Is Changing What We Read and How We Think.* Penguin, 2012.

Parry, Marc. "Reframing Black Lives Matter." *The Chronicle of Higher Education,* 23 Apr. 2017, http://www.chronicle.com/article/Reframing-Black-Lives/239833/.

Patterson, Orlando. *Slavery and Social Death.* Harvard UP, 1982.

Paul, Pamela. "As Kids, They Thought They Were Trans. They No Longer Do." *The New York Times,* 2 Feb. 2024, https://www.nytimes.com/2024/02/02/opinion/transgender-children-gender-dysphoria.html.

Pauly, Madison. "Inside the Secret Working Group That Helped Push Anti-Trans Laws across the Country." *Mother Jones,* 8 Mar. 2023, https://www.motherjones.com/politics/2023/03/anti-trans-transgender-health-care-ban-legislation-bill-minors-children-lgbtq/.

Perelman, Chaim, and Lucie Olbrechts-Tyteca. *The New Rhetoric: A Treatise on Argumentation.* Notre Dame UP, 1973.

Perkins, Kathryn J., et al. "A Right to Transition? Gender-Segregated Spaces and the Legal Construction of Transgender Identity." *Transgender Studies Quarterly,* vol. 9, no. 4, 2022, pp. 609–33, https://doi.org/10.1215/23289252-10133817.

Perry, Samuel. "President Trump and Charlottesville: Uncivil Mourning and White Supremacy." *Journal of Contemporary Rhetoric,* vol. 8, nos. 1–2, 2018, pp. 57–71.

Pew Research Center. "An Examination of the 2016 Electorate, Based on Validated Voters." 9 Aug. 2018, https://www.pewresearch.org/politics/2018/08/09/an-examination-of-the-2016-electorate-based-on-validated-voters/.

Picalini, Federico. "Evidential Reasoning, Testimonial Injustice and the Fairness of the Criminal Trial." *Quaestio Facti. International Journal on Evidential Legal Reasoning,* 4 Sept. 2023, https://papers.ssrn.com/sol3/papers.cfm?abstract_id=4561170.

Politico Staff. "Full Text: Trump's Comments on White Supremacists, 'Alt-Left' in Charlottesville." *Politico,* 15 Aug. 2017, https://www.politico.com/story/2017/08/15/full-text-trump-comments-white-supremacists-alt-left-transcript-241662.

Pritchard, Eric Darnell. *Fashioning Lives: Black Queers and the Politics of Literacy.* Southern Illinois UP, 2016.

Ramos, Santos F. "Building a Culture of Solidarity: Racial Discourse, Black Lives Matter, and Indigenous Social Justice." *Enculturation,* vol. 21, 2016.

Ransby, Barbara. *Ella Baker and the Black Freedom Movement: A Radical Democratic Vision.* U of North Carolina P, 2005.

Raskin, Jamie, et al. "Trial Memorandum of the United States House of Representatives in the Impeachment Trial of President Donald J. Trump." US Senate Documents, Congress of the United States, DigitalCommons@University of Nebraska–Lincoln, 2 Feb. 2021, https://digitalcommons.unl.edu/cgi/viewcontent.cgi?article=1005&context=senatedocs.

Reed, Erin. "June Anti-Trans Legislative Risk Map." *Erin in the Morning,* 25 June 2023, https://www.erininthemorning.com/p/june-anti-trans-legislative-risk.

Renton, David, editor. *No Pasarán! Antifascist Discourses from a World in Crisis.* AK Press, 2022.

"Republican Party Platform of 1980." *The American Presidency Project,* University of California Santa Barbara, 15 July 1980, https://www.presidency.ucsb.edu/documents/republican-party-platform-1980.

Rice, Samaria. "My 12-Year-Old Son, Tamir Rice, Was Killed by Police. I'm Not Allowed to Be Normal." *ABC News,* 13 July 2020, https://abcnews.go.com/GMA/News/12-year-son-tamir-rice-killed-police-im/story?id=71654873.

Richardson, Elaine. *African American Literacies.* Routledge, 2022.

Richardson, Elaine, and Alice Ragland. "#StayWoke: The Language and Literacies of the #BlackLivesMatter Movement." *Community Literacy Journal,* vol. 12, no. 2, 2018, pp. 27–56.

Richert, Kevin. "Amidst Student Complaints, Boise State Suspends Ethics and Diversity Course." *Idaho Ed News,* 16 Mar. 2021, https://www.idahoednews.org/kevins-blog/amidst-student-complaints-boise-state-suspends-ethics-and-diversity-course/.

Ridolfo, Jim, and Dànielle Nicole DeVoss. "Composing for Recomposition: Rhetorical Velocity and Delivery." *Kairos: A Journal of Rhetoric, Technology, and Pedagogy,* vol. 13, no. 2, 2009, http://kairos.technorhetoric.net/13.2/topoi/ridolfo_devoss/intro.html.

Ridolfo, Jim, and William Hart-Davidson. *Rhet Ops: Rhetoric and Information Warfare.* U of Pittsburgh P, 2019.

Rivas, Rebecca. "Ferguson Activist Charged with Inciting a Riot via Facebook Posts." *The St. Louis American,* 3 June 2020, https://www.stlamerican.com/news/local-news/ferguson-activist-charged-with-inciting-a-riot-via-facebook-posts/.

Roberts-Miller, Patricia. "Discursive Conflict in Communities and Classrooms." *College Composition and Communication,* vol. 54, no. 4, 2003, pp. 536–57.

ross, kihana miraya. "Call It What It Is: Anti-Blackness." *The New York Times,* 4 June 2020.

Royster, Jacqueline Jones. "When the First Voice You Hear Is Not Your Own." *College Composition and Communication,* vol. 47, no. 1, 1996, pp. 29–40.

Royster, Jacqueline Jones, and Gesa E. Kirsch. *Feminist Rhetorical Practices: New Horizons for Rhetoric, Composition, and Literacy Studies.* Southern Illinois UP, 2012.

Russell, Legacy. *Glitch Feminism: A Manifesto.* Verso, 2020.

Saad, Layla F. *Me and White Supremacy: Combat Racism, Change the World, and Become a Good Ancestor.* Sourcebooks, 2020.

Salamon, Gayle. *Assuming a Body: Transgender and Rhetorics of Materiality.* Columbia UP, 2010.

Sanchez, James Chase. "Trump, the KKK, and the Versatility of White Supremacy Rhetoric." *Journal of Contemporary Rhetoric,* vol. 8, nos. 1–2, 2018, pp. 44–56.

Sarkis, Stephanie. "Donald Trump Is a Classic Gaslighter in an Abusive Relationship with America." *USA Today,* 3 Oct. 2018, https://www.usatoday.com/story/opinion/2018/10/03/trump-classic-gaslighter-abusive-relationship-america-column/1445050002/.

Schall, Theodore E., and Jacob D. Moses. "Gender-Affirming Care for Cisgender People." *The Hastings Center Report,* vol. 53, no. 3, 2023, pp. 15–24.

Schmidt, Ana Lucia, et al. "Anatomy of News Consumption on Facebook." *PNAS,* 21 Mar. 2017, https://www.pnas.org/doi/pdf/10.1073/pnas.1617052114.

Shafie, Ghadir, and Karma R. Chávez. "Pinkwashing and the Boycott, Divestment, and Sanctions Campaign." *Journal of Human and Civil Rights,* vol. 5, 2019, pp. 32–48.

Shaye, Amaryah. "Refusing to Reconcile, Part 2." *Women in Theology,* 16 Feb. 2014, https://womenintheology.org/2014/02/16/refusing-to-reconcile-part-2/.

Shrier, Abigail. *Irreversible Damage: The Transgender Craze Seducing Our Daughters.* Regnery, 2021.

shuster, stef m. *Trans Medicine: The Emergence and Practice of Treating Gender.* New York UP, 2021.

Smilges, J. Logan. *Queer Silence: On Disability and Rhetorical Absence.* U of Minnesota P, 2022.

Smith, Mychal Denzel. "Justice for Trayvon Martin." *The Nation,* 12 Mar. 2012, https://www.thenation.com/article/archive/justice-trayvon-martin/.

Snorton, C. Riley. *Black on Both Sides: A Racial History of Trans Identity.* U of Minnesota P, 2017.

Spade, Dean. *Normal Life: Administrative Violence, Critical Trans Politics, and the Limits of Law.* Duke UP, 2015.

Spencer, Robyn C. "The Black Panther Party and Black Anti-Fascism in the U.S." *Duke University Press News,* 26 Jan. 2017, https://dukeupress.wordpress.com/2017/01/26/the-black-panther-party-and-black-anti-fascism-in-the-united-states/.

Spillers, Hortense J. "Mama's Baby, Papa's Maybe: An American Grammar Book." *Feminisms REDUX: An Anthology of Literary Theory and Criticism,* edited by Robyn Warhol-Down and Diane Price Herndl, Rutgers UP, 2009, pp. 443–64.

Steele, Catherine Knight. *Digital Black Feminism.* New York UP, 2021.

Steinmetz-Jenkins, Daniel, editor. *Did It Happen Here? Perspectives on Fascism and America.* Norton, 2024.

Stone, Sandy. "The *Empire* Strikes Back: A Posttransexual Manifesto." 1987, https://sandystone.com/empire-strikes-back.pdf.

Strangio, Chase [@chasestrangio]. "Since June of last year, I have gone to court five times. . . ." *Instagram,* 9 July 2023, https://www.instagram.com/p/Cuc896Cun8F/?utm_source=ig_web_copy_link&igshid=MzRlODBiNWFlZA==.

Swenson, Ali. "Ocasio-Cortez Didn't Lie about Location during Capitol Riot." *AP News,* 4 Feb. 2021, https://apnews.com/article/fact-checking-9951968706.

Tate, Katherine. *From Protest to Politics: The New Black Voters in American Elections.* Harvard UP, 1998.

Tekkobe, Cindy. *Indigenous Voices in Digital Spaces.* UP of Colorado, 2024.

Thomas, Ebony Elizabeth. *The Dark Fantastic: Race and the Imagination from Harry Potter to the Hunger Games.* NYU Press, 2019.

Tisdall, Simon. "Fascism Is Everywhere on the March. And It's Trump Who Sets the Pace." *The Guardian,* 20 Jan. 2024, https://www.theguardian.com/commentisfree/2024/jan/20/fascism-is-everywhere-on-the-march-and-its-trump-who-sets-the-pace.

Tomasky, Michael. "Yes, That's Right: American Fascism." *The New Republic,* 16 May 2024, https://newrepublic.com/article/181258/american-fascism-look-like.

Toscano, Alberto. "Incipient Fascism: Black Radical Perspectives." *CLCWeb: Comparative Literature and Culture,* vol. 23, no. 1, 2021, http://docs.lib.purdue.edu/clcweb/vol23/iss1/6.

United States, Congress, House. Impeaching Donald John Trump, President of the United States, for High Crimes and Misdemeanors. *Congress.gov,* https://www.congress.gov/bill/117th-congress/house-resolution/24. 117th Congress, House Resolution 24, introduced 11 Jan. 2021.

United States House of Representatives Permanent Select Committee on Intelligence. "Exposing Russia's Effort to Sow Discord Online: The Internet Research Agency and Advertisements." https://democrats-intelligence.house.gov/social-media-content/. Accessed 29 Nov. 2021.

University of Denver. "Civil Discourse Initiative." https://korbel.du.edu/scrivner/initiatives. Accessed 25 June 2024.

Vagianos, Alanna. "Read the Women's March on Washington's Beautifully Intersectional Policy Platform." *The Huffington Post,* 17 Jan. 2017, http://www.huffingtonpost.com/entry/read-the-womens-march-on-washingtons-beautifully-intersectional-policy-platform_us_5878e0e8e4b0e58057fe4c4b.

Velocci, Beans. "Standards of Care: Uncertainty and Risk in Harry Benjamin's Transsexual Classifications." *TSQ: Transgender Studies Quarterly,* vol. 8, no. 4, 2021, pp. 462–80.

Vice. "Charlottesville: Race and Terror—Vice News Tonight on HBO." *YouTube,* 14 Aug. 2017, https://www.youtube.com/watch?v=RIrcB1sAN8I.

Vick, Karl. "Perhaps the Largest Protest in U.S. History Was Brought to You by Trump." *Time,* 26 Jan. 2017, http://time.com/4649891/protest-donald-trump/.

Wachter-Boettcher, Sara. *Technically Wrong: Sexist Apps, Biased Algorithms, and Other Threats of Toxic Tech.* Norton, 2018.

Wahlquist, Calla. "Black Lives Matter Awarded 2017 Sydney Peace Prize." *The Guardian,* 22 May 2017, https://www.theguardian.com/us-news/2017/may/23/black-lives-matter-awarded-2017-sydney-peace-prize.

Waite, Stacey. *Teaching Queer: Radical Possibilities for Writing and Knowing.* U of Pittsburgh P, 2017.

Wang, Amy B. "'Post-Truth' Named Word of the Year by Oxford Dictionaries." *Washington Post,* 16 Nov. 2016, https://www.washingtonpost.com/news/the-fix/wp/2016/11/16/post-truth-named-2016-word-of-the-year-by-oxford-dictionaries/.

Ward, Ian. "The Right's Fascism Problem." *Politico,* 21 May 2024, https://www.politico.com/newsletters/politico-nightly/2024/05/21/the-rights-fascism-problem-00159265.

Washington Post Staff. "Identifying Far-Right Symbols That Appeared at the U.S. Capitol Riot." *The Washington Post,* 15 Jan. 2021, https://www.washingtonpost.com/nation/interactive/2021/far-right-symbols-capitol-riot/.

Watson, Julie. "Comparison between Capitol Siege, BLM Protests Is Denounced." *AP News,* 14 Jan. 2021, https://apnews.com/article/donald-trump-capitol-siege-race-and-ethnicity-violence-racial-injustice-afd7dc2165f355a3e6dc4e9418019eb5.

Weber Shandwick, et al. "Civility in America 2019: Solutions for Tomorrow." *Weber Shandwick,* 26 June 2019, https://cms.webershandwick.com/wp-content/uploads/2023/01/CivilityInAmerica2019SolutionsforTomorrow.pdf.

Whitman, James Q. *Hitler's American Model: The United States and the Making of Nazi Race Law.* Princeton UP, 2018.

Wilderson, Frank B., III. "Afro-Pessimism and the End of Redemption." *Humanities Futures,* Franklin Humanities Institute, Duke University, 2016, https://humanitiesfutures.org/papers/afro-pessimism-end-redemption/.

Williams, Kiyan. "Why Black People Must Hold on to Our Dreams." *The Huffington Post,* 1 Feb. 2016, https://www.huffingtonpost.com/kiyan-williams/hold-on-to-yourdreams_b_9116622.html.

Williams, Miriam F. "#BlackLivesMatter: Tweeting a Movement in *Chronos* and *Kairos.*" *Racial Shorthand: Coded Discrimination Contested in Social Media,* edited by Cruz Medina and Octavio Pimentel. Computers and Composition Digital Press, 2018, https://ccdigitalpress.org/book/shorthand/.

Wolf, Zachary B. "The American Fascism Debate Gets a Reboot." *CNN,* 6 June 2024, https://www.cnn.com/2024/06/06/politics/fascism-trump-biden-what-matters/index.html.

Womack, Ytasha L. *Afrofuturism: The World of Black Sci-Fi and Fantasy Culture.* Lawrence Hill, 2013.

Yergeau, M. Remi. *Authoring Autism: On Rhetoric and Neurological Queerness.* Duke UP, 2018.

Young, Nerissa. "My Republican Party Is Gone. America Will Follow under Trump. Ohio Dismantling Truth." *The Columbus Dispatch,* 17 June 2024, https://www.dispatch.com/story/opinion/columns/guest/2024/06/17/why-senate-bill-83-is-danger-educators-will-be-jailed/74087467007/.

Zane, J. Peter. "Trump Got It Right: In Charlottesville, Both Sides Were Itching for a Fight." *The Herald Sun,* 18 Aug. 2017, https://www.heraldsun.com/opinion/article167710407.html.

Zucchino, David. "'Wilmington's Lie' Author Traces the Rise of White Supremacy in a Southern City." *Fresh Air,* 31 Jan. 2020, https://www.npr.org/2020/01/13/795892582/wilmington-s-lie-author-traces-the-rise-of-white-supremacy-in-a-southern-city.

Zucchino, David. *Wilmington's Lie: The Murderous Coup of 1898 and the Rise of White Supremacy.* Atlantic Monthly Press, 2020.

INDEX

accountability: "both sides" rhetoric and, 79; civil discourse and, 84–85; gaslighting and, 101, 103; imagination and, 44, 49; narrative activism and, 38, 42

accumulation-based disinformation strategies, 21, 54

activism. *See specific topics, such as* Black Lives Matter (BLM) activism

Afrofuturism, 35–36, 46

Afropessimism, 10n8

Ahmed, Sabeen, 13, 110

algorithmic inequity, 52

"all sides" of an issue, seeing, 18–19

alt-right and "alt-left," 74–75

anti-Blackness: Afropessimism on, 10–11n8; as analytic, 139–40; change over time in, 11–12; US defined by, 8; violence of, 31, 39. *See also* Black Lives Matter (BLM) activism; white supremacy

"antifa," 76–77

anti-Semitism, false charges of, 68–70

"Anti-Trans Hate Machine, The" (Anonymous), 128–31

Arif, Ahmer, 53

Aristotelian rhetoric, 55

artificial intelligence (AI) technologies, 17–18

Ashley, Florence, 120–21

Awkward-Rich, Cameron, 123

Bailey, Alison, 91

Bailey, Moya Z., 20

Baker, Catherine, 77

Baker, Ella, 55–56, 59

Baldwin, James, 10

Banks, Adam J., 20, 55

Barry, Ellen, 65, 67, 70

Bellamy, Wes, 86

Benjamin, Harry, 117–18

Benjamin, Ruha, 11–12, 19, 25n13, 52

Bey, Marquis, 24, 80

"bias," 32, 79

Biden, Joe, 77, 98, 111

Biko, Cherno, 45–46

Black feminist epistemology, 55

Black insurrection and limits of testimonial, 108–11

Black Lives Matter (BLM) activism: about, 31–32; Baltimore and fake "Blacktivist" account, 60–62; *Black Futures Month* and imagining futures, 42–49; memoirs as narrative activism, 38–42; Minneapolis and fake "Don't Shoot" account, 58–60; narrative and imagination as strategies, 34–38; relational knowledge and, 55–62; restricting imagination as disinformation strategy and, 32–34; rhetoric and intersectional mission, 56–58; Russian IRA targeting of, 53–54

Black Lives Matter Global Network, 42–43, 57

Black Panther Party, 14

"Black Trans Lives Matter Too" (Biko), 45–46

Bland, Bob, 69, 70

Bland, Sandra, 32

Bonilla-Silva, Eduardo, 11

"both sides" rhetoric: after Charlottesville, 74–77; Charlottesville Unite the Right rally and Trump remarks, 72–74; civil lawsuit in Charlottesville, 86–87; civility discourse and, 84–86; as false equivalency, 73, 77–80; feminism and, 67; January 6 Capitol insurrection and, 109; naming and contextualization as strategies, 80–84; wasting time and erasing context, 73, 79–80; Women's March and, 67

Bradshaw, Jonathan L., 20–21, 54, 57, 95, 141

Bradshaw, Samantha, 66

Brock, André, Jr., 20

Browdy, Ronisha, 39

brown, adrienne maree, 36, 134

Brown, Heber, III, 60–62

Brown, Michael, 58

Browne, Simone, 19

Cameron, Shanice Jones, 22

Capitol insurrection. *See* January 6 Capitol insurrection

Carey, Tamika L., 73–74, 80, 81

Carlson, Tucker, 107–9

Carpenter, Amanda, 90

Carruthers, Charlene A., 59

Castile, Philando, 58–59

Cauterucci, Christina, 70–71

Césaire, Aimé, 14, 15

Charlottesville, VA: "both sides" rhetoric after, 74–77; civil lawsuit, 86–87; civility rhetoric and, 81, 84–86; naming and contextualization as strategies, 80–84; Unite the Right rally, 72–74. *See also* "both sides" rhetoric

Chávez, Karma, 23, 37, 55

child figure, innocent, 116–17

Cillizza, Chris, 94

circulation framework, 26–27

civility and civil discourse: "both sides" language and, 109; Charlottesville and, 81, 84–86; crisis rhetoric and, 4–6; as ideal and as mechanism of control, 16; January 6 Capitol insurrection and, 108–9; rhetoric as discipline and, 17; rhetorical exhaustion and, 21; time wasted by, 86; troubling, 15–19

Clinton, Hillary, 63, 68

Cloud, Dana L., 6–7

coalitional stances, 23–24

Cohen, Cathy, 24

Collins, Susan R., 77

colonialism and fascism, 14

Condit, Celeste, 91–92

consent, violation of, 44

conservatism, power narrative of, 41

contextualization and decontextualization: about, 137–38; BLM and, 57; "both sides" rhetoric and, 73, 79–84; gaslighting and, 92; racial rhetorical criticism and, 23; restricting imagination and, 31–32; terrorism and, 40

controlling images, 41

Cooper, Brittney, 80

co-optation: of Black language, culture, and activism, 57; fake accounts and, 62; of narratives, 37; Russian IRA and, 51, 53, 60, 62, 66

COVID-19 pandemic, 140

crisis rhetoric, 4–9

critical disinformation studies, 22

Cruz, Ted, 102, 109

Cuccinelli, Ken, 81

Daniels, Jessie, 10

Davis, Angela, 14

decontextualization. *See* contextualization and decontextualization

de-escalation, 35

dehistoricization. *See* historicization and dehistoricization

deliberative democracy, 8, 16, 67, 78–79. *See also* civility and civil discourse

DeSantis, Ron, 113

desire, economy of, 24–25

digital disinformation, analysis of, 140–41

disidentification: gaslighting and, 100–101, 106; testimonial limits and, 108; theory of, 93

disinformation: accumulation-based strategies, 21, 54; COVID-19, 140; critical disinformation studies, 22; not directly engaging with, 35, 57–58; resistance against (*see specific topics, such as* January 6 Capitol insurrection); restricting imagination strategy, 32–34; rhetorical exhaustion and, 20–21, 54, 94, 141; Russian IRA, 50, 53–54, 65–68; technology blamed for, 51–52; on trans people, 114, 126; white supremacy as co-constitutive with, 3. *See also* "both sides" rhetoric; gaslighting; post-truth politics

dissoi logoi, 88

dominant power: appeasement attempts, 41; imagination and domination systems, 44; queer epistemologies and, 93; rhetorical resources outside, 20; terms set by, 8–9, 24, 29; t4t approach and, 122

Dotson, Kristie, 92–93

Douglass, Frederick, 25n13

Drew, Kimberly, 35–36

Duca, Lauren, 89–90

Duggan, Lisa, 5n3

Duke, David, 76

Edelman, Lee, 116

Elamroussi, Aya, 87

Elster, Mikey, 119

emergent strategy, 20

emotion: civility discourse and, 85, 86; privileged tone as unemotional, 16; refusal through trans joy, 123–27; refusal through trans spite, 127–31; Russian IRA tactics and, 53–54; trans testimonial and, 130–31; trauma and, 104

enthymemes, 79

epistemic injustice, 91–94

epistemologies: beginning from marginalized knowledges, 19–21; Black feminist, 55; epistemological certainty and uncertainty, 120–21; standpoint, 93, 121

"Every Breath a Black Trans Woman Takes Is an Act of Revolution" (Hunter), 46–47

Facebook, fake pages on, 58–60

facts: civility and, 15; fact-checking and liberal rhetorics of facticity, 5–6, 9, 36, 54; imagination and, 36; ineffectiveness of fact-based appeals or debates, 57–58, 95, 141; opinions as interchangeable with, 90; revealing manufactured narratives, 130; weaponized insistence on, 74

false equivalency, 73, 77–80

Farrakhan, Louis, 69

fascism, 13–15

feminism: Black, 55, 81; standpoint epistemology and, 93; white feminism and Women's March, 63–64, 66

Fernandes, Sujatha, 37

Flores, Lisa, 22–23

Floyd, George, 31, 33

framing as violence, 32

Fricker, Amanda, 91, 92

"fringe opinions," 18

Frum, David, 4–5

Fuller, Kadeem, 47–48

futures and futurity, 42–49, 116

Gaetz, Matt, 33

Garner, Eric, 32

Garza, Alicia, 34, 38, 41–42, 57

gaslighting: as abuse, 95; anti-trans, 126; Capitol insurrection and, 89–91, 94–99, 107–10; civility discourse, limits of testimonial, and, 108–11; defined, 89; disidentification strategy, 93, 100–101, 106, 108; as epistemic injustice, 91–94; public performances of, 95, 107; structural, 91–92, 93, 109; testimonial and witnessing as

strategies against, 92–93, 99–108; trauma and, 101–7
gender-affirming care, 113–14, 124–27
Gill-Peterson, Jules, 116–17, 118
Gilyard, Keith, 55
Giuliani, Rudolph, 39
Glaser, April, 53
Gorcenski, Emily, 72–73
Graves, Clint G., 91–92
Gray, Freddie, 60
Grimm, Mica, 58–60

Harding, Sandra, 93
Harriot, Michael, 83–84
Hart-Davidson, William, 51
Hartman, Saidiya, 11
Hartzell, Stephanie, 93, 108
Henle, Amélie, 66
Heyer, Heather, 72, 76
Hill Collins, Patricia, 22, 55, 91
historicization and dehistoricization: "both sides" rhetoric and, 73–74, 79–80; civility and, 16; historicization strategy, 137–38; Hunter on Black trans women and, 46–47; racial liberalism and, 12; racial rhetorical criticism and, 23; restricting imagination and, 32
"home places," 56
hormone replacement therapy (HRT), 124–27
Hornsby, Jennifer, 92
Hsu, V. Jo, 114
Hudson, Tanesha, 81–82, 84
Huffington Post, 42–43
Hughes, Langston, 13
Hunter, Lourdes Ashley, 46–47

identity: disidentification, 93, 100–101, 106, 108; queer de-prioritizing of, 121; queer epistemologies and, 93; transness and, 118–21
imagination: as accountability practice, 49; *Black Futures Month* and imagining futures, 42–49; failure of, 36; narrative and, 34–38; restricting of, 31–34; white, 43–44
impatience, rhetorics of, 73–74, 81
incarceration, mass, 47–48
intersectionality, 22, 57, 63–64
invitational rhetoric, 17n11
Irreversible Damage (Shrier), 113

Jackson, George L., 14
January 6 Capitol insurrection (2021): civility discourse, framing of "violence," and limits of testimonial, 108–11; epistemic injustice and, 91–94; gaslighting by Trump, 89–90, 94–99; groundwork laid for, 95–96; obfuscations, denials, distortions, and rhetorical overwhelm, 90–91; Ocasio-Cortez's testimonial in response to, 99–108; restriction of imagination and, 33; Trump's actions and words on the day, 96–97; white supremacy and, 98–99, 109–11
Jefferson, Thomas, 82
Jemisin, N. K., 36
Johnson, Micah, 39
Johnson, Theodore, 53
Jones, Imara, 128
joy, refusal through, 123–27

Kelley, Robin D. G., 14, 35
Khan-Cullors, Patrisse, 34, 35, 38–41, 57
King, Martin Luther, Jr., 54
Kirsch, Gesa, 36
Ku Klux Klan (KKK), 84
Kuo, Rachel, 22

Lemieux, Jamilah, 64
LGBTQ rights movement, 8n6. *See also* trans activism
liberalism: controlling images of, 41; defined, 12; dominant social reality, racial liberalism as, 7; fascism and, 13–15; January 6 Capitol insurrection and, 109–11; neoliberalism, 5n3, 8n6; racial liberalism as rhetorical trap, 7; racialization and, 12–13; restricting imagination and, 33; solidarity and, 133–34; trans rights discourse, 115, 119–20
Licona, Adela C., 55
"Lies, Propaganda, and Fake News" (Gray), 18

Littman, Lisa, 113
live streams, 100–101
Locks, Damon, 48
López, Ian Haney, 85

Malatino, Hil, 123
Mallett, Kandist, 110–11
Mallory, Tamika, 64, 69–70
Mandela, Nelson, 39
Martin, Trayvon, 32, 57
Marwick, Alice, 22
Matthews, Shanelle, 43–44
McCarthy, Kevin, 108
McConnell, Mitch, 77
media literacy curriculum, new, 36
medicalization of trans people, 117–19
memoirs as BLM narrative activism, 38–42
messaging, narrative and decisions about, 38
Mills, Charles, 12
Mullen, Bill V., 13
Muñoz, José Esteban, 24–25, 33, 93, 108, 116
Musk, Elon, 17

Nair, Yasmin, 37, 104–5
naming: about, 23; "both sides" rhetoric and, 73–74, 82–84, 87; gaslighting and, 109–11; as strategy, 82–83, 137–38
narrative activism: co-opted, 37; imagination and, 34–38, 42–49; memoirs as, 38–42; as strategy, 138–39. *See also* testimonial
Nation of Islam, 69
neoliberalism, 5n3, 8n6
No Future (Edelman), 116
Noble, Safiya Umoja, 19, 51–52
North, Anna, 69
nostalgia: anti-trans rhetoric and, 113; "both sides" rhetoric and, 76; for civil discourse, 9, 15; crisis rhetoric and, 4; January 6 Capitol insurrection and, 96, 98; social media and, 18–19; solidarity vs., 133; white liberal, 5, 12–13

Ocasio-Cortez, Alexandria, 99–108
Olbrechts-Tyteca, Lucie, 78
Oliver, Brittany, 64
"opinions" and false equivalency, 79
Ore, Ersula, 10

Pantsuit Nation, 63
Parker, Ethan, 46
Pauly, Madison, 113–14
Perelman, Chaim, 78
Perez, Carmen, 64, 69–70
phenomenology, trans, 120–21, 127
polarization, 16
Porter, Katie, 103
post-truth, strategies against. *See* strategies, rhetorical
post-truth politics: crisis rhetoric and, 3–9; defined, 134; framed as strange mistake, 12; nostalgia as liberal response to, 15. *See also* disinformation
power. *See* dominant power
Pressley, Ayanna, 103–4
Pritchard, Eric Darnell, 55
Proud Boys, 77, 98
Purpose of Power, The (Garza), 38, 41–42

queer methodology, 24
queer rhetoric critique, 23
queerness, 23–24, 121. *See also* trans activism

racialization: of child figure, 116; civil discourses and, 16; liberalism and, 12–13; racial liberalism as rhetorical trap, 7; of trans medicalization, 116–17. *See also* Black Lives Matter (BLM) activism; white supremacy
Ragland, Alice, 37, 56–57
Ransby, Barbara, 55–56
realism, rhetorical, 6–7
Red Shirts, 1–3
Reed, Erin, 113
refusal, politics of, 80, 123–31
relational knowledge: antiracist theory of, 55–56; BLM activist rhetoric and, 56–62; disinformation campaigns and, 50–52; Russian IRA targeting of Black Americans, 53–54; slowness and specificity, 58,

62; as strategy, 137, 138; Women's March on Washington and, 62–71
Republican Party platform (1980), 4n3
Reynolds, Diamond, 58
rhetorical awareness, 58–59
rhetorical criticism, 22–23
rhetorical exhaustion, 20–21, 54, 94, 141
Rice, Tamir, 32
Richardson, Elaine, 37, 56–57
Ridolfo, Jim, 51
Robinson, Cedric, 14
Rogerian argument, 88
Romney, Mitt, 109
Roy, Chip, 102
Royster, Jacqueline Jones, 36, 56
Russian Internet Research Agency (IRA or RU-IRA), 50, 53–54, 65–68

Salamon, Gayle, 120
Sanchez, James Chase, 84–85
Sanders, Symone, 81
Sarsour, Linda, 64, 67–68, 70
Schmidt, Jalane, 86
Shrier, Abigail, 113, 121n3
Signer, Mike, 85–86
Snorton, C. Riley, 118
social media: fake accounts on, 58–62; January 6 Capitol insurrection, gaslighting, and, 95–97, 100; nostalgia and, 18–19; not engaging directly with disinformation on, 35, 57–58; as profit-driven, 17–18; Russian IRA and fake accounts on, 50, 53–54, 65–68; technology as scapegoat, 51–52. *See also* narrative activism
Spade, Dean, 120
Spencer, Leland, 91–92
Spencer, Richard, 87
Spero, Lindsey, 124–27, 131
Spillers, Hortense, 11
spite, refusal through, 127–31
standpoint epistemology, 93, 121
Starbird, Kate, 53
stasis theory, 88
Steele, Catherine Knight, 20
Stewart, Leo, 53
Stone, Sandy, 118
Strangio, Chase, 122
strategies, rhetorical: disidentification, 93, 100–101, 106, 108; emergent, 20; naming, contextualization, and historicization, 80–84, 137–38; narrative and testimonial, 34–38, 99–108, 138–39; relational knowledge, 55–56, 137, 138
structural-material model, 91–92

Taylor, Breonna, 32
technological beneficence, 52
technology as scapegoat, 51–52
terrorism, 38–41
testimonial: as gaslighting response strategy, 99–108; limits of, 108–11; live streams and, 100–101; as strategy, 138–39; testimonial exchange and testimonial injustice, 92–93, 119, 121, 124; trans, 124–27. *See also* narrative activism
t4t (trans-for-trans) approach: about, 122–23; refusal through trans joy, 123–27; refusal through trans spite, 127–31
Thomas, Ebony Elizabeth, 35
time: Black feminist refusal to waste, 81; dehistoricization and decontextualization, 79–80; queer, 80; racial politics of, 80; wasting of, 73, 79–80, 86
Tometi, Ayọ, 34
Tometi, Opal, 57
trans activism: affective knowing and, 121; anti-trans legislation, 112–13; anti-trans rhetorics, 114–15; and assumption of core cisgendered self, 115, 129; gender-affirming care and, 113–14, 124–27; impossible burden of evidence, 115, 118, 121, 125, 129; liberal rights and identity framework and, 115, 119–20; medicalization and, 117–19; narrative activism in *Black Futures Month*, 45–47; "protecting the child" rhetoric and, 116–17; refusal through trans joy, 123–27; refusal through trans spite, 127–31; t4t approach, 122–23, 126; trans phenomenology and epistemological uncertainty, 120–22
TransLash, 127–28
trauma, 39, 85, 101–7

Trump, Donald: Charlottesville and "both sides" rhetoric, 73, 74–77, 80–84; crisis rhetoric and, 3–4; gaslighting by, 94–99; impeachment of, 95–99; white women vs. Black women in 2016 election, 64. *See also* January 6 Capitol insurrection

"truth" and truth claims: anti-trans rhetoric and, 130; "equality" rhetoric and, 5n3; gaslighting and, 92, 102–3; historicization, contextualization, and multiple truths, 69–70; narrative, imagination, and, 34–38; radical narrative and, 42; radical truth-telling, 73–74; rhetorical ineffectiveness of, 6–7; structural-material model and, 91–92. *See also* gaslighting; post-truth politics; testimonial

Tyler, Sam, 58–60

"Uncaged Black Futures Now" (Fuller), 47–48

Unite the Right rally (Charlottesville), 72–74. *See also* "both sides" rhetoric

Velocci, Beans, 117–18

vernacular studies, 23

Vials, Christopher, 13

violence: of anti-Blackness, 31, 39; "both sides" rhetoric and, 83–84; false equivalency and deployment of, 77–78; gaslighting and, 94–95, 109–11; restricting and controlling imagination on, 32–33

Wallace, Chris, 77

Weigal, Moira, 22

When They Call You a Terrorist (Khan-Cullors), 38–41

white supremacy: disinformation as co-constitutive with, 3; gaslighting and, 91; January 6 Capitol insurrection and, 98–99, 109–11; as organizing principle, 10; as the real crisis, 10–12; time, control of, 80. *See also* Black Lives Matter (BLM) activism; Charlottesville, VA

"who are your people?," 55–56

"Why Black People Must Hold on to Our Dreams" (Williams), 44–45

Wilderson, Frank, 11n8

Wilmington, NC, massacre (1898), 1–3

Williams, Kiyan, 44–45

Williams, Miriam F., 35

witnessing, 94, 100–108. *See also* narrative activism; testimonial

Women's March on Washington (2017): about, 62–63; false charges of anti-Semitism against, 68–70; leadership of, 64; legacy of, 70–71; Russian IRA attacks on, 65–68; white feminism and, 63–64

Wooten, Jamye, 60

Wortham, Jenna, 35–36

X, Malcolm, 54

Yergeau, M. Remi, 17

Yiannopoulos, Milo, 67

Zane, J. Peder, 76–77

Zimmerman, George, 32

INTERSECTIONAL RHETORICS

KARMA R. CHÁVEZ, SERIES EDITOR

This series takes as its starting point the position that intersectionality offers important insights to the field of rhetoric—including that to enhance what we understand as rhetorical practice, we must diversify the types of rhetors, arguments, frameworks, and forms under analysis. Intersection works on two levels for the series: (1) reflecting the series' privileging of intersectional perspectives and analytical frames while also (2) emphasizing rhetoric's intersection with related fields, disciplines, and research areas.

Truth Be Told: White Nostalgia and Antiracist Queer Resistance in "Post-Truth" America
Laura Elliot Tetreault

The Erotic as Rhetorical Power: Archives of Romantic Friendship between Women Teachers
Pamela VanHaitsma

A Nation's Undesirables: Mixed-Race Children and Whiteness in the Post-Nazi Era
Tracey Owens Patton

Inscrutable Eating: Asian Appetites and the Rhetorics of Racial Consumption
Jennifer Lin LeMesurier

Constellating Home: Trans and Queer Asian American Rhetorics
V. Jo Hsu

Inconvenient Strangers: Transnational Subjects and the Politics of Citizenship
Shui-yin Sharon Yam

Culturally Speaking: The Rhetoric of Voice and Identity in a Mediated Culture
Amanda Nell Edgar